FINDING HARRY
A True Love Story

Judy Prescott

Brilliant Books Literary
137 Forest Park Lane Thomasville
North Carolina 27360 USA

DEDICATION

This book is dedicated to my mother Patricia Alison Amelia(Milly), the last living child of Ada and Harry Tracey.

At 82 years old, the stories of her life still enlighten me.

The more she remembers, the more I realise how much she endured as a child, and growing up.

ABOUT THE AUTHOR

Judy was born and raised in Bristol, UK, the eldest of five children. She is a mother of two grown up children, a son and a daughter, and has five grandsons. A wife to Adrian for over forty years, her husband sadly passed away three years ago.

Now living in South Wales, Judy has retired, but still loves to write and enjoys helping take care of the grandchildren.

On researching her family tree, whilst recovering from illness, the discoveries were overwhelming and she had felt that Finding Harry- A True Love Story had needed to be written. This was her first book.

THE TRACEY CURSE

The Tracey surname was spelt several different ways, Tracey, Tracy, Treacy and Traci are known to my knowledge. Census's show Tracey in one decade, followed by Tracy in another, all relating to the same family. Education years ago wasn't as it is today and the vast majority were unable to read and write.

William II de Tracy was one of the four knights who, supposedly at the behest of King Henry II, in 1670 murdered Thomas Becket, the Archbishop of Canterbury. His accomplices were Reginald Fitzurse, Hugh de Morville and Richard le Breton.

Afterwards they invaded the Archbishop's Palace plundering Papal Bulls and Charters, gold, silver, vestments, books and utensils employed for the services of the church.

Sir William II de Tracy was feudal baron of Bradninch near Exeter and Lord of the Manors of Toddington, Gloucestershire and of Moretonhampstead, Devon.

His grandfather William I de Tracy (who died around 1136) was an illegitimate son of King Henry I. The king granted William I the feudal barony of Bradninch, Devon which had escheated to the crown from William Capra, listed in the Domesday Book of 1086 as holding that barony.

The town of Bovey Tracey is derived from the River Bovey which passes through the town and from the 'de Tracy' family from Traci near Bayeux, Normandy, who settled in the area after the Norman Conquest of 1066.

Sir William rebuilt the town's church of St Peter, Paul and Thomas after 1170 as part of his penance for his part in the Archbishop's murder.

In addition he added a tower, chancel and porch to the church of Lapford, Devon, which was dedicated to Thomas Becket.

The four conspirators entered the cathedral – the three knights struggled violently to put him on Tracy's shoulders – In the scuffle Becket fastened upon Tracy's shoulders, shook him by his coat of mail, and, exerting his strength, flung him down on the pavement.

Fitzurse, glowing with rage, waved the sword over his head, but merely dashed off his cap. Meanwhile Tracy sprang forward and struck a more decided blow. The next blow was only with the flat of the sword, and again on the bleeding head.

At the third blow, from Tracy, he sank on his knees his hands still joined as if in prayer. Richard le Breton gave the final blow, a tremendous one – aimed with such violence that the scalp or crown of his head was severed from the skull, and the sword snapped in two on the marble pavement.

Before Becket died he put a curse on Tracy's family, a water curse. His family will always have too little or too much water. And believe it or not this has always happened to his family, now the Garnetts, Tracys and Coogans. Henry failed to arrest the knights, advising them to flee to Scotland.

After the bloody tragedy of Canterbury, Tracy and his three accomplices sought refuge at Knaresborough Castle, from whence they went to throw themselves at the feet of Pope Alexander III of Rome. He sentenced them to expiate their sin in the Holy Land, and they set out together on a pilgrimage to Jerusalem.

Tracy was never able to accomplish his vow, though he did begin the journey. He reached the coast of Calabria, and was siezed at Cosenza with a dreadful disorder, which caused him to tear the flesh from his bones with his own hands, but he lived to return home. The crime of having struck the first blow – was avenged by the winds of heaven, which always drove him back. The Tracys have always the wind in their faces, such is the legend.

It is believed that he returned to his estates in the West of England, where he lived 'a private life' when wind and weather turned against him, and reached the age of 90. His tormented spirit may even now, be heard moaning and lamenting on the Woolacombe Sands, where he wanders to and fro, toiling to make bundles of sand and wisps of the same, for all time to come.

CHAPTER ONE

Harry was born on the 2nd July 1901 in Shipston on Stour workhouse. What a place that was dark and depressing; damp and dreary. So much deprivation there. People working all day for a chunk of bread, cheese and water, and not much else. Sleeping in the equivalent of a prison cell. They picked oakum using a large metal nail known as a spike, broke stones and crushed bones to produce fertiliser. Female residents did various domestic duties and even the elderly were given jobs to do.

Children as young as 3 sleeping in dreadful, damp dormitories. Bathing in freezing cold water and living a life of complete discipline, not allowed to be children at play. At least they were being taught in the schoolroom, something some children outside the workhouse weren't able to do.

Education had to be paid for by relatives before 1918 and many families were unable to pay.

His mother, Martha Matilda Tracey, wasn't married, which is why they were both there. She wasn't able to give birth at home, with her parents being humiliated by others and their gossip, his mother's status, and no father on the scene. She was 22 years of age, stood at 5ft 5ins tall with dark hair falling to her shoulders. She had brown eyes and a full rounded face with somewhat childlike features. With her slight figure she looked a lot less than her actual years.

There were 6 new babies there, including Harry. Mothers sat by their cribs, feeding and changing them; cuddling and loving them, in such an awful place. There were no grandparents, aunts or siblings visiting to congratulate them on their new child. When he was asleep, his mother was working, to pay for his upkeep and food for her survival.

Nappies were limited, squares of cloth made from cotton, not always in exceptional condition. His mother tried to keep them as long as possible before changing him. They were washed in cold water and dried outside on a line, available for all to use. Sometimes items would go missing, taken by other residents, so his mother was very careful hers didn't go astray, as the workhouse wouldn't replace them. His mother breastfed him, as all mothers did, and therefore needed her meagre morsels of food and milk to be able to nourish him.

Workhouse food consisted of broth, bread and cheese. Meat, vegetables and yeast dumplings.

Soup and suet and rice pudding. Butter and potatoes was a meal of its own, and bread and gruel was also common. Food was only given if residents worked. There were no exceptions. No-one resided in the workhouse for free. The disabled and infirm, the elderly and children as young as 5 were all given chores to do.

Weeks later and Harry was now at his grandparents farm in Hidcote Boyce, Ebrington, with his mother and grandparents, George and Jane. Three of his uncles lived there too, Richard, John and Joseph. They all worked on the farm. Life was going to be hectic for Harry's mother and grandmother, with the farm duties and looking after him. His mother and grandmother attended to the domestic duties on the farm. Cooking, cleaning, milking the cows, attending to the kitchen garden. It was never ending. Life wasn't easy, but with plenty of family around, it was never dull.

The farm in Hidcote Boyce, Ebrington, was of a good size and surrounded by more farms and not much else, except for small terraced cottages scattered amongst the immense countryside. His grandfather raised sheep and cattle, for milk and meat. He had chickens, likewise for meat and eggs. He also had 2 goats. Billy the smallest, was very friendly and used to let Harry near her, but Johnny, the older one was happy to stay in the background eating the grass and running around the yard pleasing himself. Harry used to milk Billy, she was happy to let him.

Harry's grandfather and uncles were up early every morning tending the fields. Sam, the resident Collie, had followed them everywhere they went, often coming back with a rabbit in his mouth for Harry's grandmother to cook. Feeling proud, he would drop the goods in her hands, awaiting his reward.

'Okay then,' she would say and would hand him a home-made biscuit, which he demolished in no time at all, in seconds.

Harry's grandparents had 9 children (Ann, their 10th, had died before he was born, as a child, so he never knew her). Three of his uncles were married and lived locally. Uncle Walter was also married, but now lived in Worcester. Harry didn't see much of him and his family. He had many cousins who used to visit, too many to name individually.

Uncle George lived in the farm next door with his wife, Mary, and their four children. Walter and Hannah were often there with their grandmother after school. Harry thought they needed some space from their sisters, Elizabeth and Alice, who were only 5 and 2, and like himself they loved their grandmother. Walter would often help his grandfather on the farm, as well as helping his own father.

Uncle Herbert lived locally in Ebrington, too. His wife, Ann, had died in 1898, a few weeks after giving birth to their youngest daughter. He had 6 children who also visited his grandparents farm.

When Harry was 4, his mother married Frank Emms and moved to Blockley. She felt he was settled at the farm and left without him. Harry hadn't realised what was happening at the time. He had his grandparents and uncles there and saw his mother when she visited. It was strange at first, but Harry got used to life without her on a daily basis, and looked forward to seeing her on the rare occasions she did find the time to visit.

Harry rose early every morning from the age of 6, fed the chickens and collected the eggs before going to school. He was one of the lucky ones there. Not every child attended school, they were needed on their family's farm or to help out with the younger children and the domestic duties. His grandmother had insisted he went to school.

'He needs to have an education,' she would say to his grandfather.

When he returned home from school, dinner would be ready and they would all sit around the farmhouse table eating a wholesome, hearty meal. The vegetables came from the kitchen garden his grandmother used to attend to when she was younger and more able. There would be chicken, potatoes, peas, carrots, cabbage and gravy. Plenty of bread to mop up the gravy, followed by suet pudding and plenty of custard.

Rabbit stew was also very popular, followed by rice pudding. No-one ever went hungry. The home-made biscuits and cakes came out before bedtime, with a large warm drink.

Now it was Harry's job after school to pick the vegetables, remove the weeds and plant more seeds. This he did after food, ready for his grandmother the next day. She would often call him in and present him with a warm chocolate drink and a biscuit.

She would put her finger to her mouth. 'Don't tell your grandfather,' she would say and laugh.

Harry's grandfather was a very sombre man, tall, broad shouldered and he had a severe looking face, a disciplinarian. With 9 children to look after (after Ann's death) he had to be. His grandmother on the other hand was very loving and friendly, petite, cuddly and always had a smile on her face. She often gave him treats without anyone knowing, and a big hug by the roaring fireplace before bedtime.

'Now off to bed you go,' she would say. 'There's another long day ahead of you tomorrow.'

School was in Ebrington and there were about 20 pupils in the school altogether. It would take about 15-20 minutes to walk to school. His grandmother accompanied him in the mornings and he would walk back home with his school friends in the afternoon. She always had a packed lunch ready for him. Bread and cheese, an apple from the tree and a tomato, if he was lucky. She prepared packed lunches for his grandfather and uncles too, as they woke at 4 o'clock in the morning and were out in the fields by 5.

His grandfather produced some of the wool sold in the Shipston on Stour market for which the town was famous for. Sam watched over the sheep, as he knew that was his job, as well as catching rabbits. On days when it had rained the previous day, he would roll in the mud and on returning home, his grandmother wouldn't be impressed. 'In the bath you go,' she would say. 'You're not coming into the kitchen in that state.' There was a tin bath kept outside especially for him.

Harry enjoyed school and meeting his friends. He didn't have much time to play with them afterwards, as he would always be busy on the farm and at weekends. His grandmother sometimes let him bring one of them back for food with his family, but then he had his chores to do and they had to leave.

Cat would welcome him after school, showing him the mouse she had caught with pride, then off she would run looking for another! She was called 'Cat', no-one had given her a proper name but she always answered to it, happily.

Sam, on the other hand, would wait at the gate as Harry walked up the lane. He would wag his tail and bark and run alongside him to the farmhouse. He was always given his food the same time as the family, to avoid him waiting for them to give him some of theirs. His grandfather didn't like Sam in the kitchen whilst they were eating.

Harry wasn't the brightest pupil in the class, but he tried his best and his grandparents were happy with his progress. When his mother did visit, his grandmother would tell her how Harry was progressing in school. Whether she was interested, Harry was uncertain, but she was told nevertheless, and his grandmother always praised him for trying.

His grandfather died in 1910 at 73 years of age. Harry was only 9 at the time. Thankfully, uncles Richard, John and Joseph were still at home. They had never married and continued to run the farm. Then uncle Joseph died at just 45. He loved his pipe and Harry had fond memories of him relaxing, sat outside the back door of the farmhouse, puffing his pipe and smiling to himself. He had inherited his pipe from him and followed in his footsteps when he was older, sitting outside puffing tobacco on occasions, and smiling too.

In the same year, Uncle George, who lived next door to him, had died at just 52 years of age. He had been ploughing his fields, and was found next to his loyal horse, Berty, completely lifeless. No-one knew exactly what had happened as he had been on his own for most of the day. There were no marks on his body, and it was decided by the local doctor that he had had a sudden attack on his heart.

When Harry was just 16, his grandmother died. By then, Harry was labouring on the farm and had finished school. He didn't see much of his mother at all now, she had three of his half brothers and a half sister to look after. Things weren't the same without his grandmother around.

With Harry and his uncles, Richard and John, left on the farm to do everything, it was hard going, but they persevered. Food wasn't the same without a woman's touch, but they didn't starve. Occasionally relatives would bring them home-made dishes to help them out. This was very welcome and gave them more time out in the fields, attending to the farm.

By the time Harry was 18, with his grandparents and uncle Joseph now deceased, life on the farm was a solemn affair. Work was hard and long, and they now had a servant who cooked and cleaned the farmhouse and tended to the kitchen garden. Rose was in her 20's and lived locally, so was only there until 6 o'clock in the evening. She then returned to her family in Ebrington. It wasn't the done thing for her to stay overnight with only male residents on the farm. Gossip would have been all over the town and heads would have turned!

Harry's uncles also hired another farm labourer, his name was John, which could be quite confusing at times. With two Johns on the farm, they called him Joe, and he was happy to answer to it. He was 19 and became a good friend, as well as a working colleague to Harry. He had two younger brothers and a baby sister. His father worked away a lot, but was usually home at the weekend. His brothers would often walk to their farm to see him.

Joe lived locally but stayed on the farm due to the early mornings. He regularly visited his family on his day off. Harry and Joe would often walk to Shipston on Stour and have two pints of ale or cider, Harry liked his cider, in The White Bear of an evening, meet Joe's father and converse with the locals about the day they had had. They would also listen to the local gossip with interest and then head home again. On other occasions they would take a short stroll to the Ebrington Arms for a pint or two.

At 20, Harry decided to enlist in the Army. His uncles weren't too happy about his decision, but with the help of Reverend William Guerrier, the vicar in Ebrington vicarage, he was given a good reference and accepted. His grandmother had insisted that he went to church on a Sunday, but since her death the visits had become infrequent. The vicar described Harry as a respectable man with a fresh complexion and believed him to be a sober and honest man. This was quite refreshing from a man of the cloth. He was a good friend of the family and often visited his uncles, informing them of any special services being held in the parish church.

Harry often visited the churchyard in Ebrington (St Eadburgha's Church), where he would sit and tell his grandmother at her gravestone his worries, and how much he missed her. His enlisting into the Army meant he had to visit his mother with his application form, because the answers had to be precise. This did concern him as he needed to ask her who his father was.

'I wish you were here to help me,' he said to his grandmother. 'This is going to be so hard.'

This was something that had never been discussed in the family. No-one ever mentioned his father at all and as a child, he never asked. Now Harry needed to know to join the Army. This was going to be so difficult and embarrassing for him.

Harry's mother now lived in Blockley. It wasn't that far away, but he needed to catch the local bus, which wasn't very frequent. It took about 20 minutes once the bus arrived. He could walk it and did on occasions, when the weather was dry and sunny, and he'd felt the need to be on his own.

There was no proper timetable, he had to wait until it arrived, which could have been absolutely ages at times.

When Harry arrived, his mother was in the kitchen. She had two chickens cooking in the Aga and the aroma was making him feel hungry. His stepfather was at work, he worked in the timber merchants as a timber carter in Ebrington. He didn't get home until well after 5pm, plenty of time to talk to her about his application form. His brothers and sister were still at school. Albert was almost 15 now, and due to finish his education soon. Millie was approaching 14, and Frank junior was 12. Richard was 6, and John Henry a baby in his cot. Thankfully he was asleep when Harry had entered the cottage they lived in. His mother was sat at the kitchen table peeling potatoes, ready for the evening meal and still had peas to pod, and carrots to wash and peel.

'Well, don't just sit there,' she said as he sat down at the table. 'Get yourself a knife and peel the carrots for me.'

No hello or how are you? She had no time for niceties. Harry picked up a knife and started to peel and chop the carrots as he spoke.

He supposed it was easier than blurting out what he'd wanted to say. His hands were busy, so the nervousness hadn't shown as much.

Harry asked about his siblings, especially Millie. He always got on well with Millie when he saw her. He asked about John Henry and commented on how much he had grown.

Martha replied, 'They are all okay, Harry, and the baby is growing far too quickly.' The table was strewn with vegetables. There were a lot of mouths to feed and all had large appetites.

Harry had started to ask how his mother was, but she had got up from the table and was making tea for them both. She put the full cups on the table and Harry thanked her. 'No biscuits?' he asked and his mother smiled.

'Sorry, I haven't had time to do any. John Henry is so busy these days,' she replied.

Here goes! 'Mother, I need to ask you some questions to help fill in this application form. I have enlisted in the Army and been accepted. Reverend Guerrier has given me a reference, a good one. I need to know who my father is, as they are asking for next of kin on the form.'

His mother stopped peeling the potatoes and looked at him, quite shocked. 'Oh, you've taken me by surprise, Harry,' she eventually replied and got up from the table, putting the kettle back on the Aga. She was very quiet, as if trying to decide what to say. The silence seemed to go on for ever and Harry was wondering what she was thinking.

'I will pour the tea, Mother,' Harry said getting up from the table. 'You sit down, you look a bit pale.' The colour had drained from her face and Harry had never seen her like that before.

'Your father's name is Henry Westbury, Harry,' she eventually said. 'He was a friend of uncle Richard's and they used to go to The White Bear together, and sometimes The Horseshoe Inn. He would visit the farm and we became very friendly. Henry was a carter on a farm in Tredington. We started going out for walks and into the tearooms for tea and cakes, and I really liked him. By the time I realised you were on the way, he had told me that he was betrothed to Kate Tomes, the daughter of the farmer he worked for.'

She stopped for breath and continued. 'Your grandparents weren't very happy when I told them, or with your father. He was never invited to the farm again, and your uncle wasn't allowed to drink with him. I was sent to the workhouse to have you because of the stigma of being an unmarried mother. Henry was never mentioned again.' Harry could hear the emotion in her voice.

'He married Kate in 1902, not long after you were born and they have a daughter Dora May, who is now 17. Kate is a very fragile woman and nearly died having Dora, so they haven't any other children. Your grandparents made it clear he wasn't welcome, so your father was unable to see you. It took a long time for your grandfather to forgive me for what happened. He didn't really talk to me much after that, you know what he was like yourself.'

Harry could see the tears welling in her eyes, so he didn't ask any more questions. 'It's okay, Mother, I will put you down as my next of kin. I will be a good soldier, I won't disappoint you.' She knew he wouldn't, though she didn't say it in words.

Baby John Henry started crying then, so his mother got up to see to him. Harry finished preparing the vegetables for her, before his siblings returned home from school. Millie was excited to see him there and Harry informed her of his enlistment into the Army. She looked upset, but gave him a big hug and told him to look after himself. The others just nodded and walked into the sitting room. Soon afterwards, Harry left for the bus home and his mother waved, whilst holding baby John Henry.

Thankfully the bus wasn't long coming and Harry boarded it, sitting down on one of the back seats. His mind was in turmoil. It had been so hard for his mother to confide in him. She had obviously cared about his father, but hadn't been allowed to continue their relationship. Did his father really love his mother, or the lady he had married? Harry would never know the answers to these questions, but he now knew he had another sister, a half-sister, Dora May. Would he ever see her or his father in his lifetime?

Harry enlisted on the 5th May 1922 and was given his Army Number 5176743, which he had to remember, as he would be asked it constantly and would have to relay it automatically (as you would a telephone number). His regiment was the 1st Battalion Gloucester

Regiment and he was sent to Tidworth barracks in Wiltshire to do his training. This was where the Gloucester Regiment was based.

Discipline wasn't a problem for Harry. With hard work on the farm, long days every day, he knew the Army wouldn't be difficult. Training was rigorous, but Harry was in good health and although at times he was exhausted, he managed okay.

He made a good friend in Percy Bridges, who had enlisted at the same time and they slept in the same dormitory. Percy was from Farmborough in Somerset. His father had been born and raised in a place called Midsomer Norton. He had died in 1916, leaving Percy's mother with 4 children to bring up alone (Percy had a sister Dorothy and brothers Albert and Hubert).

As they shared information on their family history, it emerged that Albert was friendly with a Nellie Jarvis from Shipston on Stour, whom he had met through work. She was 8 years older than him, but they got on well. Harry thought long and hard, and realised that although he didn't know Nellie, he knew her brothers, Harold and Thomas. They were of similar ages to himself and had attended school with him in Ebrington.

Harry remarked on this and how small a world this was. After six weeks training, they were allowed a week's leave. Percy suggested staying with his family, as opposed to going back to Hidcote Boyce and his uncles.

'It would be nice to meet your family,' Harry said. 'I've heard so much about them, and it would be nice to talk to Nellie.'

When they arrived at Farmborough, Louisa, Percy's mother welcomed them. A hearty meal was ready and a warm fire lit by the huge fireplace in the kitchen. It was lovely to have a few home comforts again. Things you take for granted.

She asked them about their training and how things were going and Percy asked about things at home and the family. Harry felt very comfortable, as if he'd known them all his life. Back at the farm, conversation had been minimal after work was finished, and apart from the walk to The White Bear or The Ebrington Arms for a few pints of ale, or cider, and listening to the locals, it had been very quiet.

Percy suggested going to the cinema, which wasn't far away. 'Dorothy, my sister, can come too and bring her friend, Ada.'

'Okay,' Harry replied excitedly. 'That would make a change. We haven't a cinema in Shipston on Stour. The nearest is in Stratford upon Avon.' Dorothy was newly married. Her husband was Frederick Gay and both Ada and Dorothy lived locally.

Both Percy and Harry had learnt to drive in the Army. Percy used his brother's (Albert's) car and they picked Dorothy and Ada up and headed for the cinema. Ada was a small, slender girl with dark hair put up in a tight bun at the back. She was a pretty girl and her and Harry instantly got on well. After the film was over, all four of them finished the night in a nearby pub for a drink and a chat.

Ada was happy to talk about her family, as was Harry about his. Dorothy spoke about her mother, her husband Frederick, and generally caught up with Percy's training in the Army.

Ada was 19 years of age and living with her stepmother and her father. Her mother Lily had died in childbirth having her brother, Ernest, when she was only 9. She had several siblings older and younger than herself. Her father was a banker in the coal mines and worked long hours.

Archibald (her father) had worked as a banksman before joining the 4th Division, Somerset Light Infantry in 1914, shortly after losing his first wife, Lily. Relatives had taken over looking after the children, until her father had remarried Ethel Mary in 1915.

He had served in the Somerset Light Infantry until 1920 and was awarded a Victory Medal for his contribution in the First World War. On discharge from the Army, he had returned to the mines and his old job as a banksman. Ada was proud of her father's achievements and relished in talking about him to Harry.

Harry took Ada out the next day, only to the tearooms, but he felt even then, that he was falling in love with her. The week was taken up with home comforts at Louisa's, pub visits with Percy and the last day with Ada, walking the countryside.

He felt so at home, so alive, happy and wanted. This was something Harry had truly never felt before, not totally. His mother hadn't seemed to have any time for him and he so missed his grandmother. Going back to Tidworth came way too soon, but Ada and Harry had promised to write to each other.

CHAPTER TWO

Ada wrote to Harry every week, and every week, Harry replied. She would tell him about her family and her stepmother, who wasn't a nice person. Ethel Mary (her stepmother) was constantly adding more chores to Ada's list and also to her sisters lists. Ada seemed to have less free time to herself now. She missed Harry and was anxiously waiting for his next leave.

Harry missed Ada too, and told her so in his letters. They had only known one another a short while, but seemed to be smitten with each other. Harry wrote about his family and his duties in Tidworth and about Percy and his family. There was always something to write about.

Harry was informed by his superiors that the 1st Battalion would be serving Cologne in Germany on the 28th October that year, and would be there for approximately six weeks. He wanted to see Ada before then, as he was missing her. Thankfully, both Percy and Harry were entitled to another week's leave before heading for Germany.

Once again he spent the week with the Bridges family, seeing Ada as often as she had time to see him. His feelings towards her were becoming obvious, and with hesitation, Harry went to Ada's home to meet her stepmother, Ethel Mary, and her father, Archibald.

Ada's stepmother was a very pompous lady, kind of schoolteacher material, dressed completely in black, with a hunched back. She had a very serious looking face, not prone to smiling and laughing, Harry had surmised. It was clear by her tone of voice and mannerisms, which of Ada's siblings were hers and Ada's father's, and which were from Archibald's first marriage.

There were 5 siblings aged 7 and under from their marriage, including the twins Christopher and Kathleen, and 4 siblings living home from her father's first marriage to Lily, not including Ada. James, Ada's oldest brother, was in an institution in Chard. He had been unable to walk from birth and had been placed there after his 21st birthday. Ada's stepmother felt James, or Jim, as they called him, would be better off living with people with similar disabilities, and it helped her also.

Harry was polite to Ada's stepmother and father, and devoured the tea and scones Ethel Mary had prepared whilst she was analysing him as future husband material. Ada apologised afterwards for putting him through the afternoon, but Harry didn't mind. He was with Ada and that was what mattered.

The week finished far too quickly again, and both Harry and Percy were back on the road heading for Tidworth barracks. The regime of Army life continued and all the days were taken up with duties. Training was still rigorous and the 28th October was getting nearer. Harry had never travelled farther than Stratford upon Avon before.

This was a scary experience for him, and he thought of Ada. He would miss her letters, even though it was only for six weeks. Harry was writing his last letter before heading for Cologne, when he began to think of where he could be sent afterwards. He had enlisted for seven years as a regular, and five years as a reserve.

With pen to paper, Harry had asked Ada to marry him on his return from Germany. He knew it was right and he truly loved her, he wanted her to become his wife. Although Harry hadn't known Ada that long, he had no doubts.

He sealed the envelope and posted the letter in the mess's postbox and waited with baited breath for a reply. Hoping the answer would be a positive one, he'd also wanted a reply soon, the sooner the better. Patience was usually one of his better attributes, but not on this occasion.

Dorothy, Percy's sister, had given birth to a daughter in July, but there were health issues with the baby. They had named her Peggy, and she had died just two days later. The Bridges family were distraught. Ada, being Dorothy's friend, was so upset, and apart from her mother's death and her brother, Freddie, at aged 5, she had never encountered so much heartache. Ada had only been 11 when Freddie had died. Peggy was only 2 days old, it was heartbreaking.

Ada read over and over again the letter Harry had sent her. She thought about Dorothy and Frederick and their loss, threw caution to the wind and began replying to Harry's letter.

> *Dearest Harry,*
>
> *Yes, I will marry you. I know we haven't known each other that long, but it feels right and I think about you daily. Stepmother liked you by the way (so did father). She thinks you will be a good husband and I know father agrees. It will be one less mouth to feed, stepmother will say, though it will mean the others will have to do more work to make up for me not being there.*
>
> *It might be a good idea if I stay with them whilst you are on duties abroad, if that's okay with you, Harry. I know I will miss you so much then. I hope you are not working too hard. I await your next letter with haste, before you leave for Cologne. Take care of yourself, Harry, and give my regards to Percy.*
>
> *With love Ada.*

Strangely, Ada had never expected to fall in love at first sight. She honestly thought that had only happened in fairytales, or to other people. But it had happened to her, the minute she had set eyes on Harry, her heart had skipped a beat. She hadn't known what it was about him, his dark brown eyes, his fresh complexion or his mischievous grin, but whatever it was, it was instantaneous. She had known she was in love.

Ada hadn't encountered a member of the opposite sex quite like him. She'd been on dates before, with local boys and enjoyed herself, but this was different. She hadn't wanted the night to end, and she had wanted him all to herself, just Harry and her. Percy and Dorothy had been there at the cinema that night, but her mind had only registered the two of them. She had been in a dream, but it had been real.

When Harry had asked her to marry him, she knew her answer before writing the word 'YES' in reply to his letter. She could count the times they'd dated on one hand, but had only needed one date to confirm her feelings towards him. She had wanted to be his wife, look after him and hopefully bring Harry's babies into the world. Wherever he was, she wanted to be.

Harry received Ada's letter a few days before setting off for Germany. She had agreed to become his wife. He was so happy. He carried on with his Army duties all day with a huge grin on his face. 'What's up with you, Harry? You've been beaming all day,' Percy said to him at dinner time.

Dinner time was a noisy affair, in the huge dining room filled with soldiers sat at a long table. Tin plates, cups and cutlery clattered continuously amidst the constant chatter between each other. You could hardly hear yourself speak. Harry was still smiling though, despite the noise.

Harry could not hide his feelings from Percy. He was more of a brother to him than his own half-brothers. 'Ada and I are getting married when we get back from Germany. I asked her to become my wife in my last letter. I do love her so much. Will you come to the wedding, Percy?' Percy nodded and shook his hand to congratulate him.

That night in bed, Harry wrote back to Ada asking her to sort out the wedding date and everything else, for after his return from Cologne. He had been informed that he would be back in the UK at the beginning of December. Harry also wrote to his mother, telling her the good news. He had sent her a few letters whilst in Tidworth, asking about the family and telling her about Ada and the Bridges. She had only replied once, but it was nice to receive her letter.

Ada had received Harry's letter and realised that she had a lot of organising to do. She promptly attended the Registry Office in Clutton, and checked on dates available to suit Harry's return. The only available date was 26th December, boxing day!

'Oh well,' she said to herself and booked it there and then. She returned home and informed her father and stepmother. Her sisters, Gladys and Blanche, were really excited, as was Alice. Ada's stepmother insisted on having the reception at the cottage after the ceremony, and she didn't object. The Bridges would be there too, but Ada didn't know about Harry's family. The House sisters (Ada, Alice, Gladys and Blanche) would all work together to ensure ample food was prepared for everyone and being the day after Christmas, there would probably be plenty spare.

Windsor Cottage was a good size and had plenty of land attached to it. The House family owned cows, used to produce beef and milk for their large family. Chickens were reared for poultry and eggs. There was a kitchen garden, a small orchard and two fields. These were used for the animals, alternating regularly for haymaking and food for the winter.

Ada was so excited. She still had a month or so, but was thinking of what she was going to wear. 'You've plenty of time to worry about that,' she said to herself and decided to write to Harry in the hope he would get it whilst in Germany, or at least have the letter waiting for him on his return. She wrote slowly, so Harry could read it clearly. Sometimes her writing could be a bit like a cobweb and hard to understand. She wanted him to be able to read every word of her letter.

> *Dearest Harry,*
>
> *I could only get the 26th December, as all other dates were fully booked. I hope that is okay for you. Stepmother is organising food at the cottage after the ceremony and I've asked the Bridges to the wedding.*
> *I don't know if your mother will be coming or any of your family, I will leave you to write to them. I hope your duties aren't too hard in Cologne and the journey wasn't horrendous. I know how you were dreading the ship because of your sea sickness.*
> *I'm getting really excited, Harry. The 26th December seems too far away.*
>
> *Miss you lots, Ada.*

The letter was posted and Ada continued to prepare for her wedding with eagerness and happiness. The smiles on her face had confirmed it.

Being in the Army, Ada knew Harry's chances of being posted abroad was high, but her head belonged to the clouds. Her happiness couldn't take in the loneliness she might encounter along the way, if this became an eventuality. Ada's mind was on the here and now, and she would cope with the tomorrows of this world when she got to it. She loved Harry and he loved her, and that was all that mattered.

The days in Germany seemed to last forever, duties, duties and not much free time at all. Percy told Harry that his sister, Dorothy, was now expecting again, after losing baby Peggy. Ada had been distraught seeing her friend so upset before, and was elated for her. Louisa, Percy's mother, had sent a letter to Tidworth, which had been forwarded on to their barracks in Cologne shortly after their arrival.

Louisa and the family were all well and Ada had enjoyed a day out with Dorothy, celebrating her news. She was careful not to include any of Ada's wedding plans (Ada would want to tell Harry herself) in her letter. Louisa hoped Percy and Harry were well and looked forward to seeing them both soon.

Harry hadn't received any letters in Germany, from Ada or his mother, so had no idea that the wedding plans were all in order. He hoped Ada was sorting things, but without any correspondence was left wondering. He could trust her to organise everything, he knew, but he had wanted to see it in writing. A creature of habit, Harry was.

Harry's employment record showed him to be a clean, smart, reliable and trustworthy character and he was proud of this. He hoped he would be a good husband and father too. 'Grandmother would be proud of me,' he muttered to himself. Harry missed her so much and thought of her often.

Finally, he was on his way back to the UK and would arrive on the 5th December. Would there be a letter waiting for him?

Back home at Tidworth barracks there were two letters waiting for Harry. Both were from Ada.

The first letter was generally asking how he was, but the second letter was the one he had been waiting for. The date was set for 26th December at the local Registry Office and all was in order. All he had to do was turn up! He was brimming with delight, smiles coming from cheek to cheek. He had such a mischievous grin at times, hidden amid the solemn Army face he had to adhere to most of the time.

Percy walked into the dormitory as he was reading the letter. 'You look like the cat that's got the cream,' he said, 'Can I have some of what you've got?'

'The wedding date is set for 26th December,' Harry replied. 'Ada's stepmother is organising food at their cottage for after the ceremony. I suppose I'd better go and see the Sergeant to get leave, you too, Percy. I want you and your family there.'

Harry headed for the Sergeant's office to report his forthcoming marriage. He was given a week's leave after his marriage, but was also informed of his transfer to Aldershot, Surrey, on his return. He was offered marriage quarters in Aldershot for Ada and himself, which he duly accepted. He knew that Ada would want to be with him.

Percy was also given the same week's leave and also informed of his move to Aldershot. Things were going to be hectic to say the least. 'Everything's going well with Dorothy and the baby,' he said to Harry. 'Mother is worrying herself silly, wrapping Dorothy in cotton wool. She won't let her do anything. Only natural, I suppose. I can envisage her having a huge baby, the way mother is feeding her up.' He laughed and Harry laughed with him.

Harry set to writing to his mother, telling her about the wedding and informing her of the wedding date. Being the day after Christmas, he didn't think she would be able to attend, but he would ask anyway. She still had John Henry a toddler, though the other siblings were easier to manage now, and Millie was old enough to help out. He knew Frank didn't help much with the children, so it was hard work for her.

Harry wrote to the farm as well, telling John, Richard and Joe of his forthcoming marriage. They would be too busy to attend, but he wanted to tell them. He wanted to tell the whole world!

Percy and Harry were leaving Tidworth barracks for the Bridges residence. It was Christmas Eve, damp and miserable. They had to take all their belongings, as they would be going to Aldershot after the wedding and their week's leave. Not that they had that much, as it all fitted neatly into their rucksacks.

Harry looked at his rucksack, 'That's my whole life till now,' he said. 'The next part is going to be better.' Percy laughed at him, but Harry was deadly serious. He felt that he had a good future ahead of him.

Ada had written to Harry and so had his mother. Martha (his mother) apologised for not being able to attend the wedding, said the children were missing him, especially Millie. She wished him luck and hoped she would see Ada soon. Harry wasn't surprised, but a little disappointed.

Grandmother would have been there, he was sure. He looked up to the clouds in the sky and imagined her there, seeing her face and smiling.

Ada's letter told him that everything was ready for the big day and she so wanted to see him again on Christmas Day. Louisa (Percy's mother) was preparing a festive Christmas dinner. All the family would be there, and Harry was considered family. He'd liked that and felt special.

The Christmas meal was superb. Turkey, vegetables galore and all the trimmings, followed by Christmas pudding and custard. There were home-made mince pies and sherry to finish off with, but Harry so wanted to see Ada. He had missed her so much. Percy suggested taking his brother's car and calling in at Ada's cottage. 'If that's alright with you, Albert?' asked Harry.

'That's fine by me, Harry, but don't stay out all night, your bride needs her beauty sleep,' he said laughing.

The wedding day had arrived, and the ceremony was taking place at 11am. Ada had agreed to go to Aldershot married quarters after their marriage, but they would stay at the Bridges on their wedding night and for the week, all three of them leaving together for Aldershot afterwards.

This was going to be a huge upheaval for Ada as she had always lived in the same area, and he was taking her to some unknown part of the country. She could be on her own a lot of the time and Harry hoped she would be okay. As his wife, he wanted her by his side, but he did worry for her.

Harry was being married in his Army uniform. Louisa had kindly washed and pressed it for him, and Percy was dressed likewise. She looked at them both with pride and then proceeded to get ready herself. Dorothy had a small bump now, which she wanted to show to the world and Frederick, her husband was tastefully dressed for the occasion in dark brown trousers and a tight fitting blazer.

They all set off for Clutton Registry Office. Ada and her family were already there. Ethel Mary was ordering the family about as usual. Alice, Blanche and Gladys were there. Ernest, Phyllis and Dorothy were sat on a bench seat fidgeting, to Ethel Mary's annoyance. She had managed to find a babysitter to look after the twins and baby Roland. Archibald sat quietly in the corner, letting Ethel Mary carry on with her organising.

Ada looked lovely. She wore a smart grey suit that fitted perfectly, topped off with a small hat with netting at the front. The suit was made of pure wool and looked really warm for the time of year. The skirt sat below the knee and the jacket buttoned up the front. It had large lapels and a cloth belt around the waist. Ada's shoes were black, with a small kitten heel and a strap across the front.

She carried a small bouquet of lavender and pink chrysanthemums.

'You look lovely,' Harry said. He couldn't believe Ada was actually going to be his wife. A year ago, getting married was the last thing on his mind. He had never really had a proper girlfriend before Ada. It had only taken one, Ada, and she was stood there beside him. He couldn't quite take it in.

'You're not too bad yourself,' Ada replied.

The ceremony took no longer than twenty minutes, for which Harry was grateful. He had never been so nervous, his hands were shaking badly. The journey on the ship to Germany seemed easy compared to this. The Registry Office was decorated with flowers and was clean. The Registrar was an elderly gentleman, with a clear concise voice who seemed eager to get on with his duties in readiness for the next couple waiting. After signing the register everyone shook hands and congratulated them and they all headed for Windsor Cottage.

Ethel Mary had put on a good display of food and everyone ate heartily. There were sandwiches filled with turkey, beef and cheese. Home-made scones and small Victoria sponges adorned the table. Tomatoes, lettuce and onions from the garden were displayed separately in dishes.

The centre of the table was dominated by a wedding cake, made by Ada's sisters. It was delicately iced in white with pink and purple flowers and silver balls intricately placed around it. A silver bell stood on the top of the cake. There was ale and wine available, though Ethel Mary's eager eyes told him not to drink too much! On return from Germany, with excitement after reading Ada's letter, Harry had drank a few too many ales and been called to the Sergeant's office, charged with drunkenness. It was noted on his Army records. Not good!

Ada told Harry that she had arranged the night at a local pub where they did bed and breakfast. It was her surprise to him and he was pleased. Ada needed to pack her things ready for Aldershot, but she had plenty of time to do that. They had a full week before then.

The Bridges headed for home, the Houses were clearing up the kitchen and Ada was getting her travel bag for the evening in the bed and breakfast. Ethel Mary approached him looking rather severe.

'You will look after her, Harry, won't you?' she said in a stern but caring voice.

'Of course I will,' Harry replied. 'I love her.'

Archibald shook his hand and they both headed out of the cottage for their first night as Mr and Mrs Tracey.

Harry awoke at 6am the next morning. Ada was asleep by his side and he gave her a quick kiss on the lips and smiled. Ada woke up and looked at the clock, 'It's only 6 o'clock,' she said.

'Sorry, I'm used to getting up at this time, even while on leave,' he answered. 'What would you like to do with this week?'

'I'd like to visit your mother and family, if that's possible. I would also like to go to Frome, look around the shops and walk around Victoria Park. It's lovely there,' Ada said.

Harry was slightly taken aback, he hadn't realised Ada wanted to meet his family.

'We could catch the train to Stratford upon Avon in a few days, visit mother and my uncles. I'm sure one of them could put us up for the night,' Harry said and then became very quiet.

'Are you okay, Harry?' asked Ada. He looked in a complete daze.

'Yes, I'm fine. I was just thinking how lucky I am to have you.' He gave her another kiss and walked out of the room to visit the 'little boy's room' which was situated in the long passageway a few steps away.

When he returned, Harry suggested going to Frome that afternoon, dropping their bags off at the Bridges and seeing if Albert would let them use his car.

'Okay, I'd like that,' Ada replied.

As they left the bed and breakfast, both well fed, life seemed perfect. Harry didn't want to think past the week, it was as if he was dreaming.

Louisa welcomed them and congratulated them once again. She asked what plans they had for the day and Harry asked if Albert would mind them using the car for the afternoon.

'I'm sure he won't mind. Have a lovely afternoon. Wrap yourself up, Ada. You don't want to catch a chill out there.'

Louisa was a plump lady, completely the opposite to Ada. She wasn't tall, standing just 5ft 3ins in height. Her face was long and wrinkled, with grey coming through her dark brown hair and she had dimples in her cheeks. She didn't have a bad bone in her body.

She often spoke about her husband, George. He had died six years previous at just 45 years old. 'George would have liked you,' she said to Harry, 'and been so happy for you both yesterday.'

The weather was cold, but dry. Ada put her coat, hat and gloves on, turning up the coat's fur collar to keep her snug. Harry was dressed for the weather, though he was used to all weathers from working on the farm and serving in the Army.

Frome wasn't a great distance from Farmborough and Harry parked the car near the shops. They both did a lot of window shopping and Harry noticed Ada looking at a brooch in the jewellers shop window.

'Do you like that, Ada?' he asked.

'Yes I do, but you can't afford it,' she replied. Ada hadn't known what he could afford, if she was honest.

'Let's go and ask how much it is.' It was in the shape of a daisy, with tiny white diamonds around the petals and a large emerald gem in the centre. Harry placed it against the lapel of her coat. 'It looks lovely on you,' he commented.

Fifteen minutes later Ada walked out of the jewellers with the brooch attached to her lapel. 'Thank you so much, Harry,' she said kissing his cheek. 'I will treasure it.'

'You're worth it, Mrs Tracey,' Harry said proudly. He loved her so much.

After looking around a few more shops and picking up a sandwich each at the bakers shop, they headed for Victoria Park, finding a bench to sit on to eat them. They ate their food in silence, looking around at the flowers in bloom, arranged prettily around the huge lawn. The Hibiscus shrubs dominated the borders, neatly arranged in colours of white, red and orange. Evergreens separated the shrubs from the chrysanthemums and cyclamen. Now and then Ada could spot a red amaryllis poking its head out.

There was a sort of summer house erected in the centre of the park. Somewhere to sit and while away the time, relaxing and delighting in the views. They often had bands playing in the park.

People would sit around and listen, applauding and singing along with the music. The summer months were the best times to be there, with the sun in the sky and the bands playing. Complete relaxation after a hard day's work or on a Saturday afternoon. Harry promised to return with Ada again then.

There were a few people walking in the park, some walking their dogs. They varied from children with their mothers, couples walking arm in arm, and older ones sat on the benches enjoying the space and the views, looking so relaxed.

'Can you imagine us like that couple in years to come?' Harry said to Ada. He was pointing to an elderly couple sat on a bench holding hands and snuggling up to one another.

'Who knows?' Ada replied and laughed. 'I love this park, Harry.'

'I quite like it myself,' he replied.

They left the park and headed towards Albert's car. It was a lovely afternoon and a day they would never forget. Harry picked a flower from the border around the lawn and gave it to her. She took it and laughed.

'We'd better run,' she said. 'We'll have the park keeper after us.' They both ran to the car, smiling.

CHAPTER THREE

Two days later they were on the train, heading for Stratford upon Avon, famous for William Shakespeare and his wife, Anne Hathaway. It was about a three hour journey to Stratford upon Avon, but Harry pointed to famous locations he knew about along the way.

Ada hadn't ventured farther than Bath and Bristol in her lifetime and was fascinated with the journey. Endless greenery, fields and hills led to towns, historic buildings and areas the 1st World War had ruined. These areas had still not been repaired. Bombed and derelict houses without windows, doors and roofless, scattered helplessly around. 'Can we buy that one and live in it?' she asked. Ada had been pointing to a detached cottage in desperate need of repair. 'It so looks like it needs to be lived in,' Ada said quietly.

'It's a shame I've enlisted for seven years as a regular in the Army,' Harry said. 'We can't really find a permanent place to live, I don't know where I will be sent to whilst I'm serving.'

'It's okay, Harry, we'll manage,' Ada replied.

Harry purchased two cups of tea from the trolley. The taste was slightly weak, somewhat like dishwater. It was, nevertheless, hot and drinkable. The journey came to an end, Harry picked up the suitcase and his backpack and walked towards the exit at the far end of the platform.

Ada followed slowly. 'We will need to take a bus to mother's, it's not far,' he said. Stratford upon Avon was a large town and Ada was mesmerised by the size of it. Midsomer Norton was so small in comparison, minute in fact!

'How do you find your way around here?' she asked.

'I didn't come here often, I prefer the quieter areas, like you.' Harry stopped and asked if she wanted to look around the shops before getting on the bus.

'No,' she replied. 'Let's get on the bus, I want to meet your family before it gets too dark.'

They reached Martha's cottage around 3pm. The vegetable garden looked slightly sparse and hadn't much in it at the moment. By April the shoots would be appearing through the soil for the coming season. There was a small grassed area with a metal bench to sit on and the garden was enclosed by a stone wall, painted in white.

Martha was digging potatoes when they walked through the gate. She had heard the gate open and stopped what she was doing. She turned and wiped her hands in her apron.

'Hello, Mother. Meet Ada,' Harry said and smiled. His face was glowing with pride.

'Pleased to meet you, Ada,' she answered. 'Why didn't you let me know you were coming?' she scowled at Harry.

'Sorry, but Ada wanted to meet you and I've only a week's leave before returning to Aldershot.' They all entered the cottage and Martha put the kettle on the Aga. Harry returned to the vegetable garden and brought the bucket of potatoes in that Martha had dug.

'Thank you, Harry. Did the wedding go well?' she asked Ada.

'It was lovely, thank you. I so wanted to meet Harry's family and see where he lives.'

They were all sat around the kitchen table drinking their tea, when Millie and the boys came running into the cottage. Albert was now 16 and working in Ebrington with his father.

Millie's face froze and then she walked over to Harry and gave him a hug. 'This is Millie, Ada. My bestest sister in the world,' he laughed. 'Millie, this is Ada, my wife.'

Millie wasn't sure what to say, but surprising herself she gave Ada a big hug, too.

John Henry was 2 years old now and very busy. He had woke up as Millie and the boys had entered the cottage. Millie lifted him from his cot and placed him on the kitchen floor. He was walking and talking now, and as he looked at Millie he spoke.

'Millie, Millie,' he said and turned to look at Ada.

'What's your name?' Ada asked him.

'John Eenery,' he answered stressing the "Eenery."

'My name is Ada. Can you say Ada?'

John Henry looked at her and decided to run around the kitchen table. He held his arms up to Millie, wanting to be picked up.

'He's gorgeous, Martha,' Ada commented. She adored her younger siblings.

Ada offered to help as Martha started to wash the potatoes, but was ordered to go into the sitting room and relax. Harry remained in the kitchen with his mother. 'Can you put us up for the night, Mother?' he asked her. 'We'd like to visit uncles' Richard and John and head back to Farmborough tomorrow evening. I promised Ada I would show her where I lived and worked. I'd like to take a walk around Shipston on Stour, too.'

Millie was playing with John Henry and had overheard the conversation.

'Ada can sleep with me, Mother, and Harry can sleep in with Albert,' she said. 'Please, Mother, it would be nice to have them here.'

'Okay,' Martha answered and Millie smiled.

Millie went into the sitting room and told Ada about their sleeping arrangements. Harry followed her, looked at her and apologised. 'That's fine, Millie. We can have a girlie chat tonight,' Ada said. 'I have three sisters around my age. We often have our chats in the bedroom.'

Millie was so looking forward to it, and Ada didn't want to disappoint her. Frank, Harry's stepfather, and his brother, Albert, had walked into the cottage at about 5 o'clock. Food was almost ready. Ada was still in the sitting room talking to the boys, Frank junior and Richard. They were asking about her siblings and parents, which she had filled them in on. She told them about her brother, Jim, and her mother, Lily. They both seemed interested, and Ada asked them about their school and their education.

Frank senior introduced himself and congratulated her on their marriage. Albert looked slightly awkward, but said hello and headed for his bedroom to change his clothes. Dinner was ready and Harry had made the tea and placed the full cups on the table. Ada sat next to Harry and they all ate in silence.

Martha had prepared a beef stew with dumplings and plenty of boiled potatoes. Crusty bread was placed in the centre of the table for everyone to take as needed. 'I haven't prepared a pudding. I'm sorry, John Henry is so busy these days. I didn't have time.' She placed a bowl of fruit on the table and everyone helped themselves.

With the dishes done, the kitchen table prepared ready for breakfast the next morning, they all settled in the sitting room. John Henry was asleep in his cot. 'He's getting too big for it,' Martha remarked. 'We need to get another bed put in Richard and Frank junior's room for him.' she said loud enough to be heard, and looking at Frank.

All the boys had gone to their bedrooms, including Albert. He had an early start in the morning.

Millie was sat on the floor next to Ada, and Frank and Harry were settled on the small settee. Martha moved towards the vacant chair near the fireplace.

The sitting room was small, with a lit fire in the stone fireplace. There wasn't room for more than the two chairs and the small settee in it, but it was cosy and Ada liked it. The window looked out onto a field belonging to the nearby farm. Horses were grazing and running around. There was a newborn foal walking close to its mother.

'What a lovely view, Martha,' Ada remarked. 'That baby foal looks so cute.'

The farmer bred horses and sold them to anyone who needed them, mainly farmers for ploughing their fields. A few were sold for riding, the families with money to spare! Frank put some more logs on the fire and picked up the newspaper to read. He bought one daily on his way to work.

Millie was reading her school book and showing Ada what she needed to learn. Harry and his mother spoke about the farm, his uncles and the Army. Uncles' John and Richard weren't getting any younger and were struggling with their health. Martha didn't know how much longer they would be able to manage.

'Can't they get more hired help, Mother?' Harry asked. There had to be plenty of boys needing the work and financially his uncles could afford it. 'I will have a discreet word with them tomorrow.'

Ada joined in the conversation. 'I'm looking forward to meeting your uncles, Harry,' she said. 'I wish I'd known your grandparents.' Harry had spoken so highly about them, especially his grandmother.

'I wish you'd known them too,' he replied.

Millie started to yawn, so Ada asked Harry if he minded them retiring to their beds. Harry gave her a quick peck on the cheek and carried her suitcase to Millie's room.

'Don't go wearing yourself out with Millie's questions, Ada,' he said and winked at her. He wished them both sweet dreams and headed back down the stairs.

Harry wasn't long retiring either. They had both had a long day, with a lot of travelling. He was glad they had made the journey though, and Ada had met his mother and his brothers and sister.

Such a lot had happened since May, he could hardly believe it himself.

They both woke early the next morning. Millie had washed and dressed and was eating her breakfast at the table when Ada walked into the kitchen. 'Richard, Frank, hurry up will you,' Martha shouted up the stairs. 'The boys are always rushing for school,' she said to Ada.

Frank senior and Albert had already left for work, and John Henry was sat in his highchair eating his egg and soldiers. 'Would you like a boiled egg, Ada?' she asked.

'Yes please, but I will do it. I'm used to being busy.'

Harry walked into the kitchen as Ada was putting her egg into the pan and added another two for him. She filled the kettle and placed it on the Aga. 'How did you sleep, Ada?' he asked.

'Fine thank you, how about you?' Ada smiled at him.

'Likewise,' he answered and walked over to John Henry who was making a lovely mess with his egg.

After breakfast they both caught the bus to Hidcote Boyce, Ebrington, to visit Harry's uncles. Martha refused the invitation to join them, as she had plenty to do in the cottage. 'I will have tea ready for you both before you leave,' she said.

Uncles' Richard and John were in the far field checking on the sheep and repairing a fence that had fallen down. Joe was checking on another field and Rose was busy digging the kitchen garden. As Harry and Ada walked through the gate, Rose jumped. 'You startled me,' she said.

Harry gave her a big hug and introduced Ada. 'How lovely to meet you,' she said and walked into the kitchen to put the kettle on the fire to boil. 'How's the Army, Harry? We've all missed you here.'

'Everything's okay, Rose. I've been to Germany and I'm due back to Aldershot in a few days,' he replied.

Harry remarked on how well Rose looked and she smiled. 'You've got a man friend, haven't you?' he said laughing. Rose's face turned bright red. She was a shy girl and Harry was always winding her up.

'Don't tease her, Harry,' Ada said to him.

Rose walked them both to the far field after their tea. His uncles stopped what they were doing and introduced themselves to Ada. Richard was out of breath and glad of the rest. Harry suggested employing another farm labourer and Richard said he had been thinking about it, as he had realised things were getting more difficult. Joe was now walking towards them and Harry shook hands with his friend and working colleague. Rose blushed as Joe looked at her.

'I see!' Harry said. 'When is the wedding?'

After spending a few hours at the farm, Ada and Harry walked into Shipston on Stour. It was a long walk, but they took it steadily, stopping first at St Eadburgha's Church in Ebrington, where Harry entered the churchyard. He walked directly to his grandmother's grave and Ada followed. 'This is my wife, Ada, Grandmother,' he said looking at her headstone. 'Isn't she lovely? I'm the happiest man in the world.'

Ada blushed and bowed her head. Harry then pointed to two other headstones and told Ada who they were. 'Grandfather is buried beside my grandmother, Ada. That's where I want to be when we are gone, beside you.'

Ada became quite emotional and tried to stop the tears from showing. Harry gave her a huge hug and kissed her. They walked into the church and Ada lit a candle. They both sat down and silently prayed. He took Ada's hand in his and they stayed for what seemed ages, before leaving the church and continuing their journey.

Shipston on Stour was a small, pretty town with one main street and a few roads off of it. The shops, pubs and tea room were mainly situated on the High Street and Sheep Street. There was a church at the end of the main street and Harry entered it and sat down, while Ada looked around at the coloured windows decorating it. There was something about looking inside churches that seemed so relaxing.

After having tea and cakes in the tea room, they both headed for the bus to Blockley. Harry pointed out his school, the workhouse where he was born and the White Bear and Ebrington Arms where he would visit on occasions for his two pints of cider.

Tea was almost ready when they returned to Martha's cottage. She had prepared a salad and had chickens roasting in the oven. 'I've prepared it early,' she said. 'Frank and Albert can have theirs when they get home. Millie and the boys will be home soon.'

Millie hugged them both and promised to write to Harry. The boys waved and Martha wished them both well. Ada kissed John Henry. He was sound asleep and she didn't want to wake him.

They caught the bus back to Stratford upon Avon and then the train back to Farmborough. They both slept on the way back. It had been a long and busy few days.

There were only two days left before the three of them would be heading for Aldershot and the Army barracks. Ada needed to pack a full suitcase ready for the move, so Harry spent the next day with Percy in the local pub. Percy asked about his visit to his family, and commented on how happy he looked.

'I am, Percy,' he said. 'Perhaps you should find someone too! There's a lady out there for you.'

'I haven't found her yet, Harry. I'm happy to be here for mother for a while longer.'

Harry visited Ada's home that evening to collect her and her suitcase. Gladys, Alice and Blanche wished her luck and Ernest hugged her so tight, he didn't want to let her go. 'Please don't go, Ada,' he pleaded. 'It won't be the same without you here.'

Ada reassured him, saying she would visit soon. She looked around the cottage for one last time, said goodbye to her stepmother and her father and promised to write.

After spending a lovely evening in with the Bridges, sat around the roaring coal fire in the large kitchen, Ada and Harry retired for the night. They thanked Louisa for everything she had done for them. They needed to go shopping for a few essentials in the morning and had decided to go for a long walk in the afternoon. Harry loved walking and Ada was quite happy to accompany him.

The day had come for them all to travel to Aldershot. It was approximately two hours journey from Farmborough and they were travelling by train. They wanted to leave early to ensure getting to their destination in plenty of time. They all said their goodbyes and headed for the station.

Percy and Harry's belongings were packed neatly in their rucksacks. Ada had a largish suitcase and her handbag. She had dressed comfortably for the journey, wearing a loose knee length skirt and a blouse with a tied bow at the front. It had long sleeves and was pale blue in colour. She wore flat shoes for comfort and her coat with the fur collar for warmth.

Once again, Ada was mesmerised with the views from the window. The landscape was beautiful.

Hills, rivers and large towns passed by quickly. Before they knew it, the three of them were standing at the gate to Aldershot barracks. After reporting to the officers at the reception building, they were driven to the North Camp and the Blenheim barracks.

Percy was shown to the dormitories whilst Ada and Harry were directed to the marriage quarters and the bungalows nearby. Blenheim barracks were named in commemoration of the battle of Blenheim on 13th August 1704, they were told by the Private who was escorting them.

Aldershot barracks was a huge place, divided into North and South Camps and numerous named dormitories. You needed transport to get around it. It was a town in itself, bigger than Midsomer Norton. The barracks held a school, hospital, a reservoir, sewerage works, gas works and a power station.

There was a shop situated near the married quarters and a laundry room for the wives to use. Ada felt out of her depth. Percy headed for the dormitory. 'I will see you both later,' he said.

Harry was carrying Ada's suitcase and handed her the key to the bungalow. 'We are in number 21,' he said.

They found the bungalow and Ada turned the key, opening the door. 'Wait a minute,' Harry said and dropped the suitcase and his rucksack, picked her up and carried her over the threshold.

'You are such a romantic, Harry,' she said and kissed him.

The bungalow was very sparse and small. There was a bedroom, sitting area and kitchen and a small room housing a toilet and a sink. Furniture was minimal, but adequate. The bungalow needed an uplift, some colour, flowers etc. It needed to feel like home. Ada would turn it into one. A home for her and Harry.

Percy and Harry reported for duty the next morning, leaving Ada alone. She looked around the bungalow. It needed bright curtains, cushions and flowers. She'd needed to go shopping. It was time to check out the shop and the area. Armed with her shopping bag and her purse, Ada put her coat on and walked to the shop.

She purchased groceries for the evening meal and found curtain material and a coloured cotton to make cushions. Sewing thread, scissors and padding for the cushions were also found. It was slightly extravagant, but Ada needed to make a home for them. She found a bunch of pink chrysanthemums and bought them, too.

Back at the bungalow Ada busied herself with cleaning. It needed a good clean from ceiling to floor and she was used to housework. She needed a bath afterwards, so pulled the tin bath from the one large cupboard in the bungalow into the kitchen area.

After heating saucepans of water on the gas cooker, she pulled the curtains together, locked the doors and filled the bath with the hot water, then added some cold. Half an hour later, and she was feeling clean and refreshed. Emptying the bath and replacing it in the cupboard, she then started to prepare food for the evening meal.

It was a sunny day, very cold, but dry. Ada washed a few items of underwear in the kitchen sink and hung them on the washing line in the back garden. The garden was small and separated by fences from the bungalows either side. It wasn't very private at all.

There were clothes to be put away in the wardrobe and drawers, but she had decided that she'd done enough for the day and would start again in the morning. Her suitcase was quite full and some items would need ironing again.

It was now the 4th January and they had been married for a little over a week. They hadn't really had any time alone since their wedding night. Ada was looking forward to their evening meal that night and had prepared a casserole, which she had put in the gas oven. She had purchased a tin loaf from the shop, along with butter, jam, eggs, milk, tea and sugar.

Whilst the casserole was cooking, Ada switched on the radio and settled herself on the settee. She looked at the materials she had bought for her curtains and cushions and she was pleased with her purchases; she had plenty to occupy herself in the coming weeks.

Harry walked into the bungalow that evening. The casserole was almost ready and Ada was slicing bread and placing it on a large plate. 'Something smells good,' he said as he walked over to her and gave her a kiss. 'How have you been today?'

'I've been keeping myself busy, Harry. I've bought material to brighten the place up and given it a proper clean through,' she replied excitedly. 'I found the bath in that large cupboard and had a lovely soak. How has your day been?'

'Interesting,' Harry offered. 'I will tell you after our meal.'

They ate their meal, Ada washed the dishes and Harry sat down in the one chair in the bungalow. There was a small fireplace, but neither of them had managed to purchase any coal or firewood to light it and Harry promised to get some the next day.

Ada sat down on the settee and looked at Harry. 'Well, what is it you need to tell me, Harry?' she asked.

'I can't fool you, can I? I've been moved to the 2nd Battalion Regiment and I'm being posted to India on the 23rd of this month,' he said.

Ada was numb and speechless. They only had 19 more days together before he left. 'I can't believe it,' she eventually said. 'How long will you be gone?'

'I don't know, but going by the conversation we had, it could be years. It will take two weeks to get there on the ship, so there's no chance of leave.' Harry looked at Ada with sad puppy eyes. 'I'm so sorry, if you want to go back home I will understand.'

'No, we've still got 19 days together. Let's make the most of it.' Ada made a cup of tea for them both and they retired to the bedroom together.

CHAPTER FOUR

Harry was up early the next morning. Neither of them had slept much at all. They had spoken whilst lying in bed, both devastated about being parted so soon. 'I don't know what to say, Ada, this was a complete surprise to me. I would never have taken you away from your family if I'd known.' Harry said full of remorse.

'I know you wouldn't have, Harry, none of this is your fault,' Ada replied. 'I'm going to find some work around here, to keep me busy while you are away. I'm sure I can find something, and make some friends.'

'That's my girl,' Harry said and kissed her before leaving the bungalow to report for duty. 'I will bring some coal and firewood home with me. Have a good day, I will see you tonight.'

George V and Queen Mary were on the throne. They were the reigning Emperor and Empress of India. There was an Indian General Election due soon between the Central Legislative Assembly and the Provincial Assemblies.

Extra help was needed from the Army in case of any issues arising from the election. It was normal procedure, but training in India was also needed after the near disasters of Waziristan in 1919. Soldiers died, were wounded and many were still missing.

It was felt training had to recommence and from 1920 skills-at-arms, self-reliance, vigilance and personal judgement were put into focus.

Short lived Afghan invasion of British India in 1919 was quickly repulsed by the Army in India but the ensuing tribal rising in Waziristan (where various militias raised to Police territory had mutinied) was a far more difficult proposition. Heavy casualties were inflicted on the raw, ill-administered areas of the North-West Frontier Province and Afghanistan posed an insistent threat to the security of British India.

All Harry knew was that he would be based in Jhansi and had no confirmed dates for returning to England. 'A few years, possibly,' the Sergeant replied when he had asked the previous day. They were sailing on the 23rd and would arrive in India two weeks later, something Harry wasn't looking forward to. He didn't travel too well on water.

He felt his world was collapsing around him, but he had to be strong for Ada. She was his wife and he didn't want her upset. 'She will be fine,' he said quietly to himself. Percy had also been informed of his posting to India. Harry felt happier knowing his friend would be there with him. Percy had needed to write to his mother, as it would be a long time before they saw each other again. He would also miss seeing Dorothy's baby born. The baby was due around May.

Harry made a mental note to write to his mother, too. The thought of not seeing Ada or Millie for two years was now dawning on him, but he was in the Army and had to accept it. Letters would take longer to reach each other, but it was still a way of contact and Harry clung to that thought.

Ada was busy sewing her new curtains when Harry walked into the bungalow. There was a cottage pie cooking in the oven. Biscuits were cooling on the table and a Victoria sponge looked very inviting, almost too inviting. It had looked delicious.

'You've been busy,' he said, 'I'm starving.'

'You can keep your hands off that cake until after our meal, Harry, and the biscuits are still cooling down,' she said with a hint of authority in her voice.

Harry placed the firewood and coal next to the hearth and took a newspaper from his pocket. He put the kettle on the gas ring before kneeling down to prepare the fire. 'I can do that,' Ada said putting her sewing down on the settee.

'I will do it, you can make the tea.'

'Deal,' replied Ada with a smile.

Ada made the tea, checked the oven and placed the saucepan of vegetables on another gas ring. She cut slices of sponge and placed them on small plates, handing one to Harry. 'I'm sure you will eat all of your tea,' she said to him laughing. Harry took the plate and the tea, demolishing the cake in minutes.

She had put all her clothes away in the wardrobe and drawers, ironed what was needed and generally tidied up. She had to keep busy. A letter had been written to her father and stepmother, telling them of Harry's posting and asking how everyone was.

She had also written to Dorothy informing her too, telling her of her worries of being alone for so long, and having no friends in Aldershot. These were things Ada couldn't tell her stepmother or her father. Dorothy was her best friend, she could tell her anything.

After seeing the envelopes on the table waiting to be posted, Harry was reminded to write to his mother. 'I will do it soon,' he told Ada. 'there's plenty of time.'

They ate their meal, washed the dishes and sat on the settee in front of the fire. They listened to the music on the radio, cuddling up to one another; neither of them mentioned the oncoming post to India all night.

The bungalow was looking like a new home now, and Ada was more than satisfied with the results. The new curtains brightened the place up and the cushions made the settee more comfortable. Ada managed to purchase a small rug to put in front of the hearth, and a new eiderdown for their bed. She hadn't seen much of the neighbours at all, though she'd heard a baby crying next door, but hadn't actually seen either the mother or the baby. Ada had thought about knocking on the door, but had wanted Harry all to herself until he was posted to India. She didn't have time for others at the moment.

Ada cooked, cleaned, sewed and knitted items for Dorothy's baby. She kept herself to herself. Evenings were spent enjoying each other's company. She hadn't ventured out of the barracks. The farthest she had been was to the shop, and to the little library in the barracks. Books were swapped after reading them, so there was always different material to keep her interested.

Three days before Harry's leaving date, he was given free time to do as he pleased. 'What would you like to do, Ada? These three days are yours. Your wish is my command!' he said jokingly and bowed.

'Thank you, kind sir,' she replied laughing. 'I do love you, Harry. I would like to see outside the barracks, and the towns and villages around it. I need to know the areas around here, so I can look for work.'

'Okay. We will start early tomorrow morning.' Harry answered.

They both rose early, dressed carefully for the weather and caught the bus to Reigate, about forty minutes away. Reigate was a town constructed below a castle. The idea was for it to act as a focal point for trade and commerce, to increase the wealth of the manor owned by William De Warenne II, a knight of William the Conqueror.

The castle later fell to ruin during the reign of King James and was demolished in 1648. All that remained now was a mound with a dry moat and underground caves, which were thought to be dungeons.

Reigate was situated at the foot of the North Downs, had two parks (Priory Park and Reigate Park) and a Priory. The Priory was owned by the Howard family, including the Lord High Admiral who defeated the Spanish Armada.

Ada loved historic towns and looking at the architecture of the buildings. The town centre wasn't that big, but was more than adequate. They both wandered in and out of the shops, bought a few grocery items and household goods and took a stroll around Reigate Park.

There was a small cafe situated outside the park, so they had dinner and a cup of tea there. Harry told Ada that he would leave her money to live on and would ensure she had access to his pay via the Army barracks. She didn't want to think about it, but knew she had to.

'That's okay, Harry, I'm sure I will be fine.'

They both had onion soup and a sandwich to follow. 'I didn't know you liked onion soup, I will have to make some at home before you leave,' she said trying to lighten the conversation.

After more window shopping, strolling around Priory Park and taking in the remains of the medieval castle, they caught the bus and headed for home.

The next day was taken up visiting Guildford (the town of the ford) which is located in a gap in the North Downs, where the river Wey breaks through the hills. An ancient trackway followed the North Downs and descended to a ford, a little to the South of the town centre.

Guildford was left in the will of King Alfred to his nephew Ethelwold. Ethelwold later revolted against Alfred's successor and as a result lost his property.

They both walked up the High Street and entered the historic Angel Inn, a coaching Inn with records dating back to the 16th century. Beneath the Inn lay a 13th century undercroft. Rooms within were named after people who had reputedly stayed there. Sir Francis Drake, Oliver Cromwell, Lord Nelson and his mistress Lady Emma Hamilton and Jane Austen.

The front of the Inn led to a courtyard. Ada was fascinated by the history of the building and read every piece of information relating to it. 'It's a lovely building, Harry, don't you think?' Ada said excitedly. 'I can just imagine what it was like living here then.'

'Yes, it is. Shall we have a drink in the courtyard?'

'I would like that. A large coffee for a change, I think.' Ada was immersed in the moment. The Guildhall was a Tudor building to which a 17th century facade had been added in 1683.

There was a clock overhanging the street. 'Look at the detail in the clock, Harry. It's so intricate,' Ada commented. She felt like a child on a school outing, there was so much to look at.

At the top of the High Street there was a bookshop, Thomas Thorp's bookshop. Ada walked inside, picked up a few books of interest and purchased them. North Street was lined with butchers and fishmongers. 'Would you like some fish for your tea, Harry?' she asked. Harry nodded and Ada pointed to two large pieces of haddock, paid for them and put them in her shopping bag.

Finally they looked around St Mary's Church. It was built on a slope and the inside was on three levels. It had a Saxon tower and Norman arches and windows. 'Beautiful,' Ada said and continued walking around the back of the church.

This led to the Mill Pond, a famous pond painted by artists. They both sat and admired the scenery, whilst eating a teacake purchased from one of the baker shops. 'I've loved today, Harry. Guildford is pretty. Reigate was too. Thank you for the past two days.'

'You're welcome, Ada. Are you ready to go home?'

'Yes.' Ada replied and they headed for the bus stop to take them back to Aldershot and the barracks.

The last day had arrived far too quickly. Both Ada and Harry slept in, which was very unusual for Harry. The sun was shining through the bedroom window. Ada turned to Harry. 'We had better get up, there's a lot to do today.' she said.

'Another half an hour won't hurt. I'm comfortable here. It's nice to totally relax for a change.' Ada agreed and they lay in bed with their arms wrapped around each other, saying nothing. It felt so peaceful, no noise outside except for the chirping of the birds overhead. They had obviously woken up too, enjoying the sunshine peeping through the clouds.

'What do you need to take with you, Harry?' Ada asked. 'You can write to your mother while I pack for you,' she said.

'Okay, I do seem to have been putting it off. I will make a list of things I need. It all has to fit into my backpack.'

They ate their breakfast, drank their tea and dealt with the jobs needed doing. Harry's backpack was sorted and Martha's letter had been written, waiting to be posted. Harry explained the procedure for Ada to draw money from his Army account, after handing her a large amount of cash to keep her going. She didn't want to listen, but knew she had to.

'I am going to try to work, Harry. Any monies we can save will help towards a house when you are back home. I don't want to live here permanently. Who knows, we could have children and need something bigger.' Ada offered logically.

Ada secretly hoped that she may be pregnant. A child would keep her busy whilst Harry was away. Somebody to look after that was part of both of them. Harry looked very serious and commented, 'You've got a good point there. I will leave the finances to you. I was never brilliant with money, anyway.'

Ada started preparing the onion soup she had promised to make for Harry. She baked a Victoria sponge and a few biscuits, then settled on the settee listening to the radio. Harry sat beside her reading the newspaper. 'You're not going to India to fight, are you Harry?' Ada asked, a little concerned.

'I'm not sure what I'll be doing, the Sergeant sounded very vague about it all. I'm dreading the sailing to India, it's a longer trip than I had to Germany. I hope our letters won't take long to reach us, Ada. You will be okay, won't you?' he asked with the same concern.

'I'll be fine, promise me you will look after yourself. I'm planning on going to see my father and stepmother nearer the time Dorothy's baby is due, that way there will be plenty to write about. I can call in to see Louisa, too.'

On that note, Ada got up from the settee and set the table. They both sat down for dinner and Harry commented on the onion soup. 'This is better than my grandmother's, Ada, you're a good cook. I did well to pick you!'

'Did you want to eat the soup, or wear it?' she said with mischief in her voice, and Harry laughed. The mischievous grin she had loved so much, emerged through his laughter. 'What were your grandmother's other Christian names, Harry?' she then asked.

'Her name was Jane, that's all I knew and my grandfather was George. I don't think either of them had any other Christian names. Why do you ask?'

'I was just curious, that's all,' she replied.

Harry left the bungalow the next morning, picked up his backpack and said goodbye to Ada.

She tried to hide her sadness, but couldn't stop the tears from falling. 'Don't cry, Ada, you will have me starting too! I will write a letter to you on the ship, I'm not sure when you will receive it though,' Harry said. 'I love you so much, Ada. Take care of yourself. I will be back as soon as I can.'

Ada waved as he reported for duty. She could see Percy waiting for him and watched them walk away together. At least he had his friend with him. They were inseparable and Ada was so glad they were venturing India together. They would look after each other, she knew.

On returning to the bungalow, Ada noticed the letter Harry had written to his mother still on the table. She picked it up, put on her coat and headed for the postbox, after putting a stamp on it. She visited the library and the shop, picked up a few groceries and headed back home. 'I suppose I'd better start mixing with the neighbours,' she said to herself. 'No time like the present!'

Ada knocked on the bungalow next door and a young girl, looking no older than 17 answered. 'Hello, I'm Ada, your neighbour. I wanted to introduce myself. I've heard a baby crying, how old is your child?'

'She's 6 months old. I'm Sarah, please come in.' Ada followed her into the bungalow. It was identical to hers in size, but cluttered with baby necessities and looked a lot smaller. 'Florence is asleep at the moment. She's in the bedroom if you'd like to see her.'

Ada followed Sarah and reached over the cot, looking at the baby. 'She's lovely, Sarah. Have you lived here long?' she asked.

'Almost a year, I came here whilst pregnant with Florence. My husband is in Germany at the moment. He's due home in about a year,' she replied.

'How do you cope? Harry is off to India today, he could be away for two years. I'm dreading it!'

'You'll be okay. I'm grateful to have Florence to look after. I don't see a lot of wives around here. They keep themselves to themselves,' Sarah said. 'Would you like a cup of tea, Ada?'

'Yes please, if it's not too much trouble for you. I don't want to put you out at all.'

'It's no trouble. I could do with someone to talk to. Florence is too young to answer me,' she said laughing.

Aldershot had been a shock for Ada, having only ever been used to living in small villages since her birth. Alarm bells should have rung, but she had been concentrating on being a wife to Harry and oblivious to everything else. Whilst he was there, she knew she would be okay.

The 23rd January 1923 had came far too quickly, they had been married less than a month. Harry had been on his way to Jhansi, India for at least two years. Ada pretended well as Harry walked away, ensuring him she would be able to cope until his return, but in reality she was shaking inside, frightened in fact. Two years was a long time and Ada was now in Aldershot, completely alone.

Harry would have understood if she'd returned to her home at Windsor Cottage, but she was stubborn, determined to succeed at all costs. Ada's place was in Aldershot. She was a married woman now and would have to manage somehow, and she did.

Making a friend in the barracks was Ada's life-saver. Sarah was there for her, and Ada was there for Sarah. They would air their concerns, political or otherwise, amidst the numerous cups of tea and coffee they washed down with home-made biscuits. Loneliness could be depressing, but she had Sarah and was able to stop worrying about Harry so much. She missed Harry desperately, but had to find things to occupy herself and her mind.

Sarah and Ada became good friends and neighbours. Sarah was actually 22 years of age, 2 years older than Ada. She looked a lot younger though and Ada was slightly envious. It was strange eating alone, even after such a short time cooking for Harry. She busied herself with cleaning, cooking and knitting cardigans for Dorothy's baby, and had already finished a lemon blanket and a white shawl.

Ada would watch Florence for Sarah to walk to the shop, to save waking her up. She was enjoying her new friend and companion, but missing Harry dreadfully. Weeks passed and Ada discovered that she wasn't pregnant, and was deeply disappointed. Helping take care of Florence had had her hoping a baby had been conceived since their marriage, and a miniature Harry would have been a constant reminder of her husband.

That night in bed, Ada decided it was time to look for work. Time to save some money for when her and Harry were together again. Maybe they would be able to start their family then. Ada was planning their future. She would visit her father and stepmother in a few weeks or so, then concentrate on finding work on her return. 'I need a plan, Sarah,' Ada told her and Sarah agreed.

Ada was on the train heading for Windsor Cottage two weeks later. She still hadn't received a letter from Harry. She had written to him, but had no idea if he had received it. Ada planned to pay a visit to Dorothy and Louisa whilst at her father's and stepmother's, perhaps they could shed some light on India. She had plenty to occupy her in the meantime and put Harry to the back of her mind, though not from her heart.

Her father welcomed her home. Ernest hugged her and the girls asked how she was, and wanted to know everything there was to know about Aldershot and the bungalow. Her stepmother was quiet for a change. She wasn't ordering her about any more, she didn't live there now, but did ask after Harry and his whereabouts.

'Harry is in India. He was posted on the 23rd January and will be there for at least two years. I did write telling you,' Ada informed her. 'He had no idea about his posting when we married, but time will pass quickly, I'm sure,' she explained with hesitation.

Her stepmother gave out a huge sigh. A sigh of disbelief! 'It wasn't his fault. Harry wouldn't have let me leave here if he'd known.' Ada added. Somehow she knew her stepmother didn't believe her.

Dorothy was now huge and glowing. 'You look radiant, Dorothy. How do you feel?' Ada asked.

'I feel great. Tired at times, but otherwise fine. Mother is still feeding me up and worrying about me. The doctor says the baby is a good size and its heartbeat is normal.'

'I'm so glad, Dorothy,' Ada replied.

Ada spent hours telling Dorothy about Harry, Aldershot and the bungalow. She became tearful relaying Harry's posting and her disappointment at not being pregnant herself. Sarah, her new friend was also mentioned and baby Florence.

Dorothy loved the knitted blanket and shawl and commented on the size of the cardigans. 'They are so tiny. I love the hat and bootees too, thank you so much. You knit so well, I'm hopeless myself.'

'You're welcome, Dorothy,' Ada replied.

Frederick, her husband, entered the house after finishing a day's work in the office. He was an accountant for a local accountancy firm. He asked how Harry was and Ada's family, and gave Dorothy a kiss, patting her stomach with his right hand at the same time.

Ada thought about Harry. What would he be doing now?

Harry had managed the travelling from Southampton to India without too much nausea. He seemed to be coping better with his "sea legs" now. He had written several letters whilst on the ship and had posted them in the nearest postbox he had found on reaching India and dry land. He had given Ada an address in Jhansi to write to, and hoped he would receive post from her soon.

Jhansi was a historic city of northern India, located in the region of Bundelkhand on the banks of the Pahuj and Pushpavati river, in the extreme south of the Uttar Pradesh. The Army barracks were positioned on a large plot at the base of a hill and mountainous terrain. It held hundreds of soldiers from India, United Kingdom and the United States of America.

Numerous tanks were parked at the base of the hill of various sizes and colours. There were stables housing horses and mules, used for pulling vehicles for several different purposes. Another building held the arsenal of rifles and guns, guarded by soldiers twenty four hours a day. There was an Army hospital on the grounds too, all of which were surrounded by high secure fencing.

They were both shown to their barracks and dormitory, and were ordered to report to the Sergeant Major to be told of their forthcoming duties. Harry was placed in the stables, to learn how to groom and care for the horses and mules and Percy was to attend to transport duties. They would spend several months there, then change to other duties on the camp, on a rotational basis.

Warning bells rung in Harry's ears. How long was he going to be there? The stables and transport were only two areas of duty. There was combat duty for the front line, rifle and gun training, to name just two more! They both suddenly realised that two years in India could possibly become a lot longer.

'Don't panic, Harry,' Percy said. 'This is our first day, we will find out more in good time.'

Harry was worried though. How would Ada manage? Two years was far too long as it was. He tried to put things to the back of his mind for now.

Food was served in the huge dining area of the dormitory. Harry was starving, but hadn't realised it until then. He ate his food as if he hadn't eaten in days, and drank the tea with a thirst he needed quenching. The rest of the afternoon was free until duty began the next morning.

Harry found the building housing the post, hoping for a letter from Ada and he wasn't disappointed. There were two letters waiting for him.

There was also one for Percy, which he picked up to give to him. He headed back to the dormitory to relax and read his letters, ready for his duties the next day.

The first letter Harry opened was from his mother. She hoped he was okay in India and expressed her concern for Ada, being left alone so early in their marriage. His mother wasn't one to beat about the bush! Millie had now finished her schooling and was helping in the cottage and the garden. His mother announced that she was expecting another child at the end of the year and was suffering from severe morning sickness. His mother was 44 years old now, quite late in years to be pregnant, and needed Millie to help with the domestic chores.

Uncle Richard's health had taken a turn for the worse and his breathing was getting more difficult. He had taken on another farm labourer to help out. Joe and Rose had arranged a date for their wedding. The date was confirmed for June, and Rose was going to move into the farmhouse with Joe and Harry's uncles.

The new labourer lived two houses away, so didn't need to live in the farmhouse. His name was James and he was a widower with grown up children. He was in good health and capable of doing all the farm duties given to him.

John Henry was so busy now, a proper little boy and very quick. His mother was finding it hard to cope. He was more energetic than all of her children put together, she had said. She wished him good health and ended the letter.

The second letter was from Ada. She asked how he was, said she missed him and relayed details of Dorothy's pregnancy, Louisa and her family. She didn't feel Windsor Cottage was her home any more. Her home was with Harry now. Ada said she was ready to look for work, to keep her busy.

Sarah and Florence were mentioned and Harry was relieved that she had made a friend in the barracks. Ada hoped he wasn't working too hard and hadn't suffered too much on the journey over to India.

Harry hoped she would receive his letters soon. His eyes began to close and he realised how tired he was. Before he knew it, he was sound asleep and snoring.

CHAPTER FIVE

Ada had been back in Aldershot for two weeks now, and had secured a job in the library. Elizabeth, the librarian, had asked her if she was interested in part-time work there. Ada accepted immediately and was liking her work. She worked three mornings and was paid on a weekly basis, which she saved for Harry's return.

Harry's letters had arrived the previous week. He had told her of his voyage on the ship, telling her that he hadn't been nauseous and would be in India soon. He was looking forward to dry land, but unsure of what his duties would be. He hoped she was okay and her visit to Windsor Cottage was eventful. He promised to write again on reaching the barracks in Jhansi.

Sarah and Florence were visiting and savouring a cup of tea and a biscuit when there was a knock on the door. 'I wonder who that is?' Ada said and got up from the settee to answer it. Her sister Gladys was at the door. Ada looked surprised to see her and asked her in. She introduced Sarah and Florence, put the kettle on the gas ring and sat down. 'Are you okay, Gladys?' She looked very pale.

'I've had words with stepmother and need some space from her. Can I stay with you for a while?' Gladys asked nervously.

'Of course you can, Gladys. Stepmother can be quite demanding, Sarah,' Ada explained. 'You do look pale though, are you sure you're okay?'

'It's probably the journey, I feel so tired. I will be okay in a minute.'

Sarah excused herself and let herself out. Florence was asleep on her lap. Sarah stood up trying not to wake her. 'I'll see you later, Ada. Nice to meet you, Gladys,' she said.

Gladys was 17, a slight girl with mousey blond hair cut to her shoulders. Her pallor had always been pale, but she looked exceptionally peaky and colourless now. Ada was worried. 'Has stepmother been working you too hard? I know what she's like,' she said.

'No more than usual. She is having a spring clean at the moment. I was scrubbing the kitchen floor yesterday and felt really dizzy. I mentioned it to her, but she didn't take any notice. She just told me that the larder needed cleaning after I'd finished the floor.' Gladys continued. 'I asked father if I could come to you for a while, and he said it was okay. Have a break with your sister, it will do you good, he had said. It is okay, Ada, isn't it?'

'Of course it is. It will be nice to spend some time together.' Ada didn't question her any more. She prepared a meal for the two of them and promised to have a word with the Army doctor in the morning. Ada was worried about her sister, only natural.

They both slept in the double bed that evening, something they were used to at home. Gladys seemed to be struggling for breath at times, Ada had noticed, and her sleep pattern seemed to be out of character. Whilst living at home, Ada shared a room with her and Alice, and she had seemed fine then. After breakfast Ada left Gladys sleeping, put her coat on and headed for the Army doctor's practice. She explained Gladys's symptoms and the doctor asked Ada to bring her in for a check up that afternoon.

She called into the library to see Elizabeth, told her that her sister was with her and that she didn't seem well. Elizabeth listened and could tell that she was worried. 'I'm sure Gladys will be fine. It could be a bout of influenza,' Elizabeth said. It was Ada's working shift the next day and she assured Elizabeth that she would be there. She wasn't the type of person to let people down.

Gladys was checked over by the doctor. He sent her to the hospital for a chest x-ray and a scan. She was to report back to him in two hours for the results. They called into Sarah's for a cup of tea whilst they were waiting.

The doctor hesitated before speaking to her and Ada was concerned. 'I'm sorry, Gladys,' he said quietly. 'The scan and x-ray show a weak heart and your breathing problems confirm this. You will need to take things easier in future. No heavy work or lifting, and plenty of rest. Your heart cannot take too much and you mustn't put any strain on it.'

Ada caught hold of her sister's hand. She was in total shock. 'But she's only 17,' Ada said.

'You were probably born with it, Gladys, but the problems are only now becoming apparent health wise. You have a pale complexion, too. You must slow down,' the doctor said. It was an order.

Ada thanked him and they both headed back to the bungalow. They were both numb and neither spoke for ages. 'I am going to be okay, aren't I?' Gladys asked Ada.

'Of course you are, just take things easy. I will go back to Windsor Cottage with you in a few weeks, and you can stay here with me until then. I will explain everything to father. He will understand,' Ada replied trying to ease her worries.

Ada hoped her stepmother would be able to lose Gladys's help in the cottage, as she wouldn't be able to do the heavy domestic duties any more. 'Let's relax now. How about a shopping trip to Reigate in a few days? I've got work in the library in the morning, but Wednesday is free.'

'I'd like that, Ada,' she replied.

Reigate was as memorable as the last visit with Harry. The weather was a lot warmer and the sun was shining. Both the sisters dressed accordingly, but Ada insisted Gladys wore a scarf and warm jumper under her coat. 'You're being over protective, Ada. I'll be okay,' Gladys responded with a hint of anger. 'I know I have to be careful and have remembered what the doctor said.'

After getting off the bus they stopped in a tea room and Ada treated them to tea and a plateful of fancy cakes. Gladys was mesmerised by them and suddenly felt hungry. 'This is nice, I'm not used to going to tea rooms. You are spoiling me.'

'It's a special treat for me. I can't remember when I last left the barracks to go shopping,' Ada replied.

After a stroll around the shops, purchasing a few groceries and household necessities, Ada noticed the library and walked inside. The library was large, compared to the one in the barracks. She browsed through some books and baby knitting patterns, picked a few to take back with her and headed for the reception desk.

This was her first visit and she needed to register. She had three weeks to return the books and patterns, plenty of time. On leaving, Gladys noticed a postcard on the noticeboard, advertising a full-time vacancy, and a generous salary. She pointed it out to Ada and Ada read it with interest. 'I will have a think about it,' she told Gladys. After a walk around Priory Park and a rest on one of the benches, they both headed for the bus stop and home.

Gladys had begun to look tired and her breathing had become unsteady, though she hadn't complained. Ada was concerned, but didn't comment for fear of worrying her. Gladys thanked her for a wonderful day, relaying the fun she had had.

'I enjoyed it too, it's nice to have you here, Gladys,' she answered and meant every word.

Ada had decided against applying for the full-time vacancy in Reigate. With Gladys with her, needing to take her back home in a few weeks and hoping Dorothy would have had her baby by then, the timing wasn't right. She would need to take her library books and patterns back in three weeks' time and would check the noticeboard again then.

Two weeks had passed and Gladys had regained some colour. They both spent evenings listening to music on the radio and knitting baby clothes. Another blanket had been completed and more hats and bootees. Ada still worked three mornings in the library, whilst Gladys busied herself visiting the laundry room, though Ada insisted on carrying the basket to and from the building.

Gladys sat in the small garden and helped prepare the evening meals. She appeared happy and relaxed.

They were now on the train travelling to Windsor Cottage. Ada wasn't looking forward to telling her father about Gladys's health problems. She knew he would worry. They arrived around dinner time and walked through the back door.

Blanche and Alice had prepared vegetables ready for the evening meal and a beef joint was cooking in the Aga. They were sat at the kitchen table eating mushroom soup and crusty bread. The twins were in their highchairs and Roland was asleep in his cot. Ethel Mary was in the sitting room with a tray on her lap.

They welcomed them both and Blanche filled two more bowls with soup, placing them on the table for Ada and Gladys. 'I needed that, thank you,' Ada said after demolishing her soup and plenty of bread. 'How are things here?' she asked.

'Stepmother isn't well. She is expecting another baby,' Alice said. Ada was worried Gladys would be needed more than ever now.

'I'd better go and say hello,'

They both walked into the sitting room and asked how she was. 'Not good, I'm having another child and suffering with morning sickness,' she replied. 'You're back then, Gladys!' she said with hostility in her voice.

The others returned home from school, followed by Archibald, their father, from work. Ernest gave Ada his brotherly hug as usual, and Archibald headed for the washroom to clean the soot from his body and change his clothes. Blanche and Alice were setting the table ready for the evening meal, so Ada asked to speak to her father in private.

'What is it, Ada?,' he said.

'Gladys isn't well, Father. She has a weak heart, the doctor thinks she was probably born with it.' Ada looked at her father, then glanced over to her stepmother. 'The doctor said that she has to take things easy. No heavy work or lifting and she has to rest. She mustn't put any strain on her heart.'

Ethel Mary's face froze and she let out a sigh. 'How am I going to manage now? I can't do anything myself whilst feeling like this,' she grunted, really annoyed.

'It's not Gladys's fault, Ethel. We will look after her, Ada. She will be okay.'

'Thank you, Father. I can stay the week and help out. I've got a job in the library in the barracks now. Hopefully you will feel a lot better then, Stepmother,' she offered.

'Thank you, Ada. That will be a great help. I will be able to rest and recover.' There didn't seem to be any concerns over Gladys's health, though!

Harry was in the stables grooming Star. She needed dressing for the military parade that afternoon, as she was to pull the carriage holding Sergeant Morgan and the Sergeant Major. Harry had bonded with all the horses and mules except Blade, a 7 year old stallion. Blade would lift his front legs as Harry approached and refused to let him into his sleeping area. He was determined to tame him, Harry wasn't one to give up.

Harry had worked with horses on the farm, so was familiar with their needs and care. His duties included training the horses for parades, which involved riding them, too. He loved riding and dressing them. The mules pulled the carts laden with goods for the barracks and were used for ploughing the fields, along with some of the horses. The work was interesting, although hard work, and Harry felt the animals had learnt to trust him (all except Blade). He felt contented, but was missing Ada.

Percy was being taught how to steer the different tanks, through mountainous terrain and on flat ground. His duties included cleaning them, along with other transport vehicles. Neither of them had received any letters recently. Percy wondered whether Dorothy's baby had arrived, whilst Harry worried about Ada being alone.

Harry had received a letter from Millie a while back, a lovely letter telling him about his mother and stepfather, her daily domestic duties in the house and John Henry's antics as a toddler. Millie had neat writing, and it was carefully written without spelling mistakes. 'A lovely letter,' Percy said after reading it. 'She's growing up fast.'

'I haven't heard from Ada. Hopefully all is okay, I'm not sure if she has seen your mother. She did mention in her last letter that all was well there,'

'I know, Harry, I just worry about her being on her own. I'm sure Dorothy will call in, but Albert and Hubert work long hours and are not there all the time.' Percy replied with concern.

They walked into the dining area, where food was being prepared. They both needed it, as they were hungry. The days were hot and humid and could be very tiring at times. Food and drink was plentiful and appetising.

Harry changed into his military uniform. The horses were groomed and looking immaculate.

They wore the Gloucester Regiment's colours of red, white and blue over their saddles, and a plume of feathers around their ears and across their forehead. Star and Blaze were to pull the carriage, whilst Harry and three other soldiers working in the stables were to ride alongside them on their horses. 'Now, Star, I want you on your best behaviour,' Harry said looking at her. You could swear the horse knew what was said to her and she nodded.

Blade was not joining the parade. Harry still had a lot of work to do on him, so he remained in the stables. The parade began. Trumpeters started playing and the soldiers marched, following each other in perfect strides. They turned and stopped, raised their heads and waited for the inspection from the Sergeant and Sergeant Major to begin. Star and Blaze pulled the carriage slowly and gently. Harry was pleased with them. He was seated on his horse, along with his colleagues, guarding the carriage and its passengers. The detail was perfect. 'A good job done,' Harry acknowledged.

Each soldier was checked over by the Sergeant Major. A salute was given by each soldier as he approached, and when the inspections were fully completed, they returned to the carriage to be escorted back to the front of the parade.

The trumpeters played again as the soldiers marched away to their barracks, and Harry dismounted his horse. He was pleased with his workmanship and congratulated himself. The horses were put back in the stables, their dressings removed and placed neatly away for the next parade. After feeding the horses and the mules, Harry and his stable colleagues retired to their dormitories.

Sporting activities were the Regiment's challenges when not on duties, and Harry decided to register for the cross country running. Boxing and athletics were also available, but Harry loved his walking, and knew that this would be the best sporting activity for him. There were cups to be won and all soldiers were expected to compete in one of the sporting competitions. Harry was a good sportsman and was determined to succeed. He was a fighter through and through. A cup would be nice!

Dorothy gave birth to a baby boy two days later. He was perfect in every way. A good weight, with all his fingers and toes, and a full head of dark hair. They named him Frederick George, after his father and grandfather. The couple were ecstatic, and Louisa was now a grandmother and so excited. Ada couldn't wait to congratulate them, and visited her after her domestic duties at her father's were completed. 'He's gorgeous, Dorothy. He looks like his father, too,' Ada commented.

'I'm a mother now, Ada. That's all I ever wanted. I couldn't be happier,' Dorothy said. 'It's your turn next.' Ada hoped she was right and Harry would be back from India soon.

Ethel Mary had taken Ada at her word and she was given endless domestic duties, including tying up the cows ready for milking, collecting the eggs and digging the kitchen garden. Her stepmother remained in the sitting room reading and hardly moved. Her morning sickness was worse than ever, apparently.

Blanche and Alice were in charge of the food in the kitchen. Blanche was on her hands and knees scrubbing the floor when Ada returned to the cottage. Gladys was sat at the kitchen table peeling potatoes for the evening meal. She looked pale again and very tired.

'Are you okay, Gladys?' she asked.

'Yes, I'm fine. I didn't sleep well last night so I'm a bit tired. How is Dorothy's baby?' Gladys asked. Ada described Frederick George to everyone, from his button nose to his tiny hands and feet. Dorothy and Frederick were going to be good parents, she was certain.

Louisa had held her grandson for the first time, told him about his grandfather and uncle Percy and revelled in the moment. Dorothy was worn out after giving birth and wanted to sleep. Nellie, Albert's girlfriend, took over, lifting baby Frederick and placing him comfortably in his cot. He had the blanket Ada had knitted, wrapped around him.

Alice was now smitten with a young man living locally. His name was Henry Wheeler. Ada had met him the previous day whilst answering a knock on the door. They had been courting for a while now, and a wedding was in the air! They were both out for the evening, so Ada, Gladys, Blanche and their father spent the night playing cards. Ethel Mary had retired to her bed early, along with the rest of the family.

They spoke about Alice and Henry. He was a working colleague and was thought very highly of by the management in the coal mines. Blanche was only 15 and hadn't met her sweetheart yet.

Gladys didn't venture out much and preferred to stay at home. 'There's a dance in the church hall tomorrow night,' Blanche mentioned.

'Shall we go? It would make a nice change,' Ada replied. 'Would you like to come too, Gladys?' Gladys declined the invitation and Ada didn't push her.

Their father won all the matchsticks, their stakes for the card game, and retired to bed. The cards were packed away and after a warm milky drink everyone followed him. It had been a lovely evening and Ada was feeling relaxed. Weekends for their father was spent at Windsor Cottage and its land.

Their stepmother was in charge of the kitchen garden, but with her morning sickness and tiredness at the moment, their father and Ernest were both attending to it. Fruit needed picking from the orchard and the cows in the fields needed checking on. He paid for help during the week, for milking and generally keeping the fields in order. Summer evenings were taken up with haymaking ready for the winter. The children enjoyed helping with the haymaking and being allowed to play in the fields.

The next evening, Ada and Blanche dressed for the local dance. Neither of them owned a lot of clothes, but Blanche had two pretty dresses with dropped waists and plenty of sparkling beads sewn onto the material. Ada was the same build and height as Blanche, so they wore one each. They spent time with their faces, adding foundation, powder and a hint of eyeshadow, and a bright red lipstick.

Alice commented on how nice they both looked and they headed for the church hall. Blanche wasn't used to socialising, recognised a few local boys and blushed. Ada wasn't familiar with anyone there but loved the dancing, and both of them stepped onto the dance floor.

Two boys approached them, asked if they would like to dance and both accepted. After the music had stopped and the dance finished, they introduced themselves. They were Wilfred and Gilbert Marsh, Wilfred was 17 and Gilbert was 15.

They were from a large family living in Chew Magna. They had younger brothers and sisters. Ada spoke about Harry and his Army life, and Blanche was interested in the boys' history. They all drank orange squash, danced some more and exchanged addresses with Blanche. The boys promised to keep in touch.

They walked home feeling happy and less stressed. 'I enjoyed that, Ada,' Blanche said.

'I'm glad, Blanche. So did I.'

Ethel Mary was feeling a lot better on the Sunday and busied herself in the garden with Roland and the twins. 'It's good to get some fresh air,' she told the girls. Phyllis and Dorothy were playing with a ball, whilst the twins were running after it, before they could continue their game. 10 year old Ernest had brought his school friend to play in the garden.

Apart from Christopher and Roland, who were babies, Ernest was the only boy at home. He needed someone his age to play with. The girls were busy in the kitchen, preparing food and Archibald was busy with paperwork in the sitting room.

The week was almost up and Ada was due to return to Aldershot. She would miss the family, but was looking forward to returning to work. She needed to know if there were any letters from Harry. Time had flown and she visited Dorothy and the baby once more before packing her suitcase that evening.

Ada said her goodbyes and told Gladys to look after herself. 'Come up again later in the year for a break. I loved having you with me.'

'Thanks, Ada, I will let you know when I'm coming next time,' Gladys replied.

Her stepmother wished her well, holding her stomach with her hands, and the twins grabbed hold of her legs. Her father had gone to work. She was on the train in no time heading for Aldershot and her bungalow.

There was a letter waiting for her when she got home. Harry had been given the stable duties.

He mentioned Star and Blade and the mules. Percy was on transport duties. He described the barracks, his dormitory and told her about the cross country running competition he had entered, when off duty. He was keeping busy and Ada was glad.

He had heard from Millie and his mother and told Ada that Martha was expecting again. He wished her well and awaited a return letter from her soon. Ada replied to his letter and posted it on the way to the shop. She needed groceries, as the cupboards were completely bare. She called in to see Elizabeth in the library, and she asked about the family and how Gladys was.

'They are all okay, thank you. Stepmother is expecting again and so is Harry's mother. There must be something in the air!' she said laughing. 'I will be in tomorrow morning. I'm looking forward to getting back to normality again. It was hectic back home.'

Ada mentally listed her plans for the week. She needed to visit Reigate one of the days. Her books and patterns needed returning, as she would be fined otherwise. There was laundry to be done and the bungalow needed a clean through. She had plenty to keep her occupied.

After preparing a casserole and placing it in the oven, Ada knocked on Sarah's door. A young soldier answered it. 'Is that you, Ada? Come on in,' Sarah shouted from the settee.

'I'm Alfred, Sarah's husband,' he said opening the door wide for her to enter.

'Pleased to meet you, I'm your next door neighbour, Ada,' she replied.

Ada sat down on the settee next to Sarah. Florence was crawling around the floor and smiled when she saw her. 'Alfred got home two days ago, they sent him home earlier than expected,'

'I hope they send Harry home early too. I miss him so much.'

Alfred made them both a cup of tea. He kissed Sarah and Florence and excused himself. 'I will let you both have a girly chat,' he said.

They talked for ages. Sarah was so happy having her husband home. 'I hope he's home for a while now. He hasn't been told of any more postings yet.'

Ada spoke about Gladys and her family. She told her about Dorothy and her baby son, Frederick, her stepmother's new pregnancy and Alice's boyfriend. The dance in the church hall was mentioned, and her father's concern over Gladys. When there was nothing more to talk about, Ada excused herself and left for her bungalow. Sarah seemed overjoyed at seeing Alfred again.

The casserole was cooked, so she made herself a cup of tea, cut some bread and sat at the kitchen table eating it. It seemed strange being alone again, but peaceful. Windsor Cottage was so busy and Ada needed some space at times.

The library was busy the next day and Elizabeth had a lot of paperwork to catch up on. They didn't speak much at all. It was surprising how one week away had made such a difference.

Elizabeth was pleased she was back.

She got on the bus to Reigate the next morning to return her books and patterns to the library. After changing them, Ada glanced at the noticeboard. The full-time vacancy was still there! She enquired at the desk and was given an application form to complete. The salary was more than generous and the hours seemed workable.

On returning home, Ada read the application form and completed it. With Sarah's husband home now, she would be alone a lot more. She felt that they needed time to themselves before he was posted away again. There was a forwarding address on the application form, so Ada posted it and waited.

Work was the answer and the library would be Ada's new lease of life. Visits to Windsor Cottage helped and reunited the noise and domesticity a family brought, but she would be earning and saving for the day Harry was back with her, and she had a goal to achieve. They would need a home to call their own, as Ada wasn't prepared to live in the Army barracks for ever, and she felt she would be happier meeting people, instead of feeling alone in Aldershot.

CHAPTER SIX

Harry had made progress with Blade (or so he had thought). He was now allowing him into his sleeping area without raising his front legs. There was still a long way to go. 'One step at a time,' Harry muttered to himself. 'One step at a time!'

The mules were out ploughing the fields and Harry was grooming Star. 'Shall we go for a ride, Star?' he asked her. Star nodded and kicked her front legs in excitement. He never feared her, she was his friend. 'We will check on the mules, okay. They've got to earn their keep.'

After a ride around the fields, checking the mules and talking to the farm workers, Harry brought Star back to the stables. He wiped her over, laid some fresh bedding and fed her. He glanced over at Blade, who seemed exceptionally quiet.

Something was wrong. He walked over to him, he was still sat down on his bedding. This was very unusual, and not like Blade at all. Harry stepped closer, but he didn't move. He merely looked at him and bowed his head.

He hadn't eaten much over the past few days, either. Harry carefully stroked his head, then looked down at his hooves. The left one looked red and sore and he tried to touch it, but Blade moved it away from him immediately. 'I think we need to get that looked at, Boy,' Harry said.

The vet and the blacksmith were called and it was discovered that Blade had somehow stepped on a metal spike. These were used in the fields to separate the areas of vegetation. The wound had become infected. Blade's shoe was replaced and he was given an injection to help heal the infection. The vet would call again in a few days.

Blade looked so sorry for himself, so Harry stayed with him for a while stroking and comforting him. 'You' ll be fine. I'll see you in the morning.' The horses were his children and he hated seeing them hurt. The next morning Blade appeared a lot better.

He had started to eat again and looked a lot brighter in himself. Harry approached him slowly, he didn't want to alarm him. Blade stood up. Would he raise his front legs or let him get nearer? 'Well, how are you feeling today, Boy?' he asked. Blade stood motionless and allowed Harry to smooth him.

It was the monsoon season. The rain was coming down in sheets, but the heat was still unbearable at times. The soil had been dry and had cracked through the summer and rain was needed to cultivate the crops. Citrus fruits, wheat, pulses, peas and oilseeds were produced in Jhansi. The monsoon rains destroyed some of the crops when flooding occurred. In previous years not enough rain had also destroyed the crops.

The weather had made it difficult to take the horses very far from the campsite, though Harry would walk them around the yard several times. Harry was thinking about Blade. When the rain subsides he had decided he would take him out. He had calmed down a lot lately, and he felt it was time to ride him.

The evenings were spent playing cards in the dormitory, writing letters to family and talking with the other soldiers. Rain had stopped play for the cross country running for the time being. Harry wrote letters to Ada, his mother and Millie, and wondered how they all were.

He desperately wanted to be home to see them. He still hadn't told Ada or his mother that he could be in India for longer than two years. He hadn't officially been told how long he would be away, but somehow knew it would be a long time and he didn't want to worry either of them at the moment.

Percy had heard from Louisa and he was happy knowing she was okay. There was still no news about Dorothy's baby. Albert was now engaged to Nellie. There would be a long wait before the wedding though, as Albert wanted to finish his apprenticeship first and still had two years to completion. Albert had changed occupations, from a farm labourer to an apprentice carpenter and was thoroughly engrossed in it. He had ideas of owning his own workshop in the future.

Nellie was living locally in the farmhouse where Albert had previously worked. She was a servant there, helping the farmer's wife, Mrs Green, in the kitchen. She had 8 young children and needed the help.

Hubert worked as a farm labourer for a large cattle farm in Frome. He mainly dealt with the milking and monthly transportation to and from the cattle market. The farmer sold milk and beef locally and to the surrounding businesses. Calves were produced and reared for their meat. The hours were long and he had to be up very early each morning.

Percy wrote back to his mother, telling her about his duties and the tanks he was driving and maintaining. He looked after all the camp vehicles too, and on occasions had to drive the Sergeant Major about. This was quite daunting at times, he had told his mother. He hoped all the family were well and finished his letter, retiring for the evening.

The rain had stopped after four days of torrential downpours. The ground was soggy but thankfully hadn't flooded. The horses and the mules needed their exercise. Harry walked them around the yard, taking four at a time. Finally he was left with Star, Blaze and Blade. He called them all by name, Star and Blaze walked out without any prompting. Blade refused to move. 'Do you want some exercise, Blade?' Harry asked him. 'You've been couped up here for days. It might rain again tomorrow.' Harry checked his wound and was pleased with its healing. 'Come on, I haven't got all day.'

Blade finally decided to listen and joined the other two. He was much more relaxed now and Harry was looking forward to riding him. They had all been fed and watered, their beds had been changed and the stables looked pristine. The carriages were due for a clean after food. There was another parade soon. Harry hoped he could return to his cross country running again as well.

'I wonder what Ada is doing?' he thought to himself over lunch. 'I've plenty to occupy myself here, I hope she isn't bored on her own.' Harry had a photograph of Ada he always kept in his shirt pocket. He took it out and looked at it, placing a kiss on it before replacing it.

'You are so funny, Harry,' Percy said. 'I hope I find someone to love, like you.'

'I'm sure you will, Percy,' he replied.

Ada had received a letter from the library. She was to attend an interview in a few days for the full-time vacancy. She was a little apprehensive, as her only work had been the barracks library. Prior to that her duties were with her stepmother. She had received a small wage, but didn't feel it qualified as a job.

She needed to look neat and tidy, so searched through her wardrobe for something suitable to wear. Pulling out a woollen suit and a blouse with a tied bow at the front, she glanced at her wedding outfit hung next to it. Her thoughts reverted to her wedding day and she smiled. That day was her happiest ever and one she would never forget.

Sarah and Florence knocked on the door. Ada put the kettle on and took some biscuits from the tin. 'How are you both?' Ada asked.

'We're both fine, thank you. Alfred is being moved to Portland next week, Ada. He will be based at home for the foreseeable future. He was sent home early through sickness. Albert was suffering constant bouts of tiredness and headaches, and it was felt he needed complete rest at home,' Sarah said, sounding worried.

'He hasn't said much. I think he feels disappointed with himself. The Army doctor has diagnosed exhaustion and depression and he has recommended a long stay at home. We will be moving to Portland next week. You're welcome to visit anytime. We will let you know the address when we get there.'

Ada was going to miss them both. She still had Elizabeth, but was excited for Sarah. She had her husband back and Florence was reunited with her father. Ada made the tea and they spoke about other things. 'I've got an interview on Thursday in Reigate, Sarah. It's for a full-time library assistant.'

'I hope you get it. You need to spend more time outside the barracks,' Sarah commented, smiling.

Ada was nervous but answered all the questions with complete honesty and accuracy. She loved reading and was willing to do anything that was required within the job, and could adapt easily.

She had no family commitments and informed the interviewer of Harry's Army history and his whereabouts. Ada spoke of her family in Chilcompton and the hard work involved in helping and caring for a large family of siblings.

After a few moments assessing her, the interviewer asked when she would be available to commence work. Ada hesitated, she hadn't expected an answer the same day. 'I would need to give Elizabeth a week's notice in the barracks library,' she answered.

'That fine by me. Would you be interested in starting the following Monday?'

'Yes please,' Ada replied excitedly.

'Good, I will see you then at 9 o'clock, Ada. Call me Agnes.' Ada stood up and walked out of the library in complete shock. She had to tell Elizabeth about her new job. There was no time like the present!

Entering the barracks, Ada walked into the library first, before going home. Elizabeth was sorry to lose her, but understood her reasons and wished her luck. She promised to keep in touch outside working hours. Sarah answered the door and Ada entered.

'Well I take it the news is good, by the look on your face,' she said.

'It is, I start a week Monday at 9 o'clock. I couldn't believe being offered the job straight away, Sarah,' Ada said full of excitement. 'How's Alfred doing?'

'He's okay. A new start in Portland will help. I think he has a lot of issues in his head, but he won't talk to me,' Sarah sighed. 'I am so proud of him. He will adjust in time and make new friends in the barracks. It will be nice to have him home, helping with Florence.'

'If there's anything I can do, please ask,' Ada said to her.

'Thanks, a visit from you to Portland will help me. We can put you up for a few nights, I'm sure.'

'That's a date, Sarah.' Sarah was a good friend and Ada wanted to keep in touch with her.

She returned to her bungalow. After putting some cheese under the grill and toasting some bread, Ada made a cup of tea and retired to bed early. She felt that a good day had been had and was pleased with herself. Was life about to change for the better?

Twelve months had now passed and Ada had been working at the library in Reigate for what seemed years now! She enjoyed the job and felt privileged to be one of its employees. Cheerful customers searching for information and specific books, or just browsing and unsure of what they wanted to read next. Ada felt useful and the days passed quickly, but Harry was never far from her mind.

Her stepmother had given birth to a son, and she had named him Alfred. Blanche and Alice seemed to have no time to themselves now. With her looking after the twins, Roland and baby Alfred, there was no time for housework, cooking or tending to the kitchen garden. Gladys was getting weaker each day and was unable to help out with even the lightest duties now.

Ethel Mary wasn't amused, but her father made sure she took things easy. Alice had made arrangements for hers and Henry's wedding for March the following year. Ada was to be maid of honour, along with Blanche and Gladys as bridesmaids. Her younger sisters were to be flower girls. Alice wanted a big wedding in the local church. It was always her dream.

Martha had had a son, too. She named him Walter James, but he was known as James. Millie was coping well with John Henry and James and helped her mother out a lot. Harry's uncles weren't managing at all, health wise they were struggling and had taken on another helper on the farm.

Rose was expecting a baby early the following year and Dorothy was awaiting the arrival of a second child. Sarah had settled in Portland and was also pregnant. Frederick George, Dorothy's son, was growing fast and very mischievous, though absolutely gorgeous and Ada was so envious. She so wanted Harry's children.

Life in the Army barracks was very lonely. She saw Elizabeth occasionally when time allowed, but with a full-time job and a lot of travelling, she didn't have a lot of spare time to socialise properly. The new neighbour didn't seem to want to mingle, though Ada did try to be friendly. Harry had written three times, mainly telling her about the horses day to day activities. 'Anyone would think they were his children,' Ada muttered to herself.

He was due to be moved to transport duties soon and would miss the stables, but she was sure he would be fine. Percy was also being moved, from transport to combat duties. It all seemed to be happening in India. Ada was happy plodding along at her own pace. She read in her spare time and knitted for the babies, and there were plenty to knit for. Things seemed to be running along smoothly for her.

Ada was given two weeks off work. 'It's paid annual leave, Ada,' Agnes informed her. 'You need to take them before the new year starts,' she said. Ada thanked her and decided to pay some visits to friends and family.

She began by spending a few days in Portland with Sarah and Florence. Sarah welcomed her into her new married quarters and the accommodation was a lot bigger than the bungalow in Aldershot. Sarah's bump was now showing and Ada commented on it. 'How's baby coming along?' she asked pointing to her stomach.

'The doctor is pleased and everything seems to be normal. I did have a bout of morning sickness, but that has stopped now,' said Sarah. Ada asked about Alfred and Sarah told her that he was doing much better. He was now on transport duties and coping well. They spent the next day shopping in and around Portland.

Ada was impressed. 'Dorset has some fabulous scenery, Sarah. The beaches look so inviting. I'd be more than content living here.'

'It's lovely here for Florence. The air seems so much healthier.' Sarah replied.

'I envy you, Sarah, you're so lucky.' Sarah seemed to have it all! Her husband, Florence, a new baby due and a fantastic location to live in.

Ada caught the train from Portland to her father's a few days later and stayed for a week. Baby Alfred was very contented and hardly ever cried. He had his stepmother's features, but his father's colouring and deep blue eyes. Roland was 2 years old now and the twins were 3. The kitchen was busy with them running around after one another. Blanche and Alice were constantly having to dodge them whilst carrying heavy saucepans across the length of the large kitchen. It was an accident waiting to happen! Her stepmother was nowhere to be seen.

Gladys was resting in her room, so Ada decided to visit Dorothy and see her later. Dorothy welcomed her into her cottage. She looked really well, glowing and radiant. 'Pregnancy suits you,' Ada said. Frederick was sat in his highchair eating toast cut into soldiers.

'He's only happy when he's eating,' Dorothy said laughing. 'It keeps him quiet, though he's active enough not to get too fat.'

Ada had knitted more cardigans and a pink blanket. 'I'm hedging my bets,' she said, handing them to her. 'There have been too many boys born lately, it's time for the girls now.' Dorothy giggled and thanked her for the presents. They spoke for hours. Ada praised her job in the library and expressed how lucky she was to be working there. The only negative was the bungalow in the barracks. 'It's not the same now with Sarah and Florence gone,' she said despondently.

'Why don't you look for a place to live in Reigate, Ada? You can afford the rent and it would be less travelling,' Dorothy added thoughtfully. 'You've told me how much you like Reigate. If you were living there, the parks and castles ruins would be in walking distance on your days off.'

'You've got a point there, Dorothy.' It would be better than being confined to the barracks. 'That's something I need to think about,' Ada replied and mentally noted her suggestion.

Gladys was awake when Ada returned to Windsor Cottage. She smiled on seeing her. 'How are you, Gladys?'

'I get tired really quickly now, Ada, but I'm okay otherwise. I go to my room because it gets too noisy during the day with the children playing,' Gladys advised her.

'I'm going to see Martha and Millie for a few days after I've spent some time here, but you're welcome to come to mine when I get back.'

'Thank you, Ada. I will think about it.' Ada hoped she would take her up on the offer. Ada visited Louisa and congratulated Albert on his engagement. Hubert was still at work.

Louisa looked well and she commented on it. Ada spoke about Harry and Percy and they both shared information from their letters. Louisa was missing Percy and hoped Harry was doing okay. After a cup of tea, biscuits and a slice of Victoria sponge, Ada said her goodbyes and headed back to her father's cottage. Ada was exhausted and ready for bed. She was sure her stepmother would have plenty for her to do the following morning.

The week with her father and stepmother seemed to last forever. Ada wasn't used to all the household chores and farm work any more. Tying up the cows ready for milking, feeding the chickens and collecting the eggs. Digging the kitchen garden and picking the vegetables. The orchards had apples and pear trees, there were blackberry bushes nearby and strawberry beds. There seemed to be so much to do.

Ada didn't know how it all got done. Her father had been thinking of finishing as a banksman to concentrate on the land. He was 45 years old now, and mining was a young man's occupation. He wasn't as quick as he used to be.

He was busy doing paperwork in the sitting room when he had mentioned it to Ada. 'I think it's a good idea, Father. You're not getting any younger and the children are getting older and more busy,' she answered. Ernest was now 11 and able to help out after school and weekends.

'The other option is to sell the cottage and buy something smaller. I seem to have no time at home at all these days and I do worry about Gladys. Phyllis and Dorothy help out too now. They occupy the younger children so your stepmother can attend to the kitchen garden, but it's not ideal,' her father added with a sigh.

With so many mouths to feed, producing fruit and vegetables, eggs, milk, meat and poultry was essential. There was a lot to think about and he needed to decide soon. He was a worried man and Ada worried for him. Archibald paid Cedric and George to plough the fields, to milk the cows and attend to any repairs to fences; gates and other things, during the week.

She knew he was trying to balance the books at home and could afford to lose his workers if he attended to the fields himself. He would also be based at home, which would be a bonus. Ada wanted to say she would move back home, but she knew her life was with Harry and she needed to be at Aldershot when he returned home.

The train journey to Stratford upon Avon was stressless and Ada read a book and totally relaxed. She loved her siblings, but relished the peace and quiet too. It seemed to be organised chaos in the cottage and she was worried about her father.

She was looking forward to meeting Martha again. There was a newcomer to meet as well, baby James. The boys would be growing and Millie was a young lady now. Like Harry, Ada had a soft spot for her. John Henry would be 4 now and a proper little boy. How time had flown since meeting Harry.

Stratford upon Avon still scared her. It was so big, buildings everywhere. The shops looked inviting and Ada bought a few items of clothing. It wasn't something she had planned, but Ada felt she deserved it. The bus was punctual and within 30 minutes she was at Martha's cottage.

'It's lovely to see you,' Martha said. 'You look well, though I must say a little tired.'

'I've come from Windsor Cottage. It's complete chaos there. I think I've worked harder this last week than all year in the library,' Ada replied.

They spoke of Ada's and Martha's families and endless other topics. Harry's letters were spoken about and some were read out to each other without embarrassment. Ada liked Martha, she had decided. She may not have been there for Harry as a child, but knew she cared about him. It was plainly obvious to see.

Millie had walked to the local shop with baby James in his pram. On returning and seeing Ada her face lit up and she ran over to her, giving her a big hug. 'Ada, it's so nice to see you. Did you get my letter?' she asked.

'No, Millie, but I've been away from the bungalow for nearly two weeks. I've come from my father's now.'

'That's okay, you should get it soon. I sent Harry a letter and he replied. He mentioned it would be nice if I wrote to you,' she said excitedly.

'Thank you, I will enjoy reading it when I get back. How are you, Millie?' Ada asked.

'I'm okay, thank you,' she replied.

Ada glanced into the pram after hearing a cry. Baby James was beautiful. He had Harry's features. 'Can I pick him up, Martha?'

'Of course, you can feed him if you like and I will put the kettle on.' Ada didn't object and Millie prepared a bottle and handed it to her. Martha expressed her milk and bottled it in her own time. It meant that any member of the family could feed him and freed herself from him when preparing dinner for the family. She loved the baby, but had so much to do, even with Millie's help.

There were so many babies in the family now, Ada was feeling left out. She wanted to know when Harry would be home to be able to start a family of their own. In her next letter she would ask him if he knew, she missed him desperately. Her father's household was a nightmare at times, but it was her family and that is what she wanted so badly.

Ada stayed with Martha for two nights. She helped with baby James, played with John Henry and helped with the household chores. She accompanied Millie to the shop and pushed the pram, whilst John Henry held Millie's hand. There was a small park area nearby with a small swing, slider and a roundabout in it. There was a bench to sit on and the rest was laid to grass. They took John Henry in and Millie pushed him on the swing. Ada sat on the bench, with the baby parked next to her.

This was what Ada had wanted. She delighted in her work in the library, but wanted to be home with a family. Millie was a natural mother and she envied her. She would be a brilliant parent in the future, she was certain. Dorothy was a natural too. Ada held onto her dream of becoming a mother herself one day.

She said her goodbyes to Martha and Frank, Millie and the boys, and picked John Henry up to gave him a kiss. Baby James was asleep. She waved as she closed the garden gate and headed for the bus back to Stratford upon Avon. After picking up a sandwich and a drink in the bakers shop, Ada caught the train to Aldershot and her bungalow.

She had had an interesting two weeks. It was going to be so quiet back in Aldershot, but Ada was exhausted and looking forward to some peace, quiet and normality. The library would be missing her and she was missing the loyal customers who needed her help. She would be glad to get home.

CHAPTER SEVEN

Weeks and months passed and Ada was still in the bungalow and travelling daily to Reigate. She was used to being alone evenings now, and busied herself with her knitting and her reading. Ada had received and sent several letters to Harry. In her last letter, she had written asking him if he knew how much longer he would be in India. It had been two years already and she was becoming anxious.

Millie had sent two letters to her. Her letter writing was exemplary and Ada felt Millie could easily have secured a job in journalism or something similar. She was an intelligent girl. Ada replied to Millie's letters and wrote to Gladys.

The seasons came and went. From dark nights to summer evenings, roaring coal fires burning in the fireplace, to sitting in the garden soaking up the sunshine. She felt happy, relaxed and was enjoying life. Apart from missing Harry she couldn't have been more contented.

It was the week before Alice's wedding. Ada had travelled to Windsor Cottage a month earlier for a fitting on her outfit and hoped it would still fit now. The library work wasn't very active and Ada had put on a few pounds in weight around her waistline. She struggled to do her buttons up on some of her skirts.

Thankfully, she would be wearing a two piece outfit. A full length skirt in maroon, with a matching top decorated with pearl beads and a silk bow tied around the waist. Gladys and Blanche would be dressed in the same outfits, all topped off with a neat cream hat perched on the top of their heads.

Alice's wedding dress was only known to her. She was very superstitious and wasn't allowing anyone to look at it. The flower girls dresses were cream silk. They were decorated with embroidered maroon flowers to co-ordinate with the girls' outfits.

The church was all arranged, the flowers ordered and their stepmother was once again organising food for the reception at Windsor Cottage. Cars weren't needed, as the church was in walking distance from home. Everything was in order.

Alice and Henry had found a small house to rent in Frome and were looking forward to moving into it. Her father had decided against selling the cottage and had reduced his hours in the coal mines instead, enabling him to spend more time at home and in the fields.

Gladys was virtually housebound now. She hadn't been well enough to visit Ada after she had returned from Martha's. Her complexion was ghostly white and she spent most of her days in her room, helping out in the kitchen on occasions, peeling vegetables. This tired her out to near exhaustion, so no-one forced any duties on her.

The library had given her another two weeks leave. Ada knew she would be needed after Alice and Henry had left for their honeymoon, and was prepared to spend the week helping out afterwards. There would be a lot to do then and she could visit Dorothy and Louisa whilst she was there.

Alice looked beautiful. She wore an ivory silk dress that fitted perfectly. It fell to the hips, then flared out touching the floor, hiding most of her cream shoes. She wore a small hat similar to the girls, but hers had a veil attached to it. The veil covered most of her face, falling to her shoulders.

Henry had bought her a gold necklace with a tiny cross on it, which she wore with a pair of gold studded earrings. Her hair had been put back into a bun, showing off her pretty face. She looked fabulous, and Ada was sure Henry would be pleased with her appearance, more than pleased.

Ada helped dress the twins, Roland and baby Alfred. Kathleen looked cute in her flower girl's dress; she looked like an angel, which she wasn't. Ada then dressed herself and helped Gladys with her outfit, all walking to the church together, excited and laughing amongst one another.

The weather was dry and the sun was shining, though there was a bitter coldness in the air. Ada was taken back to her wedding day and wished Harry could have been there, watching her sister marry. The weather had been cold on her wedding day too, but she hadn't felt it so much then.

Everything went as planned. The children behaved themselves, with Ada's and Blanche's help.

Ethel Mary seemed to enjoy herself and was smiling (something she didn't do very often). Archibald was a proud man and looked a picture, walking his daughter down the aisle. Everything was perfect.

Ernest returned home and collected the wheelchair for Gladys. Her breathing had worsened and she wouldn't have been able to walk back to the cottage. She loved the ceremony though, and managed to walk the few steps needed to perform her bridesmaid's duties. Henry's parents were there and his two sisters, Mary and Ann. Mary was engaged to Richard, who also attended.

After photographs were taken, they all walked back to Windsor Cottage, Ernest pushing Gladys in the wheelchair. It was a carefree afternoon, meeting new members of the family. They discussed politics and small talk, whilst tasting the table's culinary delights.

Blanche and Gladys had excelled themselves with the wedding cake, though in all honesty Blanche had contributed to most of it. It had three tiers and was intricately iced in white, with pink flowers dominating the top tier. A bride and groom stood on top of the cake and the lower tier had a large pink ribbon tied around its base.

Alice was really pleased with it and didn't want to cut the cake. She wanted to keep it! The bottom tier was reluctantly cut for guests after the speech by the best man, Henry's friend, Joseph.

Harry had finished his duties for the day. There was a letter from Ada to read and he laid out on his bed, making himself comfortable before opening it. He was satisfied with his transport duties. Driving the tanks wasn't easy at first, but he was now getting the hang of it; slowly and surely.

He was testing out the tanks by driving them over mountainous terrain. The tanks seemed like giants, with huge dimensions. It was difficult initially to even get inside them, but more practice made perfect, and he was pleased with his achievements to date.

The Army vehicles needed to be immaculately clean, inside and out. The Sergeant Major checked them on a regular basis, the chrome on the vehicles needed to shine and you needed to see your face in it. He missed Star, Blaze and Blade though and would walk to the stables regularly to say hello to them.

Harry opened Ada's letter and read it. Ada needed to know how long he was going to be in India. He needed to give her an answer, but he knew she wouldn't like the reply. Harry had spoken to the Sergeant a few days earlier and had been told that he could possibly be in India for another two years!

How was he going to break the news to her? He didn't want to lose her, but knew four years was a long time apart. Harry was worried. How was he going to handle this? He knew Ada was working in the library in Reigate and quite settled there. She was saving money for his return and wanted to start a family.

Harry tried to word the letter in a way she wouldn't be too upset, wasn't happy with it and screwed up the letter, throwing it to the floor. Three attempts later and he still hadn't managed to complete the letter. Percy walked into the dormitory and sat on his bed. He glanced over to Harry.

'Is everything okay, Harry?' he asked.

'Not really, I need to tell Ada that I'm here for another two years. How do I break it to her, Percy?' Harry asked anxiously. Harry didn't want to lose her. This was a delicate situation.

'Let me help you, Harry. I will write to my mother, too. She needs to know, I can mention your concerns to her. Ada does visit when she sees her father and stepmother. Mother is a good listener and I'm sure she can put Ada's mind at ease.'

'Thank you, Percy. You're here for another two years also. Louisa will be worried about you,' Harry remarked. Army life wasn't easy.

'I know, but I'm not married to my mother, am I?' Percy replied and laughed. Harry saw the humour there and laughed with him. He always knew how to lighten the mood, and Harry was so lucky to have such a good friend.

Ada would not be happy after reading Harry's letter. He wouldn't have blamed her, either. Ada had married him and they had spent less than a month together in two years. He took the photo from his pocket and kissed it. Percy smiled and then laughed. 'You are so funny, Harry.'

The letter was posted, along with Percy's letter to his mother. Harry concentrated on his Army duties and his cross country running. He walked to the stables in his free time the next day. Star walked towards him and waited for Harry to smooth her. 'Well, how are you today? I hope you've been good for William.' William was the new soldier in charge of the stables.

Star nodded her head and waited for Harry to smooth her again. Blade was now waiting for some attention too, so he walked over to him. Blade was now his friend. He had managed to ride him before changing his duties and he had been on his best behaviour.

'Hello, Blade,' said Harry. 'I'm in a bit of a dilemma. It looks like I'm here for another two years and I'm not sure how my wife is going to take it. You're a man of the world, have I phrased my letter correctly, do you think?' Blade rubbed his nose into Harry's hands, waiting to be smoothed. 'I will take that as a yes then, shall I?' He couldn't leave Blaze out, so walked over to him as well, before exiting the stables. Harry loved the horses almost as much as he did Ada, and he missed his daily duties in the stables. It had been more of a hobby than a chore and he hoped he would return to stable duties in the future.

India was still hot and humid, but the rain had stopped, enabling the majority of duties and sporting activities to recommence. Awards had been won by the Regiment. Photographs were taken with the soldiers and the winning cups. They looked handsome in their uniforms and the Gloucester's were proud of their achievements.

Ada was sat at the kitchen table eating her tea. There were two letters to be read and she opened Harry's letter first. Harry started his letter as always, asking how she was and hoping all the family were well. He went on to talk about his new toys, the tanks! The Sergeant Major was impressed with the cleanliness of all the vehicles and the shine on the chrome areas. He had received a certificate for his hard work. Harry always wanted to go the extra mile, and Ada was proud of his dedication to his work.

Ada stopped eating, put her fork down on the table and re-read the second part of his letter.

Harry would not be home for another two years and neither would Percy. She sat at the table in a daze. There were no words to express how she was feeling. It wasn't anger or rage. Ada felt numb.

He apologised, saying it was out of his control. He was needed in India and as a soldier he had to stay. Ada had never envisaged Harry being away for so long, and knew she had no choice and had to get on with life on her own.

Still stunned, she opened the second letter. It was from Blanche. Blanche didn't usually write letters. Something was wrong, she knew it! Ada started to read the words, then dropped the letter on the table, putting her hands against her head and burst into tears.

Gladys had died. She was only 19 years old. Ada was so upset and she needed to go home. She would tell Agnes during work the next day. Blanche had said her heart had given up, and she died peacefully in bed. She wasn't in any pain. Ada was going to miss her so much.

She sat at the table staring into space, tears dropping continuously. Her life had been turned upside down in minutes. Her sister had lost her life and she had had everything to live for. Harry wouldn't be home for another two years. How cruel life could be at times.

Ada washed herself, undressed and put her nightdress on. It was June, but she felt cold and went to bed. She needed to write back to Blanche and Harry, especially Blanche. She sat up in bed and put pen to paper. Ada informed Harry of Gladys's death and although she was annoyed with his further absence, she didn't write it in her letter. She merely agreed that it was out of his control and she would cope. What point was there in turning it into a disagreement?

She finished Harry's letter and wrote to Blanche. She would be there as soon as possible, she wrote. Hopefully in a few days, she added. Her letter was short, but precise. She would be there to speak to her family soon.

The library was busy that morning and Ada desperately needed to speak to Agnes. It was lunch time before she was able to approach her, when the customers had dwindled down to just a few. 'I need to take some time off, Agnes,' she said. 'My sister has died and I need to go home for a while.' She told Agnes about Gladys, her illness, and her age. The whole family would be grieving and Ada wanted to be there; to be with them.

Agnes was very sympathetic and understood her urgency to return home and gave her a week's leave. She could travel home the next day. 'I can't pay you though, Ada, you've already had two weeks off this year with pay.' Ada understood and thanked her for being so helpful.

'I will see you in a week, Agnes,' she said at 5 o'clock and thanked her again.

It seemed to take ages to get to Windsor Cottage. She was in a hurry, though nothing could change what had happened. She remembered her sisters at a young age. Herself, Alice, Blanche and Gladys. So innocent and carefree. They had all been given chores to do, but they had also had their fun times, playing in the fields together, with their mother, Lily, and their father, Archibald. Blanche was only 5 when Lily died, but she had been given small tasks to do and loved doing them.

Who would have predicted then, that Gladys would have died so young. She hadn't even had chance to meet anyone, get married or have a child. At least their mother had met their father, had Ada's brother, Jim, her four girls, then Freddie and Ernest, before losing her own life in childbirth.

Reaching Windsor Cottage, Blanche answered the door and they both started crying. Her letter hadn't arrived, but she was glad to see her. Phyllis, Dorothy and Ernest had gone to school. There wasn't any point in putting them through any more heartache, they needed normality. They were all aware of Gladys dying.

Alice was there too, and put the kettle on the Aga. Archibald got up allowing Ada to sit in the armchair in the sitting room. 'Are you okay, Father?' she asked.

'She was unable to breathe at the end, Ada. She's not suffering now!' he said placing his hand on her arm.

Ethel Mary was in the kitchen garden picking vegetables. The twins, Roland and Alfred were in their bedrooms sleeping. She walked into the kitchen, noticing Ada's suitcase. Alice had made a cup of tea and asked her if she wanted one.

'I've got no time to drink tea, Alice,' she answered. 'Drinking tea isn't getting the work done.' Her words were full of hostility.

Ada shouted hello to her stepmother from the sitting room. She had put the vegetables on the table and had now entered the room. Ethel Mary asked Ada how long she was home for, and she told her that she was available for the week.

'Good, I'm behind with everything here,' she retorted. No mention of Gladys! That was typical of her stepmother.

The funeral was set to go ahead two days later. Ada busied herself helping Alice and Blanche with the food preparation for the wake. Alice went home to Frome each evening and Henry would drive her to the cottage each morning before starting work. It was an early start for Alice, but she didn't mind. Her father had taken time off from the mines until after the funeral.

Gladys was laid out in the chapel of rest and Ada visited her. She looked so peaceful and pretty, dressed in one of Blanche's evening dresses, the dress Blanche wore at the church dance with Ada. Ada spoke to her, telling her about Harry and his continued absence. 'How am I going to cope? Am I going to recognise him when he comes home?' Ada said to her laughing. She kissed Gladys on the forehead, placed a pink chrysanthemum in her hands and left. She would miss her sister.

Blanche was waiting in the kitchen with a cup of tea. 'Are you okay, Ada?' she asked.

'Yes, I'm fine thanks. We've all got to die I know, but 19 is so young. What else needs doing?' she asked, changing the subject.

The church was full and overflowing. Gladys was a popular girl in the village and liked a lot. People turned up who Ada didn't recognise, but was glad to see them. Gladys was placed next to Lily and Freddie. Archibald was trying so hard to hide his tears and Ada walked over to her father and hugged him hard. 'It's okay to cry,' she said.

The wake was a mixture of sadness, reminiscing and catching up with old friends and acquaintances. Strange faces turned out to be village friends all grown up with families of their own. Louisa and her family were there too, they were like family now. Dorothy couldn't attend as she wasn't able to find a babysitter for Frederick and her new baby, Ivy, but Ada promised Louisa she would call in to see her in a few days.

Louisa hadn't received a letter from Percy, but asked about Harry. Ada couldn't lie and told her of their posting in India for a further two years. 'I'm sorry, Louisa,' she said.

'It's you I feel sorry for, Ada. I've got Dorothy and the boys here. You're the one alone in Aldershot. Are you going to be okay?'

Ada explained that she had a full-time job in Reigate and would be fine. Was now the time to look for accommodation in Reigate and leave the bungalow in the barracks? The thought crossed her mind. She'd be a lot happier living in Reigate. There was so much more going on there and it wouldn't be so quiet. Decisions, decisions, Ada repeated to herself.

Dorothy was pleased to see her and Ada was surprised at how much Frederick had grown. Ivy was two months old and the cutest baby ever! 'I knew you'd have a girl, Dorothy. I've knitted lots of pink baby clothes,' said Ada, handing her a parcel.

Dorothy opened it and thanked her. 'I haven't forgotten you, Frederick,' she said looking at him and handed him a parcel to open. Frederick ran over to her and tore the wrapping away. Inside was a knitted teddy bear. It had a large black nose, knitted green eyes and a brown body. She had made a black jacket and dressed the teddy in it. Frederick loved it and cuddled into it.

'Say thank you to Ada, Frederick,' Dorothy prompted and he thanked her, giving her a big kiss on the lips. Dorothy handed Ivy to her for a cuddle. Ada cried whilst holding her, but it was a mixture of sadness and happiness that had brought it on. Gladys had gone, and Ivy was gorgeous.

Blanche and Ada attended the church dance the next evening. They had noticed a poster on the church door at Gladys's funeral. Gladys wouldn't want them to mourn her, she would have told them to carry on living and savour the moments. Something she would have wanted to do herself, but couldn't.

The Marsh boys were there again, but with an additional brother. Blanche walked up to them and said hello. She had been in constant touch with Wilfred and Gilbert by letter, though she wasn't that much of a letter writer, and they had met up with her on previous church dances.

The boys introduced Victor, their younger brother. Victor was 14 years old and looked very mature for his age. He was a labourer on a farm near his home in Chew Magna. Blanche seemed quite attracted to him, so Ada left them talking and danced with his brothers. Blanche was later seen dancing with him and they looked very devoted, as if they'd known each other for ages.

Walking home Blanche couldn't stop talking about Dick. 'Who's Dick?' Ada asked.

'Victor, everyone calls him Dick,' she replied. 'I like him, Ada. He's more my type than Wilfred and Gilbert. We seemed to get on well tonight.'

'I know, Blanche.' Ada said and smiled.

Ada spent the remainder of the week at the cottage. Her stepmother had asked her to clear out Gladys's clothes from her bedroom. It wasn't something Ada would have chosen to do, but felt she would be more sympathetic to her personal effects than any other member of the family.

Gladys had kept a diary and Ada opened it and read a few pages. She put the diary in her handbag to take back to the bungalow to read properly. She would give it to her father when she travelled back again.

There were a few items of clothing she liked that fitted her, so she packed them in her suitcase.

The remainder Ada put into a bag and took to the church for their charity fayres. Every penny collected from sales was donated to charity and she knew Gladys would have approved.

Her only personal items appeared to be a necklace given to her by her father on her 18th birthday, her hairbrush and matching mirror and a pretty compact with face powder in it, with a small mirror in the lid. Gladys was never a girly girl! She was more of a tomboy growing up, and never one to experiment with cosmetics or decorate her hair with fancy bows or slides.

She left them on the dressing table for Blanche. Ada was sure they would be useful to her. Dick and Blanche got on so well at the church dance, she was certain they would be contacting each other soon. There was a spark in her sister's eyes that she'd never seen before. Dick was younger than her, but there was plenty of time for them to develop a relationship, and there was nothing to hurry them, unlike Harry and herself.

When Ada had finished clearing Gladys's bedroom, she walked out into the garden and then onto the fields. The weather was gorgeous, warm and sunny with a slight breeze in the air. Her father was cutting down brambles and overgrown shrubs ready for the haymaking the following month.

He had heard her approach and stopped what he was doing. 'Are you okay, Ada?'

'Yes, Father. I've been clearing Gladys's things from her bedroom. Stepmother asked me to,' she said. 'I found her diary, I'd like to take it back with me to read. I will return it to you when I'm here next. Is that okay?'

'That's fine by me. There's probably more about you in there anyway. Gladys loved you and always said she'd like to follow in your footsteps,' her father answered.

'Really, Father. You make me out to be something special!'

'All my daughters are special, Ada, including you,' Ada smiled, she loved her father so much. They both worked at preparing the fields for haymaking until it became dark, and then returned to the cottage together.

The twins and Roland were asleep in their bedrooms. Ernest, Phyllis and Dorothy were busy doing their homework and baby Alfred was cradled in Ethel Mary's arms. He was fast asleep. She stood up and put him in his cot as they walked into the kitchen.

Their food was in the Aga keeping warm. Ethel Mary took them out and placed them on the kitchen table, then put the kettle on to make a drink. After eating their meals and drinking their mugs of tea, they both retired early. Ada had so loved working with her father, but had had a long day and felt really tired.

It was the weekend and Ada and Blanche took Ernest, Phyllis and Dorothy for a long country walk. The sun was shining and they all needed a break from the cottage. Ernest carried a rucksack filled with sandwiches, apples and cakes. He also packed bottles of water to drink for their picnic.

They walked miles, picking wild mushrooms along the way. The girls pointed to flowers, shrubs and leaves. They named them all, telling

Ada and Blanche of their Latin names. They were both learning about flowers and foliage in school.

Ernest found a football and was kicking it along the way and back. They had their picnic and rested for a while. The girls talked about school, the twins and the babies. Ernest spoke about sport, Harry and Percy, and said he wanted to join the Army when he was old enough. He was 12 and had plenty of time to think about it, Ada had said to him.

They all headed back to the cottage. They had only been gone a few hours, but Ada felt everyone had delighted in the afternoon. She told herself that she needed to do more walking when she returned to Aldershot. It would help her waistline no ends. She needed to really think about moving to Reigate.

The cows had been milked, the kitchen garden dug and all the vegetables picked. Ethel Mary had started preparing them for the evening meal. She didn't look happy. Ada sat at the kitchen table, picked up a knife and began peeling potatoes. Blanche put the kettle on the Aga and began making the tea.

The twins were sat on the kitchen floor playing with saucepans, wooden spoons and small potatoes and baby carrots. The vegetables were moved from one saucepan to the next, stirred with the wooden spoon and moved back again. They seemed to be engrossed in their play. Who needed toys?

'We will take over, Stepmother,' Blanche said. 'You go and have a rest, you look tired.'

She thanked Blanche and walked into the sitting room, sitting down in the armchair. It wasn't long before she was fast asleep and snoring.

After Gladys had died and Harry had told her that his posting in Jhansi, India, would continue for another two years, Ada had been devastated. He had already been gone for two years, and her plans for his return in the near future were no longer relevant.

She so wanted his baby. Women all around were having babies and she was so envious. It would be another two years before they could try for their own family. She accepted it though, what could she do? Harry was in the Army, and he had to serve his country.

Chapter Eight

Harry had been up early, he was going to do some running before reporting for his duties. It was light early now, and a lot cooler than waiting until after duties had finished. He prepared a bottle of water, dressed in his shorts and vest top and headed towards the hills.

Harry enjoyed his walking, but running was a lot more strenuous. He needed to stop regularly to catch his breath. More practice makes perfect, the saying goes. The stopwatch was set and Harry carried a small backpack containing a notebook and pencil to note his times down.

He needed to be quicker each session and monitoring his running was essential. There were three other soldiers entered into the cross country running competition from the Gloucester Regiment.

Percy had opted for boxing. Running wasn't Percy's best sporting achievement to date.

He passed the first marker without too much trouble, stopping to check his time. He noted it down, drank a sip of water and headed off again. His thoughts went to Ada as he was running. How did she react to his letter? He was concerned and missed her desperately. He loved the Army, but knew he needed to be home more, for his wife's sake.

The hour was up and he headed back to the barracks ready for his transport duties. He washed all the sweat from his body, changed into his Army clothes and headed for the tanks; they had needed cleaning. Two of them had been taken out for test runs the day before. Harry hadn't driven them this time, but he was responsible for their condition and maintenance.

He set to work cleaning every inch of the monster machines. Dirt was encrusted underneath the wheels. This took ages to remove and the heat was getting stronger. Harry sat down for a while and drank more water. Care was needed in this heat, it was unbearable at times.

He was a perfectionist, everything had to be exact. One small mark on the machines would not suffice for him. It might take hours, but every mark would be removed, ready for its next journey. The day was over. Harry was hungry and looking forward to his evening meal and a rest. Percy had looked exhausted as he'd walked into the dormitory. He was on combat duty and had been running, too. 'You're not drinking enough water, Percy,' Harry said at the dining table. 'You look wrecked!'

'Thanks for the compliment, Harry! I am worn out actually. I will take that on board tomorrow. I don't know how you manage to run in the mornings before doing a full shift,' Percy replied. They ate the rest of their meal in silence and headed back to the dormitory.

There were two letters waiting for them. One for Percy and one for Harry. They were both dreading opening them. 'You first, Harry,' said Percy. Harry opened the envelope slowly and started to read Ada's letter. It wasn't a long letter, but Harry sighed.

'Gladys, Ada's sister, has died. Her heart couldn't take any more and she died in her sleep.'

'I'm so sorry, how is Ada coping?' Percy had felt for his friend.

He carried on reading the letter. 'She seems to be okay. She's accepted my being here longer. There's nothing she can do about it, she says.' Harry was so glad that she had understood.

Percy opened his letter and Louisa had said much the same as Ada had, except that Percy's brothers and sister were there for company at times. Ada had no-one in Aldershot and Louisa was worried about her. She had attended Gladys's funeral and it had been such an emotional occasion.

Louisa mentioned Dorothy's new baby, Ivy, Frederick's new sister, and was overjoyed at becoming a grandmother again. She helped out whenever possible. The children keep me young, she'd said. Ada needs a family, Percy, she had written. That's the one thing missing in her life.

Harry knew she was right, but there was nothing he could do about it whilst still in India. He just prayed she would be okay until he returned home. He loved her so much, she was his only true love. Perhaps he should suggest that she moves back home in his next letter!

Ada was now back in Aldershot. She stepped off the bus and walked into the library the next morning. Agnes was glad to see her. 'The past week has been busy, Ada. How were things back home?'

She filled Agnes in with the details of Gladys's funeral, her father and stepmother and her siblings. 'It is so busy at Windsor Cottage. Coming back to Aldershot seems like a rest,' Ada replied. There was plenty to do and Agnes needed to catch up on her paperwork. Ada was left to look after the customers and replace the returned books on the shelf, as well as covering the reception desk.

She had returned to the bungalow quite late the previous evening, so hadn't been able to prepare sandwiches for her lunch.

Walking to the bakers in her lunch break, she bought a sandwich and a drink. She also picked up the local newspaper and walked into Priory Park to eat her food. Priory Park was busy that afternoon. Young children were playing on the lawn, whilst mothers sat on the benches watching them. Elderly couples walked around the paths, admiring the flowers and revelling in the sunshine.

Ada opened the newspaper and glanced at the property page. She was looking for rented accommodation in the area, and noticed there were rooms to let in Holmesdale Road. Two rooms, it said, with a shared washroom. The rent was reasonable and affordable, and there was a small garden to the front of the property, linked to the rooms being let.

It was worth a look, and she marked the page with a pen. She would find the road after work and check out the area. She had decided to seriously consider moving to Reigate. It seemed the sensible thing to do. Harry could live there with her when he was on leave, and not posted abroad.

Reigate was a lovely town and Ada needed to be back in the community again. The bungalow was okay, but she felt ready to move on. Two years was a long time and she felt decisions to her advantage needed to be made.

It was 5 o'clock and Ada left the library and hunted out Holmesdale Road. It was located within five minutes from her workplace, an ideal position. Terraced houses stood both sides of the road, three storeys high. Cars were parked comfortably outside some of the houses, and there was a corner shop selling groceries and miscellaneous goods, situated halfway down.

The area looked clean, tidy and didn't appear too noisy. Ada decided to arrange a viewing. She knocked on the door at number 49 and inquired into looking at the rooms. The door was answered by a young man, who explained that the landlord lived next door, at number 47.

Tapping on the letterbox next door, an elderly gentleman answered. Ada was to meet him after work the next day, to be shown around the accommodation being let. She caught the next bus back to the barracks, hoping tomorrow would be a good day.

Ada met Mr Smith the next evening after finishing work. He opened the front door at number 49 Holmesdale Road with a solid brass key, and asked Ada to follow him. The rooms vacant were on the first floor. Mr Smith unlocked the internal door nearest to the front of the house, and walked inside. Ada followed him and glanced around the room.

It was a large room, light and airy. She was pleasantly surprised. The kitchen area covered the entire wall opposite the large bay window. There was a large kitchen cabinet, painted green, a gas cooker and fridge, and a kitchen sink with a large drainer.

The kitchen table separated the kitchen area from the sitting room. There was a small settee and two armchairs, a small coffee table and a dresser for storage. A coal fire was set into the marble fireplace and a large mirror hung above it.

She was impressed. The room had been painted white and there was a large rug centred around the settee and the armchairs. It looked cosy, but needed a few feminine personal effects to make it look and feel like home. Through the doorway next to the dresser, the double bedroom was situated.

The room was a good size, and comfortably furnished with a bed, wardrobe and a chest of drawers. Two small rugs either side of the bed, and matching bedside cabinets completed the room. There was a small bedside light on one of the cabinets. It needed new curtains, Ada had decided.

A small washbasin was situated in the corner of the bedroom, with a bathroom cabinet and mirror above it. A curtain draped around the washbasin was needed to tidy it up, she thought. All good so far!

The small garden was accessible via the door next to the bay window, in the sitting room. It was ideal for plant pots, a small table and chair and not much else. No room for a washing line. Mr Smith advised her that a scullery was situated in the building in the back yard, and there was a washing line for everyone to use.

The communal washroom housed an antiquated shower, a large washbasin and a toilet. The room was a bit dreary, but served its purpose. With a washbasin in the bedroom, Ada was happy with the rooms and asked about the rent, electric and any other utility charges.

Mr Smith shook her hand and they agreed to meet again the next day, with a deposit to secure the rooms. There were two other occupants in the house, she was told. Both were single men, one a pensioner, and another who worked locally and had never caused any problems whilst occupying the property.

There was another washroom on the second floor, which the other occupants usually used, Mr Smith advised her. This meant that Ada would have sole use of the washroom on the first floor. She was even more impressed and thanked him, promising to see him again soon.

The next morning, Ada woke up smiling and knew she was making the right decision. She wanted to move to Reigate and make 49 Holmesdale Road hers and Harry's home, for when he returned from India. She needed to write to him soon. The spark had just returned into her life. She had a new challenge now and had plenty to keep her occupied for a while.

The day flew by in the library and she made her visit to Mr Smith in her lunch break. Handing him the deposit and a months rent in advance, she advised him that she would need to give her notice in the barracks, which she wouldn't be able to do until the weekend. Hopefully she could move in within the next week.

Mr Smith was okay with her moving in then, and handed her two keys, one for the front door and the other for the rooms. She could take things into her new home daily, on the way to work. She didn't have that much, but things would be a lot easier for her in stages.

Ada looked pleased with herself as she entered the library for her afternoon shift. Agnes commented on her mood, and was told of her future home in Holmesdale Road. Ada was over the moon, and she gave

Agnes details of the rooms she would be renting, highlighting their size and the location.

'I'll be able to walk to work and visit the parks on my days off,' she explained. 'The shops will be on my doorstep, too,' Ada was so looking forward to her move, and the excitement was obvious.

She couldn't stop talking about it.

Agnes also lived locally, she wasn't married and still lived at home. Her mother suffered badly with arthritis, so she helped out a lot when she wasn't working.

'I'm pleased for you, Ada. Perhaps we could go out on occasions during the weekends?'

'I would love to, Agnes. I know I've made the right decision already.' Ada smiled again and continued with her work. Agnes was 10 years older than her, but could become a good friend as well as her boss.

The weekend arrived and Ada handed her notice in on the bungalow. She thanked them for everything and her new address was given, and her reason for moving. The receptionist, a serving soldier, wished her well and explained the procedure for drawing funds from Harry's salary. She could deal with the bank in Reigate if she wanted to, or call back in the barracks when needed. Ada was more than happy with the arrangements and headed back to the bungalow.

There was packing to do and cleaning, so she made herself a cup of tea, a sandwich and began. She started packing her clothes, realising she needed another suitcase. With Gladys's clothes and her purchases over the past two years, she had amassed a lot more than she'd thought. There was also Harry's clothes to pack.

Ada walked over to the library and asked Elizabeth if she could borrow her suitcase. She told her of her move and invited her to visit whenever she was in Reigate. Elizabeth understood her reasons for moving and wished her well. She would bring her suitcase over to Ada when she had finished her library duties. Ada thanked her and walked back to the bungalow.

The bungalow looked spotless. All the cupboards were cleaned inside, the floors were bleached and the fireplace shone. She was pleased with her efforts. Ada was going to take her cushions with her, but leave the curtains. The windows in Holmesdale Road were much bigger, so she would have to buy new ones. The ones hanging were old and worn, and a kettle and various other household items would need to be purchased.

Ada was excited and worked until midnight without noticing the time. Tomorrow was another day of cleaning and packing and she retired for the night, sleeping more soundly than she had ever done before.

Ada was now settled in her new home. She had managed to carry a suitcase each day for the first two days, and bags with her other household items on the other days. Her clothes had been put away in the wardrobe and drawers, along with Harry's possessions. All the cupboards in the bungalow had been emptied and the property left spotlessly clean and tidy, ready for the next occupier.

She needed to take Elizabeth's suitcase back to the barracks, check the bungalow over one last time and hand in her keys. This was a job for Saturday. Until then Ada was able to find a place in her new home for her possessions, on returning home from work of an evening.

Ada had bought a kettle and a radio, items that were already in the bungalow when they had moved in. Her new home didn't have these and they were essential. She would look for curtain material later, as she wanted to stock her kitchen cabinet up with food first.

Sleeping wasn't a problem in her new home, in fact she seemed to sleep a lot better than in the bungalow. Ada had forgotten Gladys's diary until she was unpacking. On returning to Windsor Cottage, she had placed it in a drawer and not found time to read it. She decided to take it to bed with her and placed it on the bedside cabinet.

She needed to write to Harry, telling him of her move, her new address and to give him details of their new home. She was sure he would be pleased with her choice. Aldershot barracks was aware of her new address, and any letters Harry had sent would have been redirected there.

After washing herself in the first floor washroom, Ada changed into her nightdress and settled into bed. She had made sure the door was locked and turned out the main lights. With the bedside light on, Ada wrote to Harry, her father and Dorothy. She placed them in envelopes, ready to post the next day. All were similar letters, quite short and to the point, but necessary. She would send further information shortly, she had said. Once familiar with the rooms, area and Reigate as a home town, Ada would have more to write about. There were places unknown to her and others she'd noticed on the bus, definitely worth hunting out.

Sleep was beckoning her, so she turned out the light and settled into bed for the night. Gladys's diary could wait another day. So much had happened in so few days, Ada's head was in a spin. She was elated and knew things would be easier for her in the future.

Saturday had arrived and Ada was on the bus heading for Aldershot barracks. She carried Elizabeth's suitcase and the keys to the bungalow. After dropping the suitcase off in the library and saying goodbye to Elizabeth, she headed for the bungalow. On double checking everywhere, until she was certain nothing of hers and Harry's possessions were left, it was time to hand the keys in. The soldier on reception wished her luck and Ada thanked him. The return journey to Reigate was an end to yet another chapter in her life. It was quite daunting, but she'd felt excited, too!

Gladys had written lots in her diary. From how she felt about losing her mother, her father remarrying their stepmother, and their siblings being born. She seemed to pour her heart out and Ada was near to tears reading it.

She expressed how she had felt after seeing the doctor in the barracks, and being told of her medical problems, and how she was going to cope with it. She also praised Ada for her concern and taking the trouble to take her to the doctor to be checked over.

Ada was becoming overwhelmed and closed the diary promising to read more the next day. She slept soundly and awoke refreshed, ready for another day. Sunday was a day off work and she headed to the park for a walk. She couldn't contain her excitement. Was she a child all over again?

Sitting in the park admiring the view, watching the children playing, and listening to conversations from courting couples taking a leisurely stroll, took Ada back to Victoria Park in Frome. She so loved that park and had so enjoyed the day she had spent there with Harry, after their wedding night. That day would be remembered forever, top of the list for Ada.

She missed him so much and wondered when she would hear from him again. What would he be doing now? Did he have a day of rest on a Sunday in India? Ada had never asked him in her letters, only now she was thinking about it. She would mention it in her next one. She imagined he was there with her now and talking to her. Sat beside her, consuming the peace and quiet and relaxing together with their arms entwined.

A little boy had thrown a ball. It had hit her on the leg, forcing her to wake up from the cloud she seemed to be on. She threw the ball back to him, got up from the bench and walked back to her new home. Ada had never done anything like that before, why now?

Back in the rooms, she busied herself with cooking a meal and listening to the radio. She sang the songs as they played, ate her meal and smiled to herself. She felt content and more relaxed than she had ever been. The sun was shining, birds were singing and she was thinking of Harry.

There was a knock on the door. Ada got up from the kitchen table and answered it. She remembered the young man from viewing the rooms. He introduced himself as Reginald and welcomed her to number 49. Ada was taken aback with the gesture and had thanked him.

Ada opened the door wide to allow him into the sitting room and offered him a cup of tea. He accepted and sat down on the settee. He told her that he was living on the second floor and Edward Brooker lived on the top floor.

'I'm Ada Tracey,' she said.

'Really, we could be related,' he responded. 'My surname is Tracey too!'

The conversation continued for almost an hour. Ada spoke of Harry and the Army and his whereabouts. She talked about her family at Windsor Cottage, her job in the library and Gladys's death. Reginald confided in her also. He was a road sweeper in Reigate, was single and had lived at number 49 for two years. His parents lived in Guildford, not far away.

'Harry took me to Guildford before he was posted to India. It's nice there, but I prefer it here,' Ada advised him, remembering the day Harry had taken her there. She spoke about Aldershot and her bungalow in the barracks and pointed to the curtains. She needed to buy new ones to make it homely. There was something about curtains, and cushions; Ada's view on things, that was.

'A woman's touch!' Reginald said and laughed. Ada liked him, and felt she had known him all her life.

Reginald left and Ada cleared the dishes and prepared for bed. She was pleased with her day and slept soundly. She hadn't thought about Gladys's diary until she'd felt too tired to open it. There was another day tomorrow.

Work was quiet the next day, quieter than usual. She busied herself tidying up the books and dusting the counter and tables. There were a few ladies engrossed in their paperwork, not needing help. Agnes was sorting out new books recently delivered to the library, something Ada couldn't help with. Agnes had her way of doing things and she didn't want to interfere.

It was raining out, so Ada ate her sandwiches in the office at lunchtime. Agnes popped her head in and asked how her weekend had gone. Telling her about handing her keys in, visiting Elizabeth and her resident visitor the day before, Ada sounded excited. Agnes invited her to her mother's house on the Saturday for tea and cakes and she accepted, smiling.

The rest of the week flew by. She still hadn't met Edward Brooker, so walked up the two flights of stairs and knocked on his door. She needed to meet him. An elderly gentleman answered and asked her inside. 'I've come to introduce myself. I'm Ada from the first floor. I moved in a little over a week ago,' she said.

'I'm Edward and it's nice to meet you. I don't go out much, Ada, I'm retired now. I adore reading and can't walk that far, but I've got used to it. My wife died ten years ago, and we didn't have any children.'

Ada felt sorry for him. 'I work in the library, Edward. Can I pick some books up for you to read? I'd be happy to help.'

'I like historical books, the 1st World War and anything relating to it. I was in the Army when I was younger. I would appreciate that and thank you,' Edward replied.

'My husband is in India at the moment. He's in the Gloucester Regiment. I will bring some books up tomorrow.'

She hadn't been offered any tea and biscuits, so she bid him a good day and promised to see him the next evening. After preparing herself some food and a drink, she retired and returned to reading Gladys's diary.

Gladys had kept a daily detailed history of her illness after she was diagnosed by the doctor in Aldershot. Each day she seemed to grow weaker and weaker, but tried not to show it to her family.

She worried more about the extra work Alice and Blanche had to do because of her inability to help out, than she had about her ailing health. Always concerned about others, before herself. That was Ada's sister.

I can't worry Father and Stepmother, she had written, and Ada could hear her saying it. They have so much to do with the little ones and the cottage. I look forward to Ada coming home, as she has time to spend with me and we can talk and laugh with one another. I feel such a burden to everyone.

Gladys expressed her happiness on baby Alfred being born and although she wasn't able to pick him up, her father would lift him from his cot and place him on her lap for a cuddle. I will never have my own children, but I truly love my younger siblings, Gladys had said.

She hoped Alice and Ada would have children soon and Blanche would marry in the future.

Ernest had wanted to join the Army and talked about it constantly. Gladys was sure he would realise his dreams. Harry was mentioned, and she hoped he would be home soon for Ada. Gladys loved her father and didn't want any of her family to be sad on her death. Life was for living, she had said.

Her last notes were written the day before she died… I'm struggling today. I can hardly breathe.

Father has called the doctor, but somehow I don't think he will be able to help me. Blanche has brought some onion soup to my room. I've eaten a little of it. I just want to sleep. Gladys had died during the night. She'd written her last words, so sad.

Ada closed the diary and cried. She had loved her sister dearly and was missing her letters, and being able to see her on her visits home. She was going to make the most of her life, for Gladys's sake and for hers. For the first night in ages, she struggled to sleep.

There were two letters in the communal letterbox for Ada when she returned home from work the next evening. She had made herself a cup of tea and opened the first one. It was from Harry. He had received her letter telling him of her change of address, and was pleased for her. He agreed with her being nearer work and able to walk to the shops, parks and the town's facilities.

He spoke about his cross country running and how he was beating his time every day. The tanks were in immaculate condition as well as the other vehicles, and Star, Blaze and Blade were doing okay. The weather was still extremely hot, but the rainy season had stopped.

The second letter was from Sarah, inviting her to stay with her and her family over the Christmas period. It was almost September, just a few days were left in August and Ada hadn't thought about Christmas yet. Sarah now had a son, Henry, and she wanted her to meet him. Alfred was being posted to Cairo after Christmas, she had said. Ada would accept the invitation and she needed to start knitting in blue!

Walking up the stairs to Edward's rooms, she heard footsteps behind her and stopped. She turned, bumping into Reginald on the stairs. 'Sorry,' Reginald said. 'I didn't realise you were going to stop. Were you looking for me?'

'No, I am taking some library books to Edward. I introduced myself yesterday and he expressed a liking to historical books on World War 1. I've found some for him to read.'

'That's very thoughtful of you, Ada. When you've finished I will have a cup of tea and some biscuits waiting for you. Edward isn't one to make people too welcome. He's no trouble, but keeps himself to himself though.'

'Okay, I will be down soon.' Ada replied.

Edward was pleased to see her and accepted the books. He read the front covers, confirming that they were his type of book. She would call up in a few days to see how much he had read. Ada said her goodbyes and headed down the stairs to Reginald's rooms.

The door was open and Ada entered. The teapot was hot and two cups and saucers were laid out on the kitchen table. A plateful of biscuits took centre stage. Reginald was sat at the table waiting for her.

'I knew you wouldn't be up there long,' Reginald said, in a know-it-all attitude. 'I've been here for two years and he's never offered me a cup of tea.'

'I think he's lonely and used to his own company, and he's not getting any younger.' Ada replied.

Reginald poured the tea and offered the plate of biscuits. She hadn't eaten yet and gladly accepted.

Glancing around, Ada was pleasantly surprised with the room. It was clean, tidy and clutter free. For a single man, she hadn't expected it to be like it. She did notice the curtains though. 'Would you like me to make some new curtains for you, Reginald. Yours look worse for wear as mine does. I need to buy material for myself, I could double up?'

'I wouldn't say no, Ada. Would I be putting you to much trouble? I'm not any good with a sewing needle.'

'Not at all, I love being busy, Reginald. I've got baby clothes to knit as well.'

Ada's move to Reigate was a conscious one. To be nearer the library, living in a small town with more amenities, parks to walk around and to be able to make more social contact. It could be Harry's home too eventually. She had made the right decision.

Reginald and Edward were her neighbours. They lived in the same house, and she enjoyed their company. Coming from a large family, she could never ignore anyone, it wasn't in her nature. They became good friends and helped each other out.

Edward couldn't help her physically, but he would sit and listen to her bantering on and on, agreeing or disagreeing with her. He would nod his head, smile at her, shrug his shoulders or laugh at her, until Ada's mouth finally gave up.

Reginald, on the other hand was Ada's age and helped her in other ways. He would take her to the cinema, to tea rooms in Reigate and Guildford, and accompanied her home after a dance one evening. Ada never intended to give him the wrong impression, but as a single man, she couldn't blame him entirely for what had happened later.

Ada was naïve, but she liked his attention, maybe more than a little. Harry was always on her mind, but he wasn't there with her, and she needed company, and a social life of some kind.

Reginald was a companion, someone to join her on occasions where two were company, and attending alone just didn't seem appropriate.

CHAPTER NINE

The weekend had arrived and Ada had woken up early. She needed to go to the scullery (or laundry room as it is known today) before meeting Agnes at 5 o'clock for tea, with her and her mother. She placed her laundry in her trolley and pulled it through the back door and into the yard. The outhouse was situated at the end of the small garden and she used the key that she'd been given shortly after she'd moved in, to open the door.

She placed the laundry into the copper, waited for the water to heat up and added the soap flakes. The dolly was used to ensure the clothes were immersed evenly, and she continued to prod the clothes to remove the dirt. It took nearly two hours to completion. The laundry needed to be put through the mangle and then hung on the washing line to dry.

Ada usually washed her 'smalls' and individual items in the washroom, but her bedding, towels, tablecloths and tea towels needed to be put into the copper and given a hot wash. Thankfully, this was only needed on a fortnightly basis.

She was hanging the washing on the line when Reginald tapped her on the shoulder. 'Hello again,' he said.

'Hi, are you going to do your laundry?' It was a straightforward question.

'No, I could see you in the window. I was heading for the tearooms down the High Street. Well, it's more like a cafe really. They do a lovely cooked breakfast there, trust me. Would you like to accompany me?' The thought was tempting and she had almost finished.

'Come on, I will help you hang the clothes.' he said.

Ada couldn't believe how hungry she was. 'I don't usually eat so much, but I'm enjoying this.' She stopped to drink some of her tea, then continued eating her meal. Reginald had finished his and was sat opposite, staring at her.

Ada felt embarrassed and knew she was blushing. 'I'm sorry,' Reginald said. 'Anyone would think you hadn't eaten for days. I'm glad you've a good appetite, though. We must do it again.'

It was now 12 o'clock, they had been talking for ages and had ordered a second cup of tea. Ada stood up and thanked him for a lovely morning and headed back home. She'd almost skipped home, feeling alive again.

Agnes lived about twenty minutes walk away. She had changed her clothes, brushed her hair and bought a bunch of flowers to give to Agnes's mother. She didn't think she could possibly be hungry after the morning's meal in the tearooms, but was looking forward to meeting Agnes and her mother. Agnes had spoken about Mabel a lot in work.

The table was set with several different cakes, sandwiches and biscuits, all home-made. Ada commented on the display and Mabel, Agnes's mother, thanked her. She drank tea and ate whilst discussing everything from the weather, to the little girl two doors away from Mabel's house! She had never been so popular and was lapping up every minute of it.

After a day filled with socialising it had seemed, Ada returned home feeling exhausted and prepared for bed. She needed to write to Sarah, her father and Harry. Christmas was months away and knitting needed to be done for Sarah's baby. The curtain material was sitting on the bedroom chair, waiting to be cut and sewn. She was well behind with everything and needed to catch up.

After writing her letters, putting them in the envelopes and placing stamps on them ready to post, she settled for the night. She promised to start sewing the curtains the following morning, for hers and Reginald's windows. There didn't seem to be enough hours in a day.

Harry had been moved back to stable duties and had been put in charge of the parades again. Percy was now back on transport duties. They were both delighted. Combat duties hadn't been Percy's favourite and Harry loved looking after the horses. They were his babies, big ones at that.

Star, Blaze and Blade were pleased to see him back too, and walked towards him to be made a fuss of. They were his children, after all. The weather was humid, but tolerable. He placed a saddle on Blade and took him for a ride around the fields. Blade was much quieter now and co-operated with all of his riders.

They checked on the mules, stopped and spoke to the workers in the fields, and then headed back to the stables. The Sergeant was at the stables waiting to speak to him, so Harry dismounted and Blaze was put back into the stable by another member of staff. Harry approached the Sergeant and raised his hand to salute.

'There's no need, Private,' he said. 'I'm here to inform you of the next parade in two days time. I'm sure you will be able to organise everything to the Sergeant Major's satisfaction. The parade will begin at 3pm and we will need the carriage as usual.'

'Yes, Sir. I will start preparation first thing tomorrow morning,' Harry replied.

'Thank you. Have a good day,' the Sergeant said and walked away.

'Did you hear that, Star? We have a parade to organise. You and Blade can pull the carriage I think, and I will ride Blaze,' Harry had decided, looking at the three of them. Where were the horses dressings? He asked the stable staff, as he needed to check that they were in good condition and didn't need cleaning.

Back in the dormitory, Percy checked for letters. There were two for Harry and one for himself.

He put them on their beds and headed for the dining area. He was hungry and very thirsty. Harry walked in behind him, they both ate their food greedily. 'It must be the weather, Percy. It would be getting colder back home now. It's still stifling here.'

Harry opened his mail. His mother had told him that uncle Herbert wasn't well. He had retired, but didn't seem to be himself. John Henry was 5 now and attending school and James was almost 2 and into everything. Albert was still working with his stepfather and Frank junior had now moved into the farm in Ebrington to help out.

Joe and Rose had two children now and had rented a cottage nearby. Joe still worked on the farm, but didn't sleep over. Millie was still helping

Martha in the cottage and was now 18, and Richard was still at school. Things were a lot easier now for Harry's mother.

Mary Ann, George's widow, still called into his uncles farm with home-made food on occasions, but at 66 wasn't as mobile as she used to be. Martha was now cooking extra meals to send to her brothers and her son. Frank junior would visit and carry the meals on the bus, or Albert would take them in his car. James, the widower from two doors away, helped out only two days a week now.

Ada had asked how Harry was. She was interested in the weather in India and had said the English climate was becoming cold, and nights were drawing in now. She had been busy sewing and knitting and told Harry she would be spending Christmas at Sarah's in Portland.

She was due a visit to her father's on her next week off work and would call in to see Louisa then. She knew how Percy worried about her. Ada mentioned Edward and Reginald, her neighbours. Reginald was mentioned a little too often for Harry's liking, but he put it to the back of his mind.

Harry was glad Ada was okay, and coping without him. She loved her job and had made good friends since they had married. Ada had written to Millie recently, all had seemed well there. Agnes had become a good friend as well as her boss, and she was going out for lunch with her the next day, followed by a walk around the park, and Harry was pleased for her.

Percy had received a letter from Dorothy. She mentioned Frederick, her husband, and her two children. Everything was good there. She hoped Percy was doing okay too. Dorothy sent Percy a photograph of the children and he pinned it on the wall next to his bed. He studied it for ages, as he still hadn't met his nephew and niece.

The day had been hot and long and they both retired to their beds until early next morning. Harry was due a week's leave. He couldn't go home, but he could spend more time running and riding the horses. Percy had already taken his week's leave and had concentrated on his boxing and totally relaxing, something Harry could never do. He wouldn't know how to relax!

The parade went ahead without any mishaps. The horses behaved impeccably, and seemed to take great pleasure in participating in it. They revelled in the glory of being dressed for the occasion in the Gloucester's Regimental colours. Star and Blade carried the carriage housing the Sergeant and Sergeant Major to perfection. Harry was well and truly pleased with the day, and everything about the parade.

Afterwards, the dressings were carefully packed away. The carriage was cleaned and covered over, ready for the next parade. The horses were groomed, fed and watered. Harry said goodnight and headed for the dormitory and a week's leave.

He started writing a letter to Ada and asked her to send some photographs of her and their new home. Percy had a photograph of his niece and nephew pinned next to his bed, he told her, and he'd like one of her also. Harry wanted a recent one of Ada, to replace the photograph he had carried in his shirt pocket. Harry didn't know if she had a camera, but it was worth asking.

Ada had been given a week's leave from the library in the October and spent it at her father's. He looked well. The reduction in working hours in the coal mines seemed to have agreed with him. Her stepmother was no different, not that Ada expected her to be.

The twins had started school now, leaving Roland, now 3, and a mischievous Alfred left at home. Blanche was busy cleaning the kitchen and stopped when Ada entered the cottage. She had so much to tell her, and her face lit up with excitement.

Ada asked about Alice and Blanche told her that she was well. Alice normally called into Windsor Cottage twice a week. She kept herself busy in hers and Henry's home in Frome the remainder of the time. Henry worked irregular hours and Alice wanted to be there when he was home. She would see Alice before she went back to Reigate.

Blanche put the kettle on and Ada sat down at the kitchen table. 'Well, out with it, Blanche,' she said. 'You've been itching to tell me something since I walked through the door.'

'I didn't realise I was that obvious,' she replied. 'I've been to Dick's house in Chew Magna. Wilfred picked me up in his car and took me there. His parents, Walter and Alice Daisy, are lovely. So are his family, Ada. I know he's only 15 at the moment, but I'm sure he's the one for me.'

'You've plenty of time, Blanche, enjoy being friends for now. Get to know the family and spend time with them. I was never able to court Harry properly, as everything happened so quickly. You're the lucky one, Blanche.' Ada replied slightly envious. If only she had met Harry earlier.

Dick lived in Jessamine Cottage in Chew Magna. His father Walter was a labourer in the Iron Oxide works based locally. Wilfred was the oldest, followed by Gilbert, Arthur, Ivy, Hilda, Elsie and Irene. Dick came between Arthur and Ivy. Stanley, another brother, had died in 1916 at just 7 years of age. Alice Daisy was expecting again and the baby was due in the summer.

It was hectic, Blanche had said, but everyone had seemed to be happy. Walt (as they called him) and Alice Daisy loved their children and spent a lot of time entertaining them. Housework was important to them, but never a ritual, unlike the way their stepmother ran Windsor Cottage. Blanche seemed besotted with Dick and Ada wanted her to be happy.

Ada had seen most of her family in the week she'd spent there. Phyllis and Dorothy were turning into proper grown ups now. They were still only 9 and 10, but acted so mature for their ages. Ernest was his father's helper after school, and was in his element being outside in the fields. He was now in charge of milking the cows after food, during the week and at weekends, and helped with the kitchen garden.

Alice called around and told Ada that she had miscarried a child. She hadn't known, but Alice said she was fine now, and was coping with her loss. Dorothy and Louisa were both well and the children were growing fast. Ada apologised for not bringing knitted items with on her this occasion, and they spent hours talking about Holmesdale Road and her newfound friends in Reigate.

Christmas had arrived and Ada headed for Portland and Sarah's house. She had knitted several baby items in blue, including her favourite blanket. She had also made another teddy bear, for Florence this time. The train journey was peaceful and Ada read most of the way. 1925 had been an eventful year in more ways than one, both happy and sad, good and bad.

Sarah welcomed her and she headed straight for baby Henry. He was absolutely gorgeous and she immediately picked him up. Sarah wouldn't mind, she knew. Florence had grown loads and was a proper chatterbox. Alfred walked in an hour later and they were still deep in conversation. There was so much to talk about.

The dinner was cooking and Ada got up from the settee and helped lay the kitchen table. Sarah fed baby Henry and put him back in his cot. Alfred was due to leave for Cairo in a week's time, he had told her. He wasn't sure how long he would be there. Ada spoke of Harry and her disappointment at the length of time he had been in India. 'I won't be able to recognise him when he returns,' she said jokingly.

Sarah knew how much Ada was missing him and quickly changed the subject. 'I've got a small chicken and a piece of beef for tomorrow's Christmas dinner and plenty of vegetables. I've made some minced pies and a Christmas cake, Ada. I'm looking forward to it,' she said. The evening meal was ready and they all sat to the table and ate in silence.

The two days passed so quickly and Ada was back on the train heading for home. Sarah had given her a camera for a Christmas present and she was delighted. Florence loved her teddy bear and Sarah was thankful for the baby's clothes. They both promised to write to each other soon.

Ada was back in her home. Her few days at Sarah's were memorable, all good, but she was glad to be back in Reigate and felt ready for bed. She made herself a warm drink and retired. The unpacking could wait until the morning. The library didn't open for another two days, anyway.

After unpacking, Ada sat at the kitchen table and studied the camera. It was a Brownie No 2 Cartridge Hawk-eye Model B and used a film 120, which she would need to purchase when the shops reopened after the Christmas break.

She was pleased with her present and needed to read and follow the instructions. Photography wasn't something Ada was used to, she hadn't taken photographs on her wedding day, but she had her memories. Harry had wanted a photograph sent in his next letter, Ada remembered. Hopefully, she would be able to now.

There were Christmas cards in her mail on returning from Portland. Her father had sent her a card with money inside. Treat yourself Ada. You deserve it, he had written.

Likewise, Louisa had sent her a card with money inside and Dorothy had as well.

There was a new clothes shop opened in the main High Street. She would take a look in a few days. There were also cards from Edward and Reginald, so she placed them all on the mantelpiece. Harry had sent a letter and looking at the writing on the envelope, Blanche had sent her one, too.

Millie and Martha had sent cards before Ada had left for Portland. They had been looking forward to Christmas Day and had wished her a good break at Sarah's. Agnes had given her a pot plant before finishing work, which took pride of place in the bay window.

She was preparing a sandwich and a cup of tea when Reginald knocked on the door. 'Come in, Reginald. I hope you had a good Christmas,' she said.

'It was quiet. I called in to see my parents and had food with them.' he answered, but didn't volunteer any more information. Ada offered him a sandwich and a cup of tea, but he declined, telling her that he'd just eaten.

'There's a Mary Pickford film, Sparrows, on at the cinema in Guildford tomorrow. I was wondering if you'd like to see it?'

Ada hesitated before answering. 'Yes, I'd love to Reginald and thank you.'

Reginald had arranged to meet her at 6 o'clock the next day, they could take the bus to Guildford. He excused himself and headed upstairs to his rooms.

She opened Harry's letter. The Regiment had all had an early combined Christmas dinner amid the heat of the sun. The weather didn't seem to cool down a lot in India, a completely different climate to England. They had all had a good day, Harry had said.

He had enjoyed his week's leave and had concentrated on his running. The Regiment hadn't won the cup for the event, but he was pleased with his timing at the finish, and commended by the Sergeant for his dedication. Percy's group had won the boxing cup and he had loved gloating to Harry about it.

Duties were to recommence on the 27th December and Harry was looking forward to being busy again after the seasonal break. The Regiment had been allowed a seasonal drink, and they had both raised a toast to their families for the New Year, he had said. Ada laughed at his humour, he couldn't stay serious for long. That was what she loved about him!

Ada dressed for the cinema. It was still cold outside, so she put her coat with the fur collar on and her hat and gloves. Reginald knocked on the door precisely at 6 o'clock. On answering the door she commented on his punctuality.

'I'm always on time, Ada. I'm never late for anything. I'm used to routine, it keeps me going,' Reginald had replied very seriously.

'Good, I like to be on time too, though there are days I could happily stay in bed. Especially these cold mornings, I was reading Harry's letter yesterday and it's still hot in India.'

They boarded the bus to Guildford and talked about the film. Ada hadn't been to the cinema since Harry had taken her, before they were married. She was looking forward to it. Reginald paid for the tickets, and Ada handed him her share. 'My treat for the curtains, Ada,' he said. 'They look good. My rooms seem a lot cosier now.'

Ada thanked him and put her money back in her purse. The film finished and they both commented on its content. Mary Pickford was a famous actress and she had directed the film as well as star in it. It was one of her best.

They called into the tearooms attached to the cinema and Ada bought a coffee for them both. She spoke about Christmas with Sarah and her family. Ada described Henry, Sarah's baby, and Florence, and talked about them, telling him how busy they were. Reginald could tell she liked children. He briefly spoke of his parents. Somehow she was sure that they didn't see eye to eye.

They were back at Holmesdale Road. Ada thanked him for the evening and closed the door. She had enjoyed herself and Reginald was good company. After settling herself in bed, she read Blanche's letter and slept soundly.

Blanche was seeing Dick regularly now. There had been another church dance and they had met there. Wilfred was picking her up again to visit the Marsh family, and Ernest was also invited. There were siblings nearer his age in the family. Arthur was 16 and only 2 years older than him. Dick was 15, Ivy was 11 and Hilda was 7. Blanche knew he would like them.

Dorothy and Phyllis were becoming "proper little madames" and Ethel Mary was shouting at them more than usual. They needed more discipline, she had told Archibald. Her father was more lenient with the children, Ada had to agree, but they were children!

Blanche ended the letter asking Ada when she would be visiting next, and hoped it would be soon. She missed her and Alice, and thought about Gladys often. She had accompanied her father and stepmother to Chard recently, spending a few hours with Jim, their brother. Jim was okay, but missing his siblings (Blanche was excelling herself with her letter writing).

Ada didn't think about her older brother that much, but mentally noted he deserved a visit from her on her next journey home. Ernest often spoke about him when she was there, but he was rarely allowed to accompany his father and stepmother to see him. Ada would take him with her.

The Christmas period was over and everyone was back to work. The library was now open and Ada had been ready and waiting outside the library door, when Agnes approached with the key to open up. Agnes asked about her break and Ada asked about Agnes and her mother. They had both used their free time wisely, but were glad to be back at work.

On her lunch break she visited the new clothes shop to spend her monies given to her for Christmas. She found a dress she liked and tried it on. It fitted perfectly and the assistant commented on how nice it had looked on her. Ada had blushed, not like her at all.

It was a deep blue, dropped waisted dress with a low v-neck and lace sleeves. There was a silk bow attached to the bodice, underneath the neckline. The assistant picked up a hat, black in colour with a rolling brim and placed it on her head. She also picked up a pair of white above the knee stockings and Ada put them on. The dress had fallen well below the knee.

She then fastened a triple string of white beads around her neck and beckoned her towards the long mirror at the farthest end of the shop. Ada stood in front of it and couldn't believe how different she had looked. 'You look fabulous, Madame. The colour really suits you.' Ada agreed and asked the price of the complete outfit.

It was slightly more than her Christmas money, but she decided to treat herself and paid the assistant. She was well satisfied with her purchases. Ada bought a film for her camera and headed back to work for the remainder of her shift.

She was trying the outfit on when Reginald knocked on the door. Ada shouted for him to enter and walked out of the bedroom looking for his approval. 'Wow, you look gorgeous, Ada. Where did you get that?' he asked.

'The new clothes shop on the High Street. Do you like it?' Ada asked.

'Like it, I love it. You look stunning.' Reginald's eyes were almost popping out of its sockets.

The camera was on the kitchen table. Ada handed it to him. 'Can you take a photograph of me, please? I need to send one to Harry.'

'Only if I can have one too,' he answered. She agreed and Reginald took two photographs. She took some of the rooms and planned to take the camera out with her the weekend, to take some scenic photographs. She thanked Reginald and returned to the bedroom to change into her day clothes and made a cup of tea for them both.

It had rained the next day. She had taken her camera to the library hoping to take some photographs during her lunch break, but that plan hadn't materialised and she had spent her lunchtime eating her sandwiches in the office. There was another day tomorrow.

Agnes had invited her to tea on the Saturday and she was looking forward to it. Her mother always made her laugh with her comments, and Ada would always come away from their house with a smile on her face. Despite her arthritis, Mabel had never felt sorry for herself and Ada commended her for it. She was an inspiration, and Agnes was proud of her.

After several cups of tea and plenty of food, Ada left and headed for home. She had taken a few photographs in the park on the way and took a few of Agnes and Mabel to add to her collection.

There were only a handful left to take, before she needed to pay a visit to the photographers to develop the film. She could then send Harry her photograph.

Weeks passed and Ada spent her time knitting baby and children's clothes. There were so many additions to the family and within her friends, there was never a shortage of items needed and she was glad she could oblige. Her hobby had come in handy, and she'd not minded at all.

Her film had been developed and Ada was pleased with the majority of the photographs, especially the two taken by Reginald. She wrote to Harry, enclosing one of them, and the other one she kept aside to give to Reginald. She looked so different and reminded herself that over three years had passed since their wedding.

Edward was still reading books that Ada had regularly took up to him, and he relished in seeing her. She was now knocking on his door with yet more books. He answered the door slowly and looked very pale. 'Are you okay, Edward? You don't look well.'

'I'm not eating very well and feel a bit nauseous. I will be fine in a few days, Ada,' he said.

Ada put the kettle on the gas cooker, opened the kitchen cupboard and took out a tin of tomato soup. Finding the can opener and a saucepan, she placed it on one of the rings. There was a small loaf of bread in the bread bin and she cut a slice and buttered it, placing it on a small plate. Ada found a bowl, spoon and two cups and saucers.

The table was laid, so Ada pulled out a chair and beckoned to Edward to sit down. The soup was bubbling on the cooker, so she poured the red liquid into the bowl and placed the bread next to it.

Ada made two cups of tea and sat opposite him, handing him the spoon.

He didn't argue and started eating while she drank her tea. They spoke about various subjects, including the weather and he seemed to liven up. He was lonely, Ada had realised, lonelier than usual. He needed company. 'I'm going to cook a roast dinner on Sunday, Edward, and you are going to join me. I'll ask Reginald too. No arguments, I'll come and get you.' Edward nodded.

Sunday arrived and she busied herself with her cooking. She had baked biscuits and cakes as well as cooking the dinner. The table was laid and Reginald had brought Edward down with him. They all ate in silence and then settled around the coal fire for tea and biscuits. Ada and the men delighted in the afternoon. The photograph was still on the dresser for Reginald and Ada handed it to him. 'This is for you,' she said.

Reginald took Edward back to his rooms and he thanked her for a lovely time. Ada promised to do it again soon. Reginald returned and helped with the dishes. 'How about the cinema again next week? The Great Gatsby is on. It will be my treat for today?'

'Yes please, it's my birthday next week. I'll be 23. It would be nice to celebrate it,' Ada said. The Great Gatsby was very watchable and Ada had looked forward to the evening. As before, they both stayed for a coffee after the film had finished, and Reginald told her more about his family than ever before. As Ada had suspected, he didn't always get on with his parents and had an older brother and a younger sister still living at home. He didn't disclose any reasons for his family problems, but she felt he was opening up a little more to her.

Reginald was 23, the same age as herself, and always appeared serious. Ada had been used to her stepmother being the same, but her father was always smiling and tried to appear joyful to his children. He couldn't stay serious for long and Harry was similar in character.

Ada was getting too close to Reginald, but being quite a naïve person hadn't realised it until he tried to kiss her. 'What are you doing?' Ada asked and moved away from him. 'I'm married to Harry, you know that.'

Reginald walked on towards the bus stop and didn't respond. Had she given him the wrong vibes? He apologised when they were sat on the bus home. 'You must have known how I felt about you, Ada?'

'I had no idea, Reginald. You're a good friend to me, you and Edward. Can we still be friends?' Ada asked, now uncertain.

'Yes of course, but if you ever want to be more than friends, don't hesitate to let me know. You are special to me and always will be.'

They opened the main door to 49 Holmesdale Road and said their good nights. As Ada prepared for bed, she wondered whether she was to blame for what had happened. She liked Reginald, but it was Harry that she loved, and always would. Nothing was ever going to change on that score.

CHAPTER TEN

Harry had received Ada's letter and her photograph, and was overjoyed. He couldn't believe how she had changed. 'She's beautiful, Percy. That's my wife!' Percy had glanced at the photograph and agreed.

'I wouldn't put it on the wall, Harry. She will become the soldiers pin-up,' he joked and laughed.

Harry joined in the laughter.

Nothing much had changed in Jhansi. The monsoon season was due again and the farm workers were putting extra hours in daily, to harvest as many of the fruits and vegetables as possible. You could never foresee how much rain would fall in such a short time, and what proportion of crops would be ruined.

The mules and a few of the horses were working hard to plough the fields in readiness for the rain. Harry attended to the stables, ensuring there was plenty of food, water and clean bedding ready for their return at the end of the day. They would be tired and Harry always treated them with care.

There had been a few more parades giving Star, Blade and Blaze plenty to do. He was proud of his children, their behaviour had been outstanding and Harry had been awarded a class 3 certificate for his detail to his duties.

Harry and Percy were both missing England now, but still had no insight as to when they would be posted back home. Harry's siblings were growing fast. He hadn't met his youngest brother, James, at all. He was almost 2 years old now and John Henry was heading for 6. Where had the time gone? He had worried about his uncles on their farm in Ebrington, and their ailing health.

Percy hadn't met either of his sister's children, even though he had their photograph by his bed in the dormitory. He didn't have a sweetheart back home, but he was missing his family terribly.

Percy was still on transport duties, but admitted that he wasn't as meticulous with the cleanliness of the vehicles as Harry had been.

There had been rumours around the campsite that soldiers were needed in China. They both hoped they wouldn't be posted there, a lot of the other soldiers were worried too. There were so many in the campsite who were desperately homesick, and had been in Jhansi for what had seemed a lifetime.

Ada tried to put her birthday evening to the back of her mind. She liked Reginald and wanted to continue their friendship. She spent her evenings walking around the parks in Reigate, taking photographs and window shopping.

The evenings were getting lighter now, and she felt she needed to spend more time outdoors. She would sit in her small garden, either reading or knitting. Agnes was invited to her home and Ada prepared a meal and a baked a Victoria sponge, and they had had a lovely evening in, promising to go out socialising again soon. She needed to concentrate on herself now, instead of worrying about Reginald and Edward, she had told herself.

Unfortunately, this wasn't Ada's nature, and a week later she was running up the stairs to see Edward, with more books and a home-made beef casserole to ensure he was eating properly.

Edward's face lit up on seeing her, and she knew she couldn't just ignore him or Reginald. They were her neighbours, after all.

May was a lovely month. The sun was shining, the daffodils and tulips decorated the parks and looked so pretty. There was a local dance in Reigate and Agnes and herself had attended. She put on her new outfit and felt special. Agnes couldn't believe how different she had looked, and commented on it.

They both spoke to regular customers who used the library, and danced in between the conversations. Ada had noticed Reginald walk into the hall. He was with a working colleague and they both approached the ladies. That's what Agnes and Ada were, ladies! They all sat down at one of the tables.

'I didn't know you were coming to the dance,' Reginald said to Ada.

'I only decided yesterday,' she replied. 'Reginald meet Agnes, we work together.' He acknowledged Agnes and introduced his friend, Stanley.

Stanley was a few years older than Reginald and Ada hadn't seen him at Holmesdale Road before. He was a handsome man, with a mop of dark curly hair. Agnes seemed quite taken by him. They all danced together throughout the evening. The men were drinking ale, but Ada and Agnes were content with orange juice, despite being offered an alcoholic drink by them both. 'We've got work in the morning,' they both said in unison. On leaving, Stanley had offered to walk Agnes home, whilst Ada and Reginald had walked back home together.

Ada spoke about Stanley and had asked about his status, where he lived and several other personal questions. There had been method in her madness! She knew Agnes would want to know more about him the next day. They both said their good nights and Reginald had shouted down the stairs to her. 'You look gorgeous, do you know that?' She had laughed and closed the door.

Agnes was extra chatty the next morning. 'I take it you got on well with Stanley, then? When are you meeting him next?'

'You're very perceptive, Ada,' Agnes replied and smiled.

'I saw the way you both looked at one another. It's how Harry and I were when we first met.'

Agnes was meeting him again in a few days time. He was taking her to Guildford for the evening and she was looking forward to it. 'Reginald has a soft spot for you, you know,' Agnes told her.

'I know, but I need him as a friend and he lives in the same house. He knows I only have eyes for Harry.'

Ada recalled the information on Stanley she had asked Reginald about the night before, and told Agnes, and Agnes had smiled. She could hear wedding bells already and only wanted the best for her friend and her boss. She needed some excitement in her life and Mabel would be happy for her.

The mail had been delivered when Ada had returned home from work the next day. There was a letter from Blanche (she was getting good), one from Millie, and the third was from Harry. Ada was impressed. She so enjoyed reading her letters, writing and returning information back. Blanche and Ernest were still visiting the Marsh family and Wilfred was still willing to pick them up and return them home in his car, all good.

Ada wasn't sure when her next week off would be, but promised to spend it at Windsor Cottage and visit the Marsh family herself. They had sounded a lovely family and Ada knew that Blanche and Ernest were connecting with them. They both needed time away from their own home.

Millie was still working hard at home with the boys and seemed content. Martha was spending a lot of time at Ebrington with Harry's uncles. She was cooking and cleaning the house, ensuring they all had a substantial meal after a hard day's work in the fields. Frank junior was still living there, so she was able to check on him too.

Harry was pleased with Ada's photograph and informed her that she was now the soldiers pin-up! The soldiers in the dormitory had said she looked fabulous, and told Harry he was a very lucky man. Ada blushed, just reading it. The weather in India had taken a turn for the worst, as anticipated. The rain was falling in torrents and many fields had been flooded.

The campsite was back to nights in playing cards, reading and writing letters. Harry wasn't used to being inside so much, and so needed to get out. He felt claustrophobic. The horses had also felt it and were not themselves. Harry had spent many nights in the stables, keeping them company.

Percy, unlike himself, seemed to be satisfied, staying indoors. He was happy playing cards with the soldiers in the dormitory, and conversing about anything and everything. He could sleep longer and relax more, unlike Harry, who once awake had to get up. He had ants in his pants, his grandmother had used to say. He looked to the sky remembering his grandparents, Harry had said in his letter. They were both sadly missed.

Ada worried about him and wished he was back home with her. No monsoons or humid days and nights, not brilliant weather in Reigate but better than in India, she was certain. Hopefully he would be home soon and she could spoil him. He deserved it, and they needed time together again as a family. Ada was still only 23, but had felt a lot older. She knew they both needed to experience their early years together, rather than apart.

It was Reginald's birthday the next month, and he invited Ada out to Guildford for the evening.

Ada accepted, but only because he had taken her out on her birthday back in the February. They dined in a posh tea room. Ada was frightened to pick up the bone china cup for fear of breaking it, and the fancy cakes looked too delicate to eat. 'I'm not used to places like this, Reginald,' she said. 'If this is how the other half live, then I'm more than content as I am!'

'You're never satisfied are you? I bring you somewhere special and you prefer the tea rooms down the road.' replied Reginald. He wasn't laughing and sounded deadly serious.

'I'm sorry. I love it here and do appreciate it. I'm just not used to it, that's all. I feel on edge and out of my comfort zone.' They drank their tea in silence and Ada picked at the fancy cakes. You could hear a pin drop in the room, and the conversation on the other tables seemed to be minimal and down to a whisper. Ada was glad when the meal had finished and Reginald had helped her on with her coat. She gave a huge sigh of relief as they walked out of the door.

Back in Holmesdale Road, Ada had invited him in, and put the kettle on the gas cooker. She had baked some biscuits the day before, and reached for the tin, opening it. After placing several biscuits on a plate and carrying them to the coffee table next to the settee, she poured the tea and took them over.

'Sorry, Reginald. That wasn't my favourite place, but I appreciated it. Thank you for tonight and Happy Birthday.' Without thinking, Ada planted a kiss on his cheek.

Reginald turned his face towards her and kissed her full on the lips. Ada didn't stop him and she enjoyed it, if she was honest with herself. Before she knew it, Reginald's hands were all over her, and she had wound her arms around his neck. He had picked her up and headed for the bedroom.

Warning signals had entered her head, but her body was responding to his caresses and before she knew it, they were in bed and making love to each other.

Ada awoke the next morning in a daze. She was dressed only in her slip, the remainder of her clothes strewn over the bedroom floor. Reginald was sleeping beside her. She was upset and blamed herself. There was no-one else to blame. She got up, put her dressing gown on and sat on the settee. Tears fell from her eyes and she couldn't hold them in.

Reginald had felt her movement and dressed quickly. He walked out of the bedroom and sat down beside her. He put his arm around her but she moved away from him, giving distance between them. 'That shouldn't have happened, Reginald, and it won't happen again. I would like you to leave please.'

Reginald tried to console her and made another attempt to put his arm around her. He could see she was upset and wanted to comfort her. He had feelings for her and always would. He made her a cup of tea and placed it on the coffee table. She was still in tears and didn't look at him. The silence was deafening, and eventually Reginald obliged and walked out of the room; stopping to look back at her before climbing the stairs to his rooms.

Reginald kept his distance over the next few weeks. Ada was upset and he didn't want to make things any worse. He cared for her deeply, but knew she was feeling guilty, as she was married to Harry. Harry had been in India for such a long time now and feelings did change, but he wasn't sure of Ada's feelings for him.

Edward continued to receive his books from the library, and Ada still spent time ensuring he was well and eating enough. She had made certain Reginald was out of the house, before climbing the stairs to visit him. She didn't feel able to communicate with him at the moment.

Agnes's relationship with Stanley was going from strength to strength and she was pleased for them both, but she knew Agnes was concerned for her. 'You've not been yourself lately, Ada. Are you okay?' Agnes asked one day.

'I'm fine, I've just got a few things on my mind that I need to sort out,' she replied.

'His name doesn't begin with 'R' does it?' Ada didn't reply and busied herself tidying the books on the library shelves.

She was feeling more tired than usual and retired to bed earlier, even though the sun was shining through the bedroom window and it wasn't dark. She would take advantage of the lighter nights as a general rule, but found she needed more sleep at the moment.

Her knitting and reading had stopped, she'd lost interest. Sarah had invited her to Portland on her next week's holiday, but Ada had declined the offer through disinterest. She had promised to visit Windsor Cottage soon, but apart from that was more than content to stay at home.

Reginald bumped into her on the High Street a month later, and thought she looked pale. He stopped in front of her as she tried to ignore him. 'Are you okay, Ada? You don't look well,' he said with concern. Ada didn't answer, she seemed to be in a dream. He shook her and shouted. 'Ada, Ada, look at me!'

'We need to talk, Reginald. Can we walk to the park? It's important,' she said in a complete daze.

It had to be said, Ada realised, and now was as good a time as any. There would never be a right time for what she had to say.

'Okay, you seem weird.' They walked to Priory Park and sat down on one of the benches. The weather was gorgeous and the flowers were in full bloom, but Ada wasn't looking at the scenery.

'What's the matter? Please tell me, you're worrying me,' Reginald pleaded.

'I've just come from the doctor's surgery. I'm expecting a baby, Reginald. What am I going to do?' For once he was silent and in shock. He had no answers for her.

After several minutes of silence, Reginald comforted her by putting his arm around her. She didn't stop him. 'You know I'll be there for you. Harry is the problem. Are you going to tell him?'

'I've got to, I can't lie to him. I don't know how he's going to take the news or whether he'll stand by me?' Ada started to cry and reached for a tissue in her coat pocket. She didn't completely blame him, she had to take some of the responsibility.

There was no point in putting things off. It was the weekend and Ada was sat outside in the chair.

She was writing a letter to Harry. Several times the paper was discarded and thrown to the floor. How was she going to tell him about the baby? She wasn't willing to give the baby up, it was unthinkable. This baby was part of her and she would manage somehow.

Finally, Ada sealed her letter in the envelope and posted it in the letterbox at the end of the road. It would take a few weeks before she would get a reply, if she got a reply! She was crying again, so she made herself a drink and laid on her bed and slept.

Monday morning had arrived and Ada knew that Agnes would suspect something wasn't right. She looked awful. Her pallor was the colour of her bed sheet, ghostly white. Her eyes were red with the tears she'd shed over the weekend, and her weight had plummeted through not eating.

Almost immediately, Agnes ushered her into her office. 'Right, out with it, Ada. I've never seen you like this before. What's the matter with you? You look dreadful,' she said. There was no point in keeping things from her. Agnes was her friend, first and foremost.

'I'm pregnant, Agnes, and it's Reginald's. He took me to Guildford on his birthday. We went to a posh tea room and I invited him back for tea and biscuits. The rest is history!' she replied. 'Reginald knows and has said he will be there for me, but it's Harry I love. How stupid I've been, Agnes.' Agnes put an arm around her as she started to cry. She seemed to be constantly in tears.

'I've written to Harry. I don't know whether he will still want me to be his wife. I wouldn't blame him. I've messed up, Agnes. What a nightmare.'

'We are all vulnerable, Ada, and Harry has been away for a long time. Hopefully he will understand. What will you do if he doesn't?' she asked.

'I don't know. I really don't know. All I know is that I'm not giving the baby up. I may never get the chance to have children again.'

Agnes gave her the day off. 'Go home and get some sleep. You need it. Things have a way of working out, Ada. Think positive,' she said sympathetically. Secretly Agnes was worried, but tried not to show it. Stanley and her had been very close to giving into temptation on their last date. This had been a warning to her, though Agnes knew

Stanley was single and didn't have the same complications that Ada had.

Ada thanked her and headed for home. She needed to eat for the baby's sake and prepared some toast and a cup of tea, before retiring to the bedroom and yet more sleep. The baby was due in March the following year. She still had a while to go and needed to sort things out, she told herself.

Harry received her letter three weeks later. After reading it, he covered his eyes with his hands.

He wouldn't allow the soldiers in the dormitory to see his tears. He couldn't believe what he had read. Percy sat down on his bed and looked over at him. He'd just walked in.

'What's happened?' Harry handed the letter to him and Percy read it and sighed. 'I don't know what to say, except she has said she loves you and it was a mistake,' he said quietly.

'I don't know if I can forgive her, Percy. When I go back home she will have a child with her that isn't mine. I'm not sure I will be able to cope.'

'Sleep on it, Harry, you have been away a long time and you hadn't been married that long when you were posted here. You can't blame her for feeling lonely. She's an attractive lady and has probably had many admirers,' Percy replied. 'I know that's not what you wanted to hear, but it's the truth. It's been over three years now.'

Harry knew he was right but was disappointed, and for the first time in years he felt so alone. He had a wife waiting for him before, he didn't know what to think now! 'I'm going for a walk. I need some time on my own,' he said and walked out of the dormitory.

Harry walked for hours and then entered the stables to talk to the horses. Star walked over to him, waiting to be smoothed. He poured his heart out to her, and she pushed her nose into his hands. 'I love her so much, Star, I'm hurting all over.'

Eventually Harry returned to the dormitory. Percy was still awake and heard him get into his bed. 'Are you okay, Harry?' he asked. Harry didn't answer, turned away from him and tried to sleep. The next morning, for the first time ever, he didn't get up for his duties. Percy had woken him, but he just lay there motionless.

'I'm not working today,' he said. End of subject!

Percy informed the Sergeant that Harry wasn't well and was still in his bed in the dormitory. 'Thank you, Private Bridges. I will go and check on him later.' A while passed and Harry had had a visit from the Sergeant. He had explained his personal problems to him, and how mentally he didn't feel able to perform his duties. He was given sick leave, and after completing the Sergeant's necessary paperwork, was told to take things easy and report to him in a week's time.

He spent his time walking, running and visiting the horses. His mind was all over the place and working overtime! He had to reply to Ada's letter, but had no idea what he wanted to say. Life had stopped in his head, and he couldn't see a way forward.

A week had passed and the silence continued. Percy tried to make conversation, but he wasn't interested in talking. He walked around in a trance, lifeless and reserved. Percy had never seen him like that before. The Sergeant had given him another week on sick leave and was concerned. He called Percy into his office.

'I'm worried about Private Tracey, and I know you're a good friend to him. How do you see him at the moment, Private Bridges?'

'I'm concerned too. He loves his wife dearly. They had less than a month together after marrying, when he was posted here. That was over three years ago,' Percy had told him. 'He's distraught and doesn't know what to do. I've only ever seen him as lifeless as this once before, and that was the first time on the ship to Germany, when he suffered from sea sickness. He's a fighter, Sergeant, but his mind is in turmoil. I don't know what else to say.' The Sergeant excused him and Percy walked out of the office.

Percy wrote to his mother, telling her in confidence of Ada and her pregnancy. Ada would visit Windsor Cottage soon and call in to see her, he was sure. He wanted to help Harry, but didn't know how? Louisa would know how to handle the situation, she was his mother.

Harry still hadn't replied to Ada's letter. He continued to walk, run and visit the horses. They were missing him, he could tell. 'What am I going to do? I need to write to her and must make a decision. Do I forgive her or do we go our separate ways? I'm not sure how much longer I will be in India,' he babbled on to Star.

The Sergeant had called him into his office two weeks later. It was nearing the end of September and he had been on sick leave for four weeks now. 'How are you feeling now, Private Tracey. Do you feel ready to return to your duties?' he asked very sincerely.

'I need to get back to work, Sergeant. I'm still uncertain of what to do regarding my personal life, but my head is clearer now thank you,' Harry replied.

'I have received new information today, Private,' the Sergeant said. 'It has come to my attention that many soldiers will be returning home in January next year. This could include Private Bridges and yourself. It has also come to my notice that volunteers are needed in Shangai in January for several months,' the Sergeant stopped momentarily.

'This is confidential information, Private Tracey. Depending on your decision regarding your personal problems, maybe this is something to think about.' The Sergeant bid him a good day and Harry walked out of the office. He had been given a lot of things to mull over, and information he couldn't disclose to Percy. He had options now.

The new week had begun and Harry returned to the stables and his duties. The horses looked pleased to see him working again, and he didn't want to disappoint them any further. He had to pull himself together fast and he knew it. He still hadn't returned Ada's letter, or written to anyone else for that matter, and he needed to start talking to Percy and the soldiers in the dormitory again.

One step at a time, he told himself. One step at a time! Harry had to write to Ada that night, and he needed to apologise to Percy. Percy was a good friend and he hadn't deserved the way he'd been treated the past month. Harry was never a bad person, but things had to be rectified, for everyone's sake.

After the evening meal was finished, they returned to their dormitory. Percy was silent and undressed ready for bed. 'I'm sorry, Percy. I haven't been fair with you. I've made a decision now, and I'm going to write to Ada tonight. My head's been all over the place, but that's no excuse for my behaviour.'

'You've had a lot to think about, Harry. It can't have been easy. Whatever you've decided, I'm behind you.'

'Thank you, Percy. You're a true friend. I couldn't ask for anyone better.' He removed his writing pad and pen from his locker and started writing.

Percy didn't ask any questions about his decision, Harry would tell him when he felt ready to. This had to be one of the hardest things ever, and he was glad it wasn't him having to decide. Harry was talking now, and that was a start in the right direction. Time would tell how the future turned out. Mistakes had been made, but no-one was perfect.

Ada wasn't sure that Harry would ever forgive her, once he'd found out she was expecting. She wouldn't have blamed him if he'd never set eyes on her again. She was at fault, no-one else, and Harry was busy serving the country and working hard. Four years had seemed like forty at times, but he was her husband and she had to cope, somehow. Her love for Harry would never change, He was her true love, and there would never be another.

CHAPTER ELEVEN

Ada wasn't doing too well with her pregnancy. She knew what morning sickness was all about now. Martha and her stepmother had spoken about how they had felt whilst pregnant, and now she was feeling it too. It wasn't good, and all she wanted to do was sleep. She was so tired. Agnes tried to give her sitting down jobs in the library; nothing too strenuous and no climbing or heavy lifting.

Ada looked so delicate, Agnes was being careful for hers and the baby's sake.

Harry's letter finally arrived and it was an ordeal in itself. Ada sat at the kitchen table, made herself a sandwich and a cup of tea before opening it, hesitating several times. She wasn't sure what to expect and didn't deserve any form of support from him. The guilt was hers and hers alone.

He started the letter telling her of his disappointment at what had happened. The weeks on sick leave and confusion in his head had also been included, along with his guilt at the way he had treated Percy, his good friend. He understood her loneliness and regretted the length of time he had been away. It had been out of his hands, he'd written.

Harry finally concluded his letter, telling her that he had made his decision. China was looking for volunteers in January, for several months, and he had put his name forward. He loved Ada and always would, but wasn't sure he could cope, returning home to her and a child not belonging to him.

He needed more time, and volunteering for China would give him that. The Sergeant had disclosed that Percy would probably be home in January, but Harry would be posted to China instead. This was the only way he could handle it, he had said. He'd apologised to Ada, but had stood by his decision.

Ada didn't cry, she couldn't blame him. She was the one in the wrong and she could understand his reservations at bringing up another man's child. This child was hers too and she couldn't give him or her up, mistake or not.

She decided to leave it a while before writing back, but was going to ask Agnes for a week's leave, to go home and tell her father. None of her family knew about the baby yet. It would be a complete shock to them all.

Reginald had called in to see her, he was worried about her. She was truthful to him from the start. She had liked him a lot, but she loved her husband, Harry. Nothing would ever change there. If Harry couldn't accept them both, she would manage on her own. Reginald had feelings, she knew, but this was her final decision. It was Harry or no-one, she'd told him.

On August 1926, Sun Chaunfang's Army, now close to the Yangtze, launched an all-out attack upon the Nationalist Forces. The worst hit was the First Route Army, defending the strategically placed city of Longtan, vital to the supply of Nanking via Shanghai.

On August 30, the full night of the Second Route Army attacked Longtan and by late afternoon, recaptured the city. Sun's Army, with losses to 2/3 of their original strength, fled across the Yantze in defeat. The Northern Expedition opened the way for another war between the Kuomintang and Guominjun during the Kuomintang Jihad in Gansu (1927-1930)

The Shanghai Massacre of 1927 was the massacring of the Communist Party in Shanghai midway in the Northern Expedition. 12[Th] July 1927 was the violent suppression of Communist Party Organisations in Shanghai by the Military Forces of Chiang Kai-shek and conservative factions in the Kuomintang.

By July 15th, the Wuhan Regime had expelled the Communists in its rank effectively ending the Kuomintang's four year alliance with Soviet Russia and its co-operation with the Chinese Civil War. With the failure of the Guangzhou uprising the Chinese Communist Party's eclipse was complete.

It was two more decades before they were able to launch another major urban offensive. That incident was a key moment in the complex sequence of events that set the stage for the first 10 years of the Nationalist Government.

Ada spoke to Agnes the next day in the library. Agnes was worried about how she was going to cope, but tried not to give her advise. Ada's decision had been made and nothing could change her mind at the present time. The library would not be able to continue to employ her once her pregnancy was in full view. Tongues would be in full force, in light of Harry not being around. It hadn't been mentioned yet, but there was plenty of time.

The majority of the customers in the library knew of Ada's husband being in India, and would easily put two and two together. People loved to gossip and Ada would be in the forefront of it all, she was certain. She wasn't aware of this, at the moment she was oblivious to what was ahead.

Thankfully, she had requested a week's leave to visit her family. Agnes had approved it and she could travel on the weekend. She didn't look well. Her colour had still not returned, but Agnes knew she needed to get away from Reigate.

Ada sat on the train wondering how she was going to tell her family about her delicate situation, without creating a storm. There was never going to be an easy way around it, but she didn't want a full blown confrontation. She still looked pale and had lost a lot of weight. It wouldn't be difficult to analyse her condition.

She hadn't sent a letter this time, so wasn't expected at the cottage. Ada walked through the kitchen door to find Alfred and Roland running around the table. The kitchen floor was covered with playthings and Blanche was sat at the table, peeling vegetables.

Blanche jumped up and ran over to her, full of excitement. 'Ada. Why didn't you let me know you were coming? You haven't sent a letter for ages,' she said slightly annoyed.

'I'm sorry, I've had a lot on my mind. I'm here now, though,' she replied smiling. Blanche filled the kettle and put it on the Aga to boil.

'Where's Father and Stepmother, Blanche? I need to talk to them.' It was now or never. She wasn't looking forward to it.

'Stepmother is in the kitchen garden. Father is in the fields. Are you okay, Ada? You don't look well.' Ada didn't answer and walked towards the fields and her father.

Archibald noticed Ada approaching and stopped what he was doing, heading towards her. 'What's up, Ada? You look pale, and you've lost weight.'

'I need to talk to you, Father. What I need to say isn't easy for me,' she said. They sat down on the grass and she spilled it all out, not stopping for breath.

Archibald looked shocked, but didn't shout at her. 'Do you want to come home? You know you can,' he said.

'What about Stepmother? What will she say?'

'Leave her to me, no-one would know anything here. They would assume the baby was Harry's and he'd been home on leave. In Reigate it might be a different story, and plenty of people will talk, Ada.'

'I hadn't thought about that, Father. You are right though. I don't know what to do? Reginald has a right to see his child, I have told him it's Harry I love and always will. It was a mistake, he's a good friend and nothing else.' Archibald caught hold of Ada's hand, beckoning her to the kitchen garden where her stepmother was digging potatoes.

Ethel Mary took one look at Ada and guessed the situation instantly. 'Don't shout at her, Ethel. What's done is done. We have to deal with it now,' Archibald said with a hint of dominance.

'I'm not giving the baby up, Stepmother. I may never get another chance. Harry has volunteered to go to China in January. He's going directly from India. He can't face things here at the moment,' Ada said quietly.

'There's no choice then, you need to come home. Hopefully Harry will come to you in time,' her stepmother replied and continued to dig the potatoes. No sentiment there, not that she had expected any. Ada needed to think, and walked back into the kitchen for her cup of tea.

Blanche had a right to know and looked shocked when Ada had spoken to her. She needed to speak to Alice and Dorothy, too. There was another day tomorrow. Louisa would no doubt be aware of the situation, Percy would have written to her. How was she going to handle this? She was worried about what people would think of her and it was still early days.

Ada didn't sleep well and awoke early the next morning to find Blanche already up and in the kitchen eating her breakfast. 'You're up early, Blanche,' she said.

'Yes, I couldn't sleep. I was worried about you, Ada,' she replied.

'I'll be okay, I'm sure things will turn out fine. How are the Marsh family? Are you still keen on Dick?' she asked.

Blanche talked for ages about Dick and his family. Things were obviously progressing. Ernest was still accompanying her and enjoying the break from Windsor Cottage. 'I'm going to visit Jim in Chard today. As it's Sunday, Ernest can come. Would you like to come too, Blanche?' asked Ada.

'Yes please, Father and Stepmother never take us.'

Ernest and the other children were up and dressed within the hour. Ernest was looking forward to seeing his older brother. Their stepmother didn't seem too pleased about their visit, but Ada knew Jim would be missing his siblings. He deserved to see them.

The three of them caught two buses to reach their destination, but it didn't take too long. Jim recognised them all immediately and welcomed them with a huge smile on his face. He introduced his friends and carers to them and seemed well enough. Ada promised to visit again soon and bring her baby with her. Jim understood and patted her stomach with his hand.

They headed back home and Ernest expressed his concern, and how he wished Jim was still at home; that was where he really belonged, with his family. Ada agreed wholeheartedly, but it was out of their hands. Jim was being cared for and living with others with similar disabilities. He was comfortable and contented, in his own way.

Ethel Mary was preparing dinner when they returned home. The twins were in the sitting room drawing pictures and colouring them in. They didn't always keep to the lines on the pictures, but they did try their hardest. Roland and Alfred were sleeping, and Dorothy and Phyllis had gone to help their father in the fields. Ernest immediately walked up to see him. Blanche and Ada helped lay the table ready for food.

'How was Jim today? Your father always worries about him when we're about to leave. He seems to get upset.'

'He seemed fine today. I promised to take the baby in to see him, when it's born,' Ada said.

'Really, Ada. You shouldn't make promises you might not be able to keep.'

'I will be able to keep it, Stepmother, I'm certain of that,' Ada responded and walked out of the kitchen.

They all ate in silence. Ada and Blanche cleared up and the twins asked to go on the swings. They were almost 6 years old now and very busy. 'Okay then, I will take you both. Shall I take Roland too?' she asked her stepmother.

'Yes please, it will give you some practice, Ada,' her stepmother replied sarcastically.

The small park was less than five minutes away, but Ethel Mary rarely had any time to take the children. It was a special treat for them and they were excited. It was dry but very cold out, but with their coats, hats and gloves on, the children didn't complain. It was nice to see the smiles on their faces. Ada needed to make sure her baby got its "special" times.

She walked the children back to the cottage. It was a school day the next morning, and her stepmother was ironing the children's clothes in preparation. Archibald had retired to the sitting room, and was almost asleep in the armchair. He had had a busy day and was shattered. There never seemed to be enough hours in a day at Windsor Cottage.

Dick had arranged to meet Blanche the following evening at his parent's home. 'You promised to come, Ada, will you come tomorrow night?' Ada couldn't refuse and agreed. She decided to visit Dorothy and her children in the afternoon. She also needed to see Louisa, but was not looking forward to it. She was under no illusions, and knew that Percy would have told her about the baby.

Alice had called in to see the family and was surprised to see Ada. After a lengthy conversation Alice wished her well, and promised to do anything she could to help her. Ada thanked her, knowing how hard it must have been after losing a child herself. She still hadn't made a decision whether to return home and bring the baby up there. She would decide when she was back in Reigate. There was plenty of time, she'd thought.

The visit to Louisa's was better than she had anticipated. She was very understanding and promised to help her wherever possible. Ada confided in Louisa completely, something she couldn't do with her stepmother. The tears fell easily and she removed a tissue from her handbag to wipe her face.

'Do you think Harry will ever forgive me, Louisa? I love him so much. He would have been home in January if I hadn't been so stupid,' she said. 'He's volunteered to be posted to China instead. He can't face up to our problems at the moment. That's what he said in his letter.'

Louisa made a fresh pot of tea and poured a cup for Ada and herself. 'Thank you, Louisa, you are so kind to me,' she said full of emotion.

Louisa had agreed to write to Percy, who hopefully could talk to Harry. There were no guarantees, but it was the only option at the moment. Harry had been born to an unmarried mother, Ada relayed to her. There was never a father around, only his grandparents. His mother had left him with them when she married Frank Emms, his stepfather, four years later.

This was going to be difficult, but Louisa knew that they truly loved each other. Mistakes happen and hopefully they would be able to overcome them. Ada was going to need to be very patient. The baby would keep her busy and there would be support in the House family. She was one of the lucky ones.

The visit to the Marsh family in Chew Magna was hectic. Children of all ages walking around the house. The word "quiet" didn't exist in the household, but everyone appeared contented. There was no squabbling amongst the children. Dick's parents were adorable. Alice Daisy was in the kitchen preparing food, and Ada offered to help. 'Blanche and Ernest love it here, they get on well with all of the children. I love seeing them,' she said.

They spoke about both families whilst laying the table ready for the meal. 'Would you like to join us, Blanche and Ernest always do?' Ada accepted and in minutes the family were seated at the table eating. It was the only place she had been, where silence wasn't expected at the dinner table.

After clearing the dishes, Wilfred drove them back home. The car was slow and not in brilliant condition, but he was proud of it and was forever cleaning it. He didn't have a girlfriend, and doted on his car. Blanche had arranged another visit for the next week, and waved as he pulled away from the cottage.

Ada had met Dorothy and her two children and they had decided on a country walk, for a change. They seemed to have walked for miles. She poured her heart out to her best friend and Dorothy tried to console her. The baby was hers and she was going to bring it up, with or without Harry, she reiterated to her. She would work as long as she could in the library and wait to hear from Harry, however long it took.

Back in Reigate, Ada unpacked and prepared a sandwich and a cup of tea. She had called into the local shop before going home to her rooms. Her laundry had been done at Windsor Cottage prior to coming back, and Ada was relieved. She was still feeling so tired.

Her clothes were getting tight on her now, and she rummaged through her wardrobe for skirts and dresses with a fuller waistline. She didn't have many and needed to visit the clothes shop again soon. Ada retired early in readiness for work again the next morning.

There was a knock on the door, just as she had got into bed. Ada shouted through the door and Reginald answered, so she put on her dressing gown and opened the door for him to enter. 'I heard you come in and wanted to check you were okay. You look tired! How did your father and stepmother react to your news?' he asked.

'Father was brilliant, Reginald. He said I could move back home and bring the baby up there. He's concerned about how Reigate's residents will react towards me once my figure changes. The library customers know Harry is still in India,' Ada said rubbing her well rounded belly.

'What are you going to do? I don't want you to go, Ada,' said Reginald in a concerned manner.

She told him that she hadn't had time to think about it yet, and he would be the first to know when she had come to a decision. She knew how much he cared. They both enjoyed a cup of drinking chocolate and Reginald said goodnight, leaving Ada to return to her bed.

The library was quite busy the next morning. The weather wasn't exceptional and more reading was done on dull and rainy days. A few customers asked about her week back home, and welcomed her back to work. Agnes was keeping an eye on the customers and listening in to their conversations, for any gossip spreading regarding Ada. So far, so good!

Lunchtime had arrived and Agnes popped her head around the office door and asked about her week, in confidence. Ada could see her glancing at her stomach and she tried to hold it in. 'I'm going to buy some bigger clothes in the shop on the High Street next week, Agnes,' she said. 'I know you are concerned about gossip among the customers.'

Agnes didn't answer and headed back to the reception desk. She knew it wouldn't be long coming and was worried for her. After all, she was a Reigate resident herself. Perhaps another invitation to tea with her mother would help, Mabel would know what to say. She would ask her later.

Ada accepted her invitation to tea on the weekend and headed home after a busy day. Before entering her rooms she climbed the stairs to check on Edward. He was pleased to see her and asked her about her visit home and hoped everyone was well.

He didn't look well and Ada put the kettle on and opened the kitchen cabinet to check on his food content. 'You haven't been looking after yourself, have you? There's not much here to eat Edward,' she said unhappily.

'I haven't felt like going out, Ada, or been very hungry. I haven't been reading much either,' he replied.

Ada opened a tin of baked beans and put some bread under the grill. 'I think it's time for another visit to mine on Sunday. You like my roast dinners and Victoria sponge,' she said.

'I don't want to put you out, not in your condition,' Edward said looking at her stomach and she blushed.

'I'm pregnant, Edward, not ill. I'm no different than any other woman and I can manage. I worry about you, and you are a good friend and neighbour.' Ada realised that she needed to confide in him about her pregnancy. She couldn't lie to him and it wasn't in her nature to, anyway.

They both sat at the kitchen table, Edward eating his beans on toast and Ada drinking her tea.

She told him everything and he became very emotional. Edward could see how heartbroken she was and understood her worries for the future. He also realised her love for Harry, and her concerns over Reginald, as the father to her unborn child.

'I'm here if you want to talk or have a good cry with someone. You're a lovely lady, Ada, and such a caring person. You deserve the best life can offer.' Ada got up from the chair and gave him a big hug.

'Thank you, Edward. I will be taking you up on that, I'm sure. I will call up in a few days to check on you and Sunday is a date, okay?' After washing the dishes and making sure Edward was comfortable, she returned to her rooms and bed.

It was Saturday and Ada walked to the clothes shop on the High Street. She needed new skirts and dresses, but knew she had to be careful with her money and prices were important, now especially. The assistant was very helpful and picked out two skirts and a dress with a simple style, which had ample room for her growing figure. All the items were on the sale rack.

The skirts had elasticated waists and were very versatile, being a longer length and in black and grey. The assistant also showed her another similar skirt in dark blue, which wasn't a sale item. Her clothes had to last and after looking at the price tags, purchased all three skirts and the dress. They would suffice until the baby arrived.

After returning to her rooms and preparing a snack and a drink, she changed into her new dress and walked to Agnes and Mabel's house for tea. She was slightly apprehensive about today, somehow she felt a lecture was in store for her.

The table was laid with various cakes and sandwiches and a bowl filled with salad items. The chocolate cake looked delicious, oozing with cream separating the layers of sponge. Agnes commented on her new dress and Mabel immediately begun chatting away, as if there were no tomorrows. After pouring a cup of tea, Mabel cut a slice of chocolate cake and handed it to her.

'How did you know I wanted the chocolate cake?' she asked laughing.

'Two reasons, firstly the look on your face when you noticed it on the table, and secondly your condition. Chocolate was my craving when I was expecting Agnes,' Mabel replied.

Ada blushed and waited for her lecture, but she didn't get one. Mabel was very sympathetic and understanding, but did advise her to expect others in the area to be less accommodating. 'Try not to worry too much, concentrate on getting things ready for the baby. Time flies by so quickly and before you know it, he or she will be here.'

Walking back to her rooms, Ada realised that Mabel was right. She had nothing at all for the baby and would need to start purchasing items in readiness for his or her arrival. Knitting would need to be done as well. Blankets, a shawl, cardigans, hats and bootees. She had a busy few months ahead of her and Christmas was getting closer.

After Edward's visit for Sunday lunch, Ada started knitting again. She had plenty of wool and needed to make several items for her baby, Dorothy's children and Sarah's. There were Christmas presents to be knitted, as well as items for her baby, and she didn't have a lot of time left. There were also letters to be written.

Sarah still hadn't been told of her pregnancy and Martha needed to be informed as well. Both were difficult letters to write, and Ada decided to wait until she had retired to bed before putting pen to paper. Harry hadn't sent another letter, though somehow Ada knew it would be a long time before he did. He was a proud man and a good soldier, and he would need time to come to terms with the situation. Ada could only wait and hope for the best.

The letters were written and posted on the way to work the next morning. She wore the new dress and Agnes felt happier. It was November now and Ada was five months pregnant, she wouldn't be able to continue working in the library for much longer, and the dress helped hide her protruding stomach.

Ada thanked her for Saturday's invitation and Mabel's help with the situation. 'I've started knitting again and need to look for baby items. If you know anyone getting rid of or selling any, please let me know, Agnes,' she said. Agnes promised to do so. Ada had finally realised things had to be sorted quickly. It was another busy day, and she was glad to sit down and relax when she arrived home after her working shift.

Reginald called in to see how she was and stayed a while. Being a road sweeper by trade, she had asked him to pick up anything he could for the baby, and he was pleased to help. He could probably find things quicker than her. Second-hand was fine, she was used to that at Windsor

Cottage. Reginald smiled, he felt useful at last. 'Have you come to a decision yet regarding moving back home?' he asked.

'I am going to stay here for the moment, work until I need to finish and see how things go here. This baby is yours, as well as mine, Reginald. You're entitled to see it,' she replied.

'Thank you, Ada, I appreciate it. I'll do all I can to help.' Ada knew he would.

Weeks went by and it was now a few days before Christmas. Ada declined offers to spend it with Sarah or her father. She had so much to do at home now. Agnes had advised her to finish at the library, so she was not returning after Christmas. She was upset, but knew Agnes was right. It was time to concentrate on the baby.

A few customers had noticed her changing figure, but hadn't said anything. No-one had been heard talking about her, but Ada knew it wouldn't be long. She needed to stay focused now and concentrate on the future. Reginald had managed to obtain most of the items needed for the baby and Ada felt on top of things, finally.

Her knitted items were piling up and she had posted more clothing to Dorothy's children and Sarah's family, promising to see them all soon. Mabel had also sent babies clothing to her, for which she was grateful. Agnes was a very thrifty person and found baby bargains galore. Ada had found true friends in them both.

Agnes and Stanley were now engaged and saving for their wedding the following year. Stanley seemed content and agreeable to moving into Mabel's house with Agnes, after their marriage. He got on well with Mabel and knew Agnes wouldn't want to leave her, with her health issues.

Christmas passed by quietly. Ada had received plenty of Christmas cards and as usual, her father and Dorothy enclosed money to spend on her and the baby. Blanche and Sarah had sent letters, wishing her a good Christmas and New Year, and so had Louisa. There were no letters or cards from Martha or Harry though, and she was disappointed.

Ada wondered how Harry was, and sent him a letter a few days after Christmas, wishing him a good journey to China in the near future. She told him that she had now finished working in the library, and hoped to hear from him soon. She added her love and signed it. Ada missed him so much, and worried about his sea sickness and the long journey from India to China. How long the actual journey was, she'd no idea.

Harry and Percy had celebrated their Christmas as usual in the huge dining room in the Jhansi camp. They had toasted their families back home with ale and ate a hearty meal of turkey, stuffing and various vegetables. Christmas pudding and mince pies were prepared by the Army chefs. Harry tried to appear happy, but Percy knew of his heartache.

Percy had been informed of his return to England at the end of January, and was looking forward to seeing his family. Harry was to embark the ship H.J.Vasna from Bombay to Shanghai on the 27th January.

Percy had tried to dissuade him from volunteering for China and returning to England instead, but Harry wouldn't change his mind, and he was determined to put as much distance as possible between himself and Ada. He wasn't sure he would be able to cope with things back in England, and he didn't feel able to write to her at the moment, either.

Louisa had sent a letter to Percy, telling him about Ada's visit and her offer from Ada's father to return home to bring up the baby. She was still living in Reigate, and hadn't taken him up on it at the moment. Ada was a very proud person and had her reasons for remaining where she was. Percy was due back to Aldershot barracks on his return from India, and Louisa suggested he make a visit to her whilst on leave.

Percy didn't disclose the contents of his mother's letter to Harry, as he would decide when he had returned to England. They both belonged together, that much he knew. Four years was a long time apart and people did change, and not always for the better.

Percy wouldn't know how much Ada had changed, if at all, until he had made that visit. He had so much to catch up on in England, and he was hoping the Army would give him immediate leave on returning home. This was going to be a long three weeks. He would worry about Harry though, that he was certain about.

Chapter Twelve

Reginald Anthony Tracey arrived on the 5th March 1927 at 49 Holmesdale Road, Reigate. He was perfect in every way and Ada was overjoyed. Reginald was sat on the settee in her rooms whilst the midwife attended to her needs in the bedroom.

Reginald had heard the baby's cry and ran into the bedroom to meet his son. He couldn't contain himself and kissed her on the lips. The doctor was present and congratulated them both on their new arrival, and would call in to check on them both in a few days.

Reginald let him out and returned to the bedroom. 'I know we are naming him Reginald Anthony, but I want to call him Tony,' Ada said and handed the baby to him for a cuddle.

'He's beautiful, so tiny, but perfect. How are you feeling?' Reginald asked.

'I'm a little sore, but otherwise okay. A cup of tea would be nice,' she hinted. He obliged and stayed a few hours with them both.

Reginald didn't want to leave Ada, but she insisted she was fine. There had been enough siblings born at Windsor Cottage since her stepmother had married her father. She knew how to handle newborn babies. This was her child though, and a different situation altogether.

Agnes and Stanley visited a few days later to see and spoil Tony with presents. Ada promised to call around and see Mabel soon. Edward was like a grandfather visiting his grandson, and couldn't hide his smiles when looking at him. Ada felt happy inside and was devouring motherhood.

When the baby allowed her some quiet time, she wrote her letters to her family and friends, announcing Tony's birth. She used her camera and took some photographs, too many in fact!

Reginald checked on her daily and she liked the company and the pampering, but she was true to Harry. He would always be her true love. No-one would ever take his place.

Three weeks passed and Ada felt ready to show Tony to the outside world. She'd also needed some fresh air herself. Reginald had purchased a second-hand pram and the baby was settled comfortably into it, ready for his first tour of Reigate. Ada needed a few grocery items and called into the shop in Holmesdale Road before heading for the park.

It was still cold with a bitter wind in the air, so she had wrapped up well and Tony was dressed accordingly. She pushed the pram around the park, pointing out the new buds in the flower borders to a sleeping baby. Passers by stopped and took a peek into the pram, others took no notice of her and quickened their pace to avoid her, stopping to whisper to other passers by.

These were the first signs of gossipmongers and Ada could do nothing about it. There would be more to come and she would have to deal with it. When she called into the library to see Agnes, faces turned to stare at her, then turned away. A few approached her and looked at Tony, commenting on how tiny he was. She had a lot to get used to and couldn't hide in her rooms all day.

Agnes picked Tony out of the pram for a cuddle. Some customers looked away in distaste.

Agnes was a loyal friend and Ada knew she would help shield her from the gossipmongers. 'Is it okay to call on your mother, Agnes?' she asked.

'Of course, she is waiting to see the baby. Mother will spoil him for sure,' said Agnes.

After visiting Mabel, they headed home and Ada gave out a huge sigh. She didn't want another day like that again, but knew it was inevitable. Things weren't going to be easy from now on and she had to make the most of it, for both their sakes.

Life for Harry had changed. He was now in Shanghai and working as a military policeman.

Things seemed strange. Percy wasn't there with him and he wasn't the best at making new friends. He kept himself to himself and got on with his duties. He wrote to Percy at Aldershot barracks and his mother, and Millie. He had received Ada's letter before he was posted to Shanghai, but hadn't replied to it.

Percy hadn't been given immediate leave on returning to Aldershot, as he had hoped. It was the end of March before he was finally given two week's leave, and he had decided to make his first visit to Ada. Harry had sounded very subdued in his last letter and Percy felt he needed to see her. He knocked on the door at 49 Holmesdale Road, hesitating at first.

Ada's rooms were closest to the main front door, so she usually answered it. She heard the knock and got up from the settee and headed for the door. On opening it her face lit up. 'Percy, how lovely to see you. Please come in.' Percy followed her into the sitting room and sat down.

Tony was asleep in the bedroom, so Ada put the kettle on the cooker. 'How are you, Percy? I want to hear all about India. I'm so glad to see you,' she said. There was so much she wanted to know and Percy could see the hurt in her eyes. She so wanted to know about Harry. She was still wearing her wedding ring, he had noticed.

To lighten the mood, Percy commented on her figure and mentioned her pin-up photograph in India, laughing. 'I take it you've had the baby, Ada?' he said.

'Yes, he's in the bedroom sleeping. Go and take a peek at him, but don't wake him up.' Percy walked into the bedroom and glanced down at a wide awake baby, just about to cry.

'He's not asleep now, Ada. What shall I do?' he shouted.

Ada asked him to pick Tony up and bring him into the room. 'He probably needs changing. He's not due for a feed yet.' Percy hesitated before picking the baby up, but obliged and carried him delicately to Ada's arms.

The tea was made and she had placed biscuits and cake on the coffee table next to the settee. 'Help yourself to whatever you'd like while I change him,' she offered. After dealing with Tony, she sat beside Percy and introduced them. 'This is Reginald Anthony, known as Tony. Tony, this is Percy, Harry's best friend.'

'Pleased to meet you little one. He's gorgeous, Ada,' Percy replied.

They both started talking seriously and Ada explained everything to him, telling him that Reginald and her were not together. Harry was her husband and always would be, nothing had changed there. Percy spoke of Harry and his dilemma and Ada understood, but she was prepared to wait for him. She had missed him so much.

Percy was heading for Louisa's the following day. He now had his own car and offered to take her and the baby to Windsor Cottage for the week. 'Really, Percy! I would love to go. Father and the family haven't seen Tony yet. Are you sure you don't mind?'

Percy understood her loneliness during Harry's absence, and her mistake. Tony was the result of something she couldn't give away, someone so precious. He didn't blame Ada or Harry, he blamed life, and life could be so cruel at times.

He agreed on a time to pick them up and Ada thanked him for everything. Her thoughts went to Harry. Why did he volunteer for China? She needed him so desperately here. He would be so alone without Percy, and she worried about him. He was her husband after all, and she was allowed to worry.

Ada walked into the cottage carrying Tony. Percy kindly carried her suitcase and Tony's bag of baby necessities. Blanche ran to her and held out her hands to hold the baby. Ethel Mary was also in the kitchen and helped Percy with the luggage. 'Thank you, Percy. I'm so grateful. Would you like a drink before you go to Louisa's?' Ada asked.

'No thank you, I'll pick you up again in a week. No doubt I'll see you at mother's and my sister's.' Percy was certain of it.

Blanche was excited to see her, and couldn't take her eyes off Tony. Her stepmother had put the kettle on the Aga and continued preparing food for the evening meal.

'Percy is back in Aldershot and came to visit me yesterday. He asked if I wanted a lift here. He's home for a week and has his own car now,' Ada said, looking at her stepmother.

Alfred was the only one home now, as the twins and Roland were now at school. Ernest had finished school and was helping in the fields with his father. Things seemed to be quieter during the day. Ada handed Tony to her stepmother for a cuddle, and finished preparing the tea. She poured three cups from the teapot and sat down at the table.

Her stepmother didn't say a lot, but Ada could tell she delighted in holding the baby. 'Where did the name Tony come from, Ada? It suits him though. I can see your father in him,' she commented.

'His full name is Reginald Anthony Tracey, but I call him Tony. He's a good baby and I'm coping well,' Ada explained. 'Say hello to your grandmother, Tony.' Tony gave her one of his vacant stares. 'Shall we go and find your grandfather?' Ada asked. Ethel Mary realised she was now a grandmother. It sounded good and she smiled.

Ada finished her tea and headed for the fields with her son. Archibald and Ernest were busy checking the cattle. There had been a few additions since her last visit. There were potatoes growing in one of the fields, and several other crops. Her father had more time now and produced goods for the market to increase his income.

On seeing Ada, he stopped and walked towards her. Ernest followed and gave her his usual hug. 'Say hello to your grandson, Father,' Ada said. Archibald was taken aback and tears came to his eyes. 'His name is Tony. What do you think?'

'He's beautiful. You make me so proud. Can I hold him?' he asked.

'Of course you can.' Ada handed him over and she could see the emotion in her father's face.

How could she have given her baby up she asked herself, and knew her decision was right.

Phyllis and Dorothy loved the baby, the twins and Roland said hello and Alfred wanted to play with him. Ada fed him in the bedroom, changed him and put him down in Alfred's cot for a sleep. They all sat down to their evening meal and Ada felt a part of the family again. She loved her home in Reigate, but loved being at Windsor Cottage, too.

Alice called in the next day and was surprised to see Ada there. She cuddled the baby and became very tearful.

'Your time will come, Alice,' Ada said.

'I hope so, Ada, it's just not happening at the moment.' Alice was keeping herself busy and still living in Frome. She had good friends in the area, but so wanted a child of her own.

Ada and Blanche made the journey to Chard first, to visit Jim. Ada had promised to take the baby to show him. He was so elated at seeing them and for the first time since he had been placed there, Ada knew that he should be home and not in an institution.

They called in on Louisa next, and finally Dorothy. Feeding Tony wasn't a problem at theirs, and she was given privacy to do so. It had been a long day for everyone. Ada was glad to get back to the cottage. She would stay at home the next day and help with the domestic duties.

The sun was shining in the morning, so she carried Tony to the churchyard and showed him where her mother, brother and sister, Gladys, were buried. She placed some flowers on each of their graves and headed back to the cottage, returning to help Blanche and her stepmother in the kitchen. It felt good to be home.

Blanche told her that Dick and her were still seeing each other, and the Marsh's seemed like family now. Dick would often call on her, and they would spend the evening at the cottage. Ada was pleased for her. No-one mentioned Harry, and Ada declined to bring him into any conversation. She was hurting, but had her priorities now.

The week flew by and Percy was ready to return to Aldershot and take her back to Holmesdale Road. She was sorry to leave and was having second thoughts about returning home to live. But there was Reginald to consider. She didn't know what to do!

Ada thanked Percy for the lift and allowing her to see her family.

'It's the least I can do, Ada,' Percy said. 'You haven't changed at all and I hope Harry sees things clearer soon. I'll see you when I'm on leave again.' He helped her into her rooms and left for the barracks.

Reginald and Edward were overjoyed to see them both. They both commented on how much Tony had grown in a week. Routine was back to normal and Ada busied herself with baby duties, cooking and cleaning. Visits to Edward were now occurring daily and seeing baby Tony was compulsory for him. His eyes lit up when he saw him, but Ada knew he wasn't well.

She took Tony out for some fresh air on a daily basis, weather permitting, but still received the stares and overheard neighbours gossiping. It was hard, but she put it all to the back of her mind and carried on with her day.

It was Agnes's wedding the following week and she'd been invited. The ceremony was to be in the local Registry Office, followed by a reception at Mabel's house. Stanley and Agnes had booked a week's honeymoon in a hotel in Devon. Ada needed to check in her wardrobe for something to wear for the occasion. With no salary coming in from her work in the library, her savings were being used to live on and dwindling quite fast. She was devoted to the baby, but financially it was a struggle, although she was very thrifty and wasn't an impulsive buyer.

Her own wedding suit was a possibility, but it needed more decoration. She found a silk scarf in a pale lemon whilst window shopping, and decided that that was the answer. She purchased it, took a stroll around Priory Park and headed home. She had a hat that would blend with the outfit perfectly, and thankfully her weight had returned to her pre-baby figure. She was lucky there.

She wanted to give them a wedding present. They were good friends and she felt it was customary to do so. After purchasing white linen from the drapers, she made a tablecloth and matching placemats, all embroidered with red roses. It had taken a lot of time and was very intricate, but Ada was thrilled with the result and sure that Agnes would love them.

The wedding went ahead without any hitches. Reginald was Stanley's best man and both men looked very handsome in their suits. Agnes looked stunning. Her hair had been put away from her face and she wore a small hat tilted to the side of her head. Her suit was in a deep blue and well fitted, and brought out her rosy complexion.

Ada felt satisfied with her suit, though she felt emotional wearing it again and thought of Harry.

The silk scarf and her hat completed the outfit. Tony was dressed for the occasion and received plenty of attention from the wedding guests. Mabel took charge at the reception and everyone enjoyed themselves. It was a quiet affair, but beautiful, and there were a few tears of happiness amongst the guests, including Ada. The newly-weds left for Devon and their honeymoon.

Reginald walked back to Holmesdale Road with Ada and the baby, and the gossipmongers were about, in full force it seemed. This was something Reginald hadn't encountered before. 'Is this what you have to put up with on a daily basis, Ada?' he asked.

'Yes, and it isn't easy. Talk will be about us together after today now,' she replied. 'I'm so sorry, I didn't realise.'

She had had a lot to put up with, and none of it was nice.

It was now Christmas and Ada had moved back to Windsor Cottage with Tony. The months after Agnes's wedding in Reigate, had been awful. At times she hadn't wanted to leave her rooms. Gossip amongst the residents had escalated, and got well out of control. Fingers were pointing at Ada everywhere she went. She'd hated it.

This wasn't fair on Tony or Reginald, and Reginald had to continue living there. Financially, Ada was struggling, and her savings had almost disappeared. She could have gone to Aldershot barracks and withdrew some monies from Harry's salary, but felt that as Tony wasn't his child, it wasn't up to him to keep them.

Edward had become more solitary and disinterested in anything life had offered him. He seemed to have given up and had died in his bed after retiring for the night. Ada was so upset, he was a second father to her, and another grandfather to Tony. The funeral was a quiet affair and Ada and Reginald ensured he was laid to rest next to his wife.

She regretted letting Reginald down, as he wouldn't be able to visit his son, but she promised to send him photographs as he grew. 49 Holmesdale Road wasn't the same any more, with Edward gone, the heart of the house had been lost, and she didn't feel welcome in Reigate, either. Ada was ready to move on.

Percy had paid a visit on his last leave, and she had asked him if he minded moving them back home. He was happy to oblige and knew she would be better placed there, for obvious reasons.

Reigate had been her home for a long time and she was sad to leave, but things had changed and the residents of Chilcompton village wouldn't know of Tony's true father and didn't need to know.

Tony had Ada's siblings to play with, and plenty of outdoor areas to allow him to grow into a proper little boy. She knew it was the right decision. Losing her independence was a small price to pay, considering the circumstances.

Percy had told Ada that Harry was now back in India. He had returned in the August after serving seven months as a military policeman in Shanghai. He was now back in the stables in Jhansi with Star, Blaze and Blade.

Ada wrote to him, telling him of her return to Windsor Cottage, and hoped he was well. She added her love, and promised to wait for him. Harry hadn't replied to any of her letters after Tony's birth. Hopefully he might respond this time. It was worth a try. Anything was worth a try!

Ada wrote to Martha and Millie, and although she hadn't received any correspondence initially, Martha had replied a few weeks later. Harry's uncle Herbert had died. He hadn't been well and Martha had looked after him to the end. Martha hoped all was well at Windsor Cottage and wished her the best. Her letter detailed Harry's siblings and what they were all doing now.

Ada felt Martha's response was somewhat sympathetic and less hostile than her previous letter (before Tony was born). Perhaps she had forgiven her and moved on. She could only hope! Perhaps being away from Reginald had impacted on her change of heart, or she had realised that Harry had also been conceived by another man and not her husband, even though it was before her marriage to Frank.

Percy had no idea how much longer Harry was likely to be in India, but had said he seemed more himself in his letters. Ada was relieved, and turned her wedding ring around her finger, thinking of him. She looked at Tony and smiled. How could she be sad and miserable with him around? He was a little bundle of joy, brightening up every day. It wasn't possible, and with so many people living in the cottage, she didn't have time to be lonely, either.

Harry was happier back in Jhansi. He loved his horses and all his duties relating to the stables.

His "children" were excited to see him back and the days never seemed dull. He received Ada's letter telling him of her move back home and he read the words over and over again. She was now back at Windsor Cottage, no man in tow! Just her and Tony and her own family.

He looked at Star and started talking to her. 'What do you think, Star? Can I cope with bringing up Tony when I go home? My life is with Ada, I'm certain, but I'm still apprehensive about it all.

Any suggestions?'

Star rubbed her nose into his hands and Harry smoothed her head. 'Well, you're not much help are you! I will have to work this out for myself,' He had some thinking to do.

He started by writing to his mother and Millie, perhaps they could advise him, or at least lead the way to a final decision. He also wrote to Percy. His friend had now met a young lady he was keen on. Her name was Lily and she was from Cornwall. She had friends in Frome, where they'd met, and Percy seemed besotted. He had had a lot to say about her in his last correspondence and Harry wanted to know more.

The Christmas festivities had come and went in Jhansi, nothing had changed except Percy wasn't there to celebrate with Harry. There were a few soldiers in the camp he confided in, but he mainly kept himself to himself and was satisfied with his own company.

Harry had missed the monsoon weather whilst in Shangai and was now involved in the boxing event, and wasn't getting on too well. Boxing wasn't his sport, but it kept him busy. He read Ada's letter again that evening and pondered. 'What shall I do?' he said to himself. She deserved a reply, that was certain and he would write back this time.

After asking the Sergeant about postings back to the UK, he was advised that he could possibly be back in England by the end of 1928. This meant another year in Jhansi. The Sergeant made a point of stressing that this was only a guideline, and nothing was confirmed.

He'd sent letters to his mother and Ada. Percy had told him of his future marriage to Lily, in July the following year. Harry was pleased for him, but wouldn't be able to attend, and he was disappointed. Lily had sounded a lovely lady, and he was looking forward to meeting her. It seemed he had a long wait.

The letter to Ada was difficult. Harry was nervous about making a solid commitment to return to her and Tony. He had decided to return to his mother's cottage initially and meet with Ada afterwards, when he'd worked out what he was going to say to her. Martha and Frank had moved back to Ebrington, to be nearer his uncles and Harry's brother, Frank junior. It was a short walk from their farm. He still had a year at Jhansi and his mind could be changed before then, but as things stood, this seemed to be the best solution.

Knowing Ada had moved back home had made Harry think differently towards the situation. She wasn't working now and had a baby to care for. Ironically, he felt more comfortable about her position, though he had initially been okay about her working in the library.

Harry had been away for a long time and she had needed something to occupy herself, but he realised jealousy could have become an issue. He had to give them another chance and despite everything, he still loved her.

Life carried on as usual and he put thoughts of England to the back of his mind. The horses needed attending to and another parade was looming. There was a lot to organise and things had to be perfect. Harry wasn't interested in any other result. Failure wasn't negotiable, not at all.

Time passed quickly for both Ada and Harry. They both got on with their separate lives and thought about each other often. Percy and Lily's wedding was a small affair, but beautiful nevertheless. They were renting a small cottage in Tellisford and Lily was preparing their home, ready for his discharge from the Army in May. Percy was now based in Gravesend, but thankfully had not been posted abroad again.

Tony was growing fast and Ada appreciated how busy her stepmother had been with her younger siblings. She needed eyes in the back of her head! Blanche helped a lot and she was grateful. Most of her money had gone, but her father didn't ask her for anything. She helped in the cottage and in the fields, and no-one complained.

It was nearing Christmas again and Harry had been told he would be back in England on the 26th December. He was to be posted to Gravesend barracks, where Percy was now stationed. After over 6 years away, he couldn't have been more delighted. He was going home! His discharge from the regular Army was to mature in May, too soon for him to be posted abroad again.

Letters had been sent to his mother, Percy and Ada. They all knew of his return to Gravesend shortly after Christmas, and they couldn't have been more pleased. Ada still had no idea if Harry would return to her and Tony, but she hoped things would work out for the better, and in her favour. She was excited and worried at the same time, but daren't show her emotions, for fear of being disappointed. He had mentioned travelling to Martha's once he had been given leave.

Harry's mother had a small thatched cottage, a short stroll away from his uncles' farm. It was located in the heart of the tiny village. The children were older now, James was 4 and John Henry was 8. They went to the local primary school, where Harry had been educated as a child himself. Ebrington was nearer Frank and Albert's work, in walking distance in fact.

Archibald and Ethel Mary silently prayed that Ada and Harry would be able to repair their marriage. They hadn't really had a chance in 1922, being together for less than a month before Harry's posting. They deserved to be happy. Only time would tell.

Having said goodbye to his "children", Star, Blade and Blaze, he had felt quite emotional, and would miss the horses. He knew they would be looked after, but couldn't guarantee they would be given the individual attention he had paid them. He had two weeks travelling by ship ahead of him, and didn't think he would ever get used to travelling by sea. 'I'm not looking forward to it,' he said speaking to the three horses.

He was now in Gravesend barracks and given a few days off to adjust, before commencing his duties. The climate was the most dramatic change for him, after 6 years in a hot and humid country. Gravesend was freezing in comparison and would need some adjusting to, a lot in fact.

After reporting for duty a few days later, the Sergeant announced his discharge on the 20th April, in lieu of leave owing. He could have jumped for joy, but kept his cool and thanked the Sergeant.

Percy had managed to locate Harry, but they were not in the same dormitory or on the same duties. They spoke whilst off duty, and Percy handed a photograph of his wife, Lily, to him. Lily was a pretty girl, petite with a fresh complexion and shoulder length mousey blond hair. 'She looks lovely, Percy and I hope to meet her soon,' he said.

'Ada is waiting for you, Harry. Don't leave it too long,' Percy replied.

'I'm going to my mother's when I'm discharged. I finish here on the 20th April and I don't need to return. I'll write to you whilst I'm in Ebrington.'

'Take care, Harry. Lily and I are happy, you and Ada are made for one another, too. You've been away for a long time, maybe you need to court each other again.'

'Now there's a thought. Maybe you are right, Percy. You've given me something to think about for sure. Thank you,' Harry said.

CHAPTER THIRTEEN

Alice announced that she was expecting her first child. She had passed the twelve weeks stage and felt confident that she wouldn't lose it. Henry was being very careful and ensured she didn't do anything strenuous. He wouldn't allow her to lift anything, or do any heavy domestic duties.

Ada was elated and their father was really excited. He loved babies and this would be a second grandchild. 'He or she will be another play partner for Tony, and nearer his own age,' Ada said.

Louisa announced that Lily was expecting a baby too, and was overjoyed for both Percy and Lily. 'Who's next, Louisa?' Ada wondered. 'It usually comes in threes!' It was time to get her knitting needles out again. More baby clothes to make, but she loved knitting. It was more than a hobby to her. Tony needed new jumpers; he was outgrowing his so quickly, she didn't know where the time had gone.

Sarah had sent Ada a letter and had invited her to Portland for a few days. Tony was older now and able to travel by bus and train, so she accepted. It would be a change and there was so much to talk about. It had been arranged for April, which was only weeks away.

Harry had just weeks left in Gravesend, before taking his leave and discharge. Percy wouldn't be far behind him. Things were happening very quickly now and both men were eager to move on with their lives. Seven years had passed by since they'd first met. It hadn't seemed possible. Where had the years gone?

Ada and Tony headed for the bus to Portland and were looking forward to seeing Sarah and her family. Harry was travelling to Ebrington and his mother's home, though Ada was unaware of it. Neither of them knew of each others plans. Letters hadn't been exchanged for a while.

Sarah welcomed them both, and was excited to see them. Alfred had been posted abroad and had been away for six months. Florence and her brother, Henry, were growing up and no longer babes in arms. Florence was in school now, and Henry attended a play group with Sarah a few mornings a week.

They talked non stop for hours, recalling their lives since their last meeting, good and bad moments, and the children. All children had their own personalities, their own ways, comments and comical situations. No two children were alike and they both laughed and smiled, remembering their own offsprings characters, mishaps and sayings.

They walked around Portland pointing out Portland Castle to the children, built for defence against attacks by the French in the 16th Century. The lighthouse stood out, with it's distinctive red and white striped exterior. It had been built in 1906 and stood 115 foot high.

The children enjoyed running towards the water's edge and looking at the odd shaped rocks, especially the Pulpit Rock, a natural solitary rock located north-east of Portland Bill lighthouse, which had slowly eroded over time to form a stack. Ada and Sarah had their wits about them, ensuring they didn't venture too far to the edge to cause concern.

Ada loved the Dorset countryside and the coastal views, and felt relaxed whilst with Sarah and the children. She was sorry to leave and the last few days had flashed past far too quickly. They both reluctantly said their goodbyes and promised to meet up again soon, and headed for the bus back home.

It had been a tiring experience for Tony, and he slept in Ada's arms most of the way back. It must be the sea air, she'd decided. She'd felt tired herself, but she was happy and had been thoroughly satisfied with her break. It had been nice visiting her friend and unloading her troubles onto her.

Dorothy and Sarah were loyal friends, and she could freely talk to them about anything, and she usually did!

Harry reached Ebrington to a welcome from his family and a kitchen table packed with food, awaiting his arrival. Hugs were readily given and handshakes from the older generation. Frank senior was sat by the fireplace and didn't look well.

His uncles had been plagued with health problems, but they didn't complain. Martha's cottage was small, but big enough for the family left at home, and Harry liked it. He preferred it to the property they'd had in Blockley. There wasn't so much land around it, but they didn't need it.

Fruit and vegetables came from his uncles farm, and Frank junior would bring them to the cottage after his days work, although he still lived with his uncles. Martha would cook extra meals to send back, or they would eat with them, there.

Martha prepared a cup of tea each for the family and they all sat at the table and ate. Frank senior remained by the fireplace with a tray on his lap. 'Frank isn't well, he hasn't been for a while now and I'm worried,' she said to Harry. 'He has no energy and hasn't been to work for the past few weeks.'

'Is there anything I can do, Mother?' he asked.

'No, Harry, your job is to visit your wife and rectify your relationship there. Ada has been alone far too long,' Martha replied.

'Things aren't that simple, Mother. There is a child there now, I'm not sure I will be able to cope.'

Martha put her fork down on the table and her face changed to a scowl. 'You love Ada and you've got a chance to be with her now, as a family. I never had the chance with your father. I love Frank, but he wasn't my first love, Harry. Don't let pride stand in your way.'

With the lecture over, she continued eating and they spoke about his Army life and his siblings. Martha was a strong willed person and had had a lot to deal with. Harry appreciated that, but missed his grandmother and her loving ways. Millie was quiet, and had grown into a pretty young lady. She didn't say anything, but Harry knew she was thinking a lot more. He would speak to her later.

His uncles kept him up to date with the farm activities, Ebrington and Shipston on Stour.

Nothing much had changed. He would visit his old haunts soon and check on anyone he knew still living in the vicinity. Harry was excited, but slightly apprehensive. Tomorrow would be soon enough.

After visiting the churchyard and discussing his problems with his grandmother, Harry took a slow walk into Shipston on Stour, and entered the White Bear. There weren't many people in there and no-one he knew, but he ordered his usual pint of cider and sat down on one of the seats.

Joe and his family approached him and sat down next to him. 'I thought it was you walking in front of me. Your uncles gave me the day off to meet you. How are you, Harry?' he asked.

'I'm doing okay. You look well, Joe. How are Rose and the children?' he asked with interest.

'We have three now, two boys and a girl. Rose is well, thank you. It's nice to see you home again. Have you decided what you are going to do now?'

'Not really, Joe. I need to see Ada, but it's going to be difficult. I'm thinking of travelling down in a few days, but want to spend some time on the farm until then. I was just checking out my locals, seems strange after all this time.' Harry reminisced and smiled.

Joe told him of Frank senior's health problems and it didn't sound good. 'Perhaps I ought to stay here with Mother for a while. What do you think, Joe?'

'Your mother wants you to visit Ada, she will manage with Frank until then. She's a strong lady and will cope, whatever happens.' Harry knew Joe was right.

The Ebrington Arms deserved a visit, so Joe, his uncles and his older siblings joined him for a well deserved pint. He was revelling in his homecoming, but his mind was working overtime. The worry was beginning to show, now. He would spend a day helping out on the farm, and then make that important journey to Windsor Cottage.

Harry knocked on the kitchen door of Windsor Cottage. He was nervous, tense and his hands were shaking. He remembered his wedding day and the same nervous tension. Blanche answered the door, seven years older, but recognisable. She couldn't contain herself and threw her arms around him screaming, and pulled him into the kitchen.

Ethel Mary was preparing vegetables and wondered what the noise was all about and looked up from the table. Her face was a picture as she headed towards him and shook his hand. 'It's lovely to see you, Harry. Ada is in the fields with her father. Would you like a drink?' she asked. Harry accepted and sat down at the table.

After asking about the family and how things had been during the past seven years, well almost, Harry finished his tea and started walking towards the fields. He wasn't sure his legs would carry him there. They had felt like jelly as he walked. He had never felt so nervous and frightened.

Ada wasn't afraid of hard work and was busy with Ernest clearing the weeds from one of the fields. Haymaking would be upon them soon and everything needed to be ready. Preparation was the key. Archibald was checking on the cattle, after milking the cows.

Ernest saw Harry approaching and nudged his sister. She stopped what she was doing and walked towards him. He hadn't changed, looked slightly weary, but he looked like Harry! It was as if she'd seen him yesterday. Ada hadn't changed much either. She had always looked younger than her years, had a few more lines on her face, but no different otherwise.

As they met, Harry's eyes melted and he stood staring at her, for what seemed ages. Ada didn't speak and was mesmerised. Archibald was the first to speak and broke the silence. 'Harry Tracey, it's lovely to see you. I hope you've been well and the Army hasn't wore you out too much.'

Harry turned to look at him and shook his hand. 'No, Sir. I'm fine. It was a long six years away though, and India was so hot.'

'Less of the Sir. This isn't the Army now!' Ada laughed and Harry's smile emerged at last.

Archibald signalled Ernest to follow him and they both went back to the cottage, leaving Harry and Ada alone. They walked to one of the benches in the field and sat down. Ada was the first to speak. 'It's so nice to see you. I've missed you so much, Harry. You look well and haven't changed.' A tear fell from her eye and she raised a hand to hide it.

Harry caught her hand to stop her, but she couldn't control her emotions. Through her tears she apologised over and over again. 'I love you so much, Harry. I never meant to hurt you.'

'I know, Ada. I'm partly to blame. Six years is a long time, seven in the Army. I shouldn't have married you and left you for so long.' he said sympathetically.

They aired their problems in detail and hugged each other, finally deciding to find a place to live and try again at their marriage. 'I won't leave Tony here, he's my child and he belongs with us, Harry. Your mother had her reasons for leaving you with your grandparents, but I can't leave Tony. You will love him too, I'm sure,' she said with puppy eyes, looking so elated.

'I understand, Ada. I will do my best to bring him up as my own, I promise,' he replied.

Ada's heart had skipped a beat and her head had spun, as Harry had walked towards her, after six years apart. Her mouth wouldn't move, and she was speechless. Harry hadn't changed at all, and her love for him had been stronger than ever. Had he come back to her? She had truly hoped so, she'd been waiting for so long, for ever it seemed.

Holding him again, kissing him and looking at his handsome face, she couldn't take it in at first.

Her Harry was back, and they were going to find somewhere to live and continue, or start, their marriage. All her wishes had come true at once, and she was in heaven. She wasn't letting him go again, ever.

Archibald and Ethel Mary offered to have Tony for the night and they stayed in the bed and breakfast, their honeymoon venue in 1922. It was as if they'd never been apart, and they were so in love. The next morning they caught the bus to Victoria Park in Frome, revisiting their past and the pretty park, full of flowers in bloom and the band playing next to the summerhouse.

There were couples walking hand in hand admiring the views, enjoying each others company and still so much in love, it was plainly obvious. Children playing on the grass, accompanied by loving mothers, and others deep in thought sat on individual benches.

'Thank you, Harry. I haven't been here since our last visit,' she said.

'I said I would bring you back sometime, and I always keep my promises, Ada,' Harry replied and kissed her. They were like teenagers on a first date. No-one would have known they'd been married for six years!

Their house-hunting begun the next morning. They checked newspapers and shop windows for local rentals. Ada didn't want to move too far from her father. Blanche had paid her weekly visit to the Marsh's and told them of a small cottage available in Norton Malreward, approximately twelve miles from Chilcompton and three miles from Chew Magna, where they lived.

The location was near enough to Ada's family, yet far enough away to be able to have time on their own. A viewing was arranged with the owner's for the next morning. Norton Malreward was a small village close to the town of Bristol.

Ada informed Harry that she had no savings towards the rental, but had not withdrawn any monies from his Army salary whilst living in Reigate. Harry was surprised and he still hadn't checked his account since returning from India. He had no idea how much was in it. 'You haven't taken anything from there since you started work?' he asked in complete amazement, surprised.

'No, Harry, I managed on my salary and saved a little. It's almost gone now, though,' she explained. 'I didn't starve. I know how to be careful with money, coming from a large family.'

Harry couldn't envisage a problem in managing the rent on the cottage. The salary accrued over the past six years would be more than adequate. He had withdrew some monies whilst on leave in India and China, but nothing extreme, but he would need to look for work soon.

The cottage was compact, but big enough for the three of them. There was a small sitting room, small kitchen and scullery, and two bedrooms. The washroom had a bath, toilet and small washbasin, and there was an enclosed back yard, ideal for Tony.

The cottage was surrounded by green fields and trees and was very picturesque. The Post Office and a few village shops were only minutes away. They both liked the cottage and agreed to rent it. It was partly furnished and needed a few more items of furniture to make it a home.

The conversation that evening was all about the cottage in Norton Malreward and their excitement was more than obvious. After the paperwork was completed they hoped to move in by the beginning of the next week. Harry spoke about his mother and stepfather. He needed to return to Ebrington soon, to check on Frank.

Ada understood and was more than happy for him to return once they had moved into the cottage. She was used to being on her own with Tony and didn't mind. Martha was concerned for Frank senior and Harry felt he needed to be there, but also knew he needed to be with Ada. He was trying to bond with Tony, but was finding it difficult. Hopefully things would be easier in their own home.

Ada was scrubbing the scullery floor, after giving the cottage a spring clean. Although it looked clean, she insisted on giving it a thorough going over. She wouldn't be satisfied otherwise. Harry had purchased the essential pieces of furniture needed, a double bed, a single bed for Tony and a settee. There were wardrobes in each bedroom and a chest of drawers in the main bedroom.

The small kitchen had a gas cooker and fridge, a kitchen cabinet, sink and a small table with two chairs. Harry managed to purchase a further two chairs to set around the table. There was already a kettle there and Ada still had her radio from Holmesdale Road.

Her father helped out with various household items and bedding. Tony's toys and clothes filled the cottage, he had far too many for his age. As usual, Ada wasn't enamoured with the curtains and needed cushions to liven the cottage up, but she was otherwise satisfied.

Harry stayed the week and with Ada's agreement returned to Ebrington to check on Frank. He promised to look for work on his return. Things were getting easier between Tony and Harry, they would play together in the back yard and Harry would take him for a walk in his pushchair. At 2 his little legs didn't walk far.

Nothing was really said about India or China, they concentrated on being a couple and spending time together. They were in love, a couple, and the cottage suited them. Harry loved his walking and would often take a long walk whilst Ada prepared food for the evening meal.

The journey to Ebrington seemed to take forever. Harry wanted to get there and return the next day, but somehow knew that wasn't going to happen. He hadn't received any correspondence from his mother, and had no idea how Frank, his stepfather, was.

Frank was on the mend, he had spent weeks in bed with influenza and had contracted pneumonia, but thankfully was a lot better. He was 53 years old and the doctor had said he had been lucky. His mother was still nursing him, but things were a lot easier in the cottage. Harry had been so worried and felt so relieved.

Millie was helping out with the younger boys, so Harry spent a few days helping his uncles out on the farm. He socialised in the Ebrington Arms with his family, and spoke about Ada and Tony and the cottage in Norton Malreward.

Martha was overjoyed, hearing of their life as a couple and being back together again, and Harry seemed really contented. 'You were right, Mother. Ada and I are meant to be together, until death,' he said. 'I can't live without her, and Tony is so like her.'

Harry busied himself on the farm, took walks around the countryside and spent a few evenings in with his siblings, talking with Millie and making certain Frank senior was okay. He hadn't returned to work as yet, but was getting bored and fidgeting now. It wouldn't be long before he was back on his cart again, loading the timber.

A week had passed and Harry was travelling back home, to his wife and stepson. He knew Frank would be okay now, and he could concentrate on his family at last. His smile had returned and he looked so mischievous at times, especially when he was smoking his pipe.

Back in Norton Malreward, Tony was playing in the back yard, whilst Ada was hanging clothes on the washing line. She hadn't been feeling too well, and had spent time the last few days playing with Tony, instead of dealing with her chores. This wasn't like her at all.

Harry walked through the front door of the cottage and headed directly for the back yard, after hearing voices. Tony ran to him and shouted 'Daddy, Daddy.' Ada was taken aback and couldn't believe how Tony had taken to him. '

'Did you hear that, Harry? He called you Daddy!' she said excitedly.

Harry was shocked too and picked him up and carried him to Ada's side. 'How are you? I've missed you both and I'm so glad to be home.' He kissed her and they all went inside the cottage. Ada put the kettle on the cooker and took two cups from the cupboard.

'How are Martha and the family? How is Frank?' Ada asked.

'Frank is much better now. I don't think it will be long before he's back to work. The doctor said he was lucky. The pneumonia could have been fatal. He was getting bored when I was there, that's a good sign.'

'I'm so glad, Harry. I was worried about him and was thinking the worst. Martha needs him and so does his children. Millie would be devastated if anything happened to her father, I'm sure. She is a daddy's girl, I noticed.'

'You're right, Ada. She's the only girl too. He will be okay and things should be back to normal soon,' Harry replied and smiled.' I would like to make regular trips to see them, if that's okay with you, Ada?' Ada agreed and she felt he needed to see his family more often. He had been away for several years, far too long.

Ada made the tea and sat down on the settee, then she suddenly became nauseous, and her eyes had lost their focus. Harry noticed and asked if she was okay. 'I haven't been well for a few days, a lot of the chores have been overlooked. I'm sorry, Harry,' she said full of apology.

Harry babysat Tony the next morning for Ada to visit the doctor. Harry had insisted on it the night before, and she hadn't argued. The doctor examined her, asked a few questions and Ada left the practice with a huge smile on her face.

On reaching the cottage, she could hear Harry and Tony laughing. They were bonding and she was over the moon. Ada walked through the doorway, as the front door was open. Harry was sat on the settee, Tony was on his lap and being tickled. Tony was smiling and laughing, whilst Harry continued to tickle his belly. They looked so happy.

'I'm back,' she said. 'Who's for a cup of tea and a sandwich? I'm starving.' Harry got up from the settee and walked towards her.

'Well, what did the doctor say? Is everything okay?' Ada didn't answer and Harry looked worried. 'Ada, talk to me. What's wrong with you?'

She couldn't keep it up any longer and suddenly produced a huge grin on her face. 'You're going to be a father, Harry. I'm pregnant!' Harry was numb and speechless. He looked at her, but didn't move. 'Well say something. Are you pleased?' she asked.

'Pleased, I'm ecstatic! I love you so much, Ada.' Harry kissed her and hugged her, bringing Tony into the embrace.

They visited Archibald and Ethel Mary the next day and announced their good news. 'I knew there would be a third baby, but I never expected it to be me,' she said to her father. Blanche was overjoyed, she loved babies. Archibald pulled Harry to his side and they headed for the sitting room.

'Is everything okay, Archibald?' he asked.

'Yes, I have a proposition for you, Harry. I've finished working in the coal mines now, and will be working in the fields full-time. The workers I had here beforehand have also finished and I was wondering if you would be interested in working here, with Ernest and myself? You would receive a salary and I know you were looking for work. With baby number two on the way, you need a job,' Archibald pointed out.

Harry accepted and agreed with Archibald. 'I need to get some transport though. I was thinking perhaps a small motorbike, to be able to get from here to the cottage daily. It would be easier than buses, and I don't want to leave Ada again. With transport I could be here as early as you need me to be here. Do you know anywhere I could get something reasonable?'

He found his transport in Frome. The motorbike wasn't new, but in good condition. After purchasing the compulsory accessories, Harry rode it home and showed it to Ada. There was room at the side of the cottage for the motorbike, and Harry was more than satisfied with his investment.

Alice visited the cottage, after hearing of Ada's news. 'Our babies are going to be so close in age, Ada. I'm so excited, they will be like twins and we can babysit them between us,' said Alice.

'I've got Tony too, Alice. He won't be left out and I'm glad he is going to have a sibling to play with.' Alice didn't think at times, but Ada knew she hadn't meant to omit Tony.

'I'm sorry, Ada, I wasn't thinking straight. Of course Tony will be included.

They drank tea and talked about everyone and everything from morning sickness to baby accessories, to Henry, Harry and Windsor Cottage. 'I suppose I'd better get my knitting needles out again. There's three babies to knit for now!' They both laughed.

Life seemed to be back on track and Ada couldn't be more elated. Harry had got himself into a routine. He worked five days a week at Windsor Cottage, giving him two free days with Ada and Tony. He was getting on well with his stepson, but there were times Ada worried that perhaps things might change when his true son or daughter arrived. Only time would tell!

CHAPTER FOURTEEN

Lillian Peggy Tracey was born on the 6th February 1930 and a welcome addition to the Tracey family. Ada and Harry were both overjoyed and couldn't take their eyes off her. Tony was almost 3 years old and was looking forward to playing with his little sister.

They had decided to call her Peggy after Dorothy's first daughter, who had died at just 2 days old. Dorothy and Frederick were delighted; it had meant so much to them. Alice had given birth to a son, Allan James Wheeler, on the 6th December, and Gerald George Bridges was born on the 1st December to Lily and Percy. All babies were perfect.

Harry couldn't stop smiling. His cheeky grin now more prominent than ever before. He was a father to a daughter, and his life was complete. Archibald now had three grandchildren and doted on them all. He was still a child at heart, babies brought out the clown in him and he adored playing with them.

Ethel Mary didn't say much, but you could tell she was proud of them all. Life had slowed down somewhat and the rush at Windsor Cottage had gone. She was often seen in the fields with Archibald, relaxing and admiring the views; something unknown to her in previous years.

Alice, Ada and Lily met up on a weekly basis. They took turns in visiting each other's homes for a baby meeting, coffee morning and a gossip. Tony was thoroughly spoilt by all of his aunties.

Harry was still working five days a week for Archibald, and riding his motorbike to and from Windsor Cottage. Once a week, Ada would get the bus to her father's and stay until Harry had finished work.

Everything seemed perfect. That was until Harry was informed of his training in Portland for the Army reserves. Training was compulsory and had to be done on a regular basis, whilst he was still in the reserves. There was over four years left to complete.

The cottage was getting a little cramped with Tony and Peggy's toys and baby accessories, and they both knew there wouldn't be enough room in Tony's bedroom for Peggy as well. She was sleeping in her cot in their room at the time. They would need a bigger premises, soon.

Ada suggested finding a place to live near Portland, nearer to his training centre. After staying with Sarah, Ada had fallen in love with Dorset and was more than happy to relocate there. Harry could find work in Dorset, she was certain. Archibald was okay about the decision and would hire another labourer to replace him.

Being born and raised in Belchalwell in Dorset, Archibald made some enquiries with family there and found accommodation near Wareham, not far from Portland. Ada would be able to visit Sarah and her family. With the decision made, the Tracey family moved South, in time to discover that baby number three was on the way!

Dorset was famous for being the native county of author and poet, Thomas Hardy. Explorer Sir Walter Raleigh had lived in Dorset for a time. Its high chalk hills had provided a location for defensive settlements for millennia, with neolithic and bronze age burial mounds on almost every chalk hill in the county, and a number of Iron Age forts also.

The residence was in East Creech, three miles from Corfe Castle and four miles from Wareham town. The river Piddle ran through the pretty village and added to the beauty of it. Quaint cottages, some with thatched roofs, were scattered about the area and flowers of all sorts adorned the well kept gardens. The location was idyllic, quiet, and in the heart of the countryside.

Ducks could be seen swimming in the river, adding an air of peacefulness and tranquillity to the area. The village was situated at the Northern foot of the Purbeck hills and close to the picturesque village of Corfe. Ada, Harry and the children were elated with the location, and even more so when they reached the cottage they were renting. It was ideal for their growing family.

The accommodation was spacious in comparison to the small cottage in Norton Malreward. There were three steps from the path to the front door and another door led to an outhouse/shed. The sitting room was a good size with a large feature fireplace, the kitchen leading from the sitting room. This too was perfect, and the scullery was situated opposite the kitchen.

There was plenty of cupboard storage and a decent sized washroom. Three good bedrooms and a single toilet upstairs, and a large garden. The only downside seemed to be the slope of the garden, which could only be reached by many steps. It wasn't a garden used for growing vegetables, as Ada was used to, and she had concerns leaving the children to play outside unsupervised.

Peggy was too young at the moment and Tony was a climber, a proper little boy. With another child on the way, she would have to be careful. Nevertheless, she was excited about their new life and busied herself making the cottage a home, with Harry's help.

Harry found work around the area, cutting the grass in the gardens, repairing walls and fences and general gardening, as well as labouring in the farm locally. He was a good handyman, repairing and fixing, painting walls and numerous DIY jobs. There were more elderly residents than younger ones in the village, and they all needed a helping hand somewhere along the line. Harry was an all rounder and could put his hand to most things.

Ada missed him when he was on training duties, but paid several visits to Sarah and her family, when he wasn't at the cottage. Sarah now had another daughter, Edith, and Alfred was now home again. They enjoyed their meetings together, amidst their busy lives with the children, but Ada couldn't have been more settled. Harry still had his motorbike, but had now added a sidecar to it, to take his family out on sunny days.

The visits to Ebrington had suddenly became more frequent for Harry, and he stayed for four weeks at a time, helping on the farm. Martha and his uncles were indebted to him and Ada never complained, even though she had missed her husband dreadfully. They were his family, after all. Dick now had his own car, and both him and Blanche would spend weekends in East Creech with Ada and the family, when Dick wasn't working, that was.

Walks into Corfe, and Corfe Castle was a treat for the children, until Ada reached her eighth month in her pregnancy, and had to rest more. Harry took over and Tony joined him on his walks, pushing Peggy in her pushchair.

Baby number three entered the world in the form of a daughter, known as Milly, and named after Harry's sister. Her full name was Patricia Alison Amelia Tracey, and she was born on the 6th November 1931. They couldn't wait to share the news with their families and friends. Financially things were harder, but they coped, as all families did then.

Time flew and Tony had started school. Ada was able to spend more time with the girls, and Harry worked away a lot to earn more money to keep his family. With his visits to Ebrington, training in the Army reserves and working away, Ada didn't see much of Harry, but wouldn't dare complain. He was being loyal to his family and ensured food was put on the table.

Millie married Henry Vernon in 1932. Henry, known as Frank, was originally from Birmingham, but moved to Bidford with his family as a child. He was a brickmaker by trade and he moved into Martha's cottage after their marriage. Harry attended the wedding, but Ada remained at East Creech. The children were too small to travel such a distance.

Hubert, Percy's brother, also married the same year. His wife was a local girl from Paulton and her name was Gertrude. They hadn't known each other that long, but like Ada and Harry, knew it was right, instantly. Percy drove to East Creech to collect them the night before the wedding. He wanted his best friend and his family there, and they spent a few days afterwards at Windsor Cottage. Archibald and Ethel Mary were so pleased to see them both, and the grandchildren. They were missed around the area.

Blanche and Dick married in September 1933 and settled in Chew Magna. His parents helped find a cottage for them to rent, and eventually purchase, and they were more than content there.

Their residence was an open house to relatives, old and young, and they always accommodated any visitors. The more the merrier, Blanche would say; she was so much a people person.

Ada lost three babies after Milly. They were all stillborn, fully formed and perfect in every way, but had not reached their full term. Harry and Ada were both heartbroken, but tried to carry on for the sake of the children. Tony, Peggy and Milly were perfect; any more in the future would be a blessing, but they were more than thankful for the three children they had.

Milly turned 4 years old and all three children were now in school, Milly was attending part-time. Ada was expecting again and the pregnancy seemed to be going okay this time She ensured no chances were taken and took things a lot easier. Harry helped when he was at home.

Tony was now 8 years old and tried to help his mother out as much as possible. The logs were kept in the outhouse, located at the side of the main entrance to the cottage. He often chopped them, ready for the coal fire in the large ornate fireplace. He had been busy creating more firewood when Peggy had run into the outhouse and placed her hand on the table. Tony had the chopper in his hand and dropped it onto the log in place. It had hit Peggy's hand and her little finger was severed.

Blood was everywhere and the hospital staff were unable to stitch it back on. Peggy was just 5 years old and Tony blamed himself, but Ada reassured him it was an accident, and she would survive without her little finger. Harry had been away at the time, and tried to cut his journeys down to spend more time at home after that. He had felt guilty for being away, and knew he should have been there to help his wife.

Ernest had enlisted in the Army, his childhood dream fulfilled, and Ada was elated, over the moon for him. He had spoken about nothing else for years. Her father was managing, but had to take on yet another labourer. Christopher, one of the twins, and Roland, helped out after school. Archibald was never one to complain and plodded on, in his own way.

Mary Vera Tracey was born in Poole hospital in December 1935, the doctors weren't taking any chances after Ada had lost the last three babies, but she was perfect, a healthy baby girl. They were both thrilled to bits, happy to become parents again. Vera was a welcome sister to Tony, Peggy and Milly, and Harry's time in the Army reserves had now finished. The family were on the move again.

They now lived in Norton St Philip, near Frome, not far from Windsor Cottage. Tellisford was in walking distance and where Percy and Lily lived. The cottage belonged to Upper Farm and the landlord was a Percy Wadman. Harry wasn't too keen on him, there was something about him he didn't like, but he couldn't put his finger on it, not at that precise moment in time, anyway.

Ada was employed to milk the cows, collect the eggs and feed the chickens. In the summertime she helped with the haymaking. This secured the rent on the cottage. She was more than able to attend to the farm duties, so Harry had looked for work locally.

He sat in the Fleur de Llys pub nearby, enjoying his pint of cider, looking out of the window towards the George Inn opposite, thinking. Norton St Philip was a lovely village, small and picturesque with a few shops, a church and not much else. Scattered cottages and farmland, pretty gardens and peace and solitude. Harry knew he was home at last and his life felt complete.

'I remember my past, Grandmother,' Harry said, sat in the church speaking out loud. The church was empty, so no-one was there to listen to him.

St Philip and St James was built in the 14th Century and was located centrally in the village.

Samuel Pepys visited the church in the 17th Century and described the tomb of one of the knights templar, which is now thought to be that of a lawyer or merchant from 1460. The north aisle was added in the 17th Century and a major Victorian restoration was undertaken by George Gilbert Scott in the 1840's.

The memorials in the churchyard, included one of a soldier slain in Norton St Philip in 1643 during the English Civil War and there were further military casualties in the village during a skirmish in the Monmouth Rebellion.

'I have been through a lot and will never forget my home with you and my grandfather. You both raised me well. Mother is having a hard time in Ebrington now and trying to look after everyone, everyone else before herself.' After placing his hands together, as if praying, Harry continued. 'I've found my piece of heaven at last, Grandmother. My life is in this village, this is where I belong. It feels so right here, I have Ada and the children and have never felt more settled. I want to thank you for my upbringing, and the love you bestowed on me. This is where I'm going to end my days, this is home, Grandmother.'

Harry left the church, after lighting a candle for his grandparents and donated a shilling in the church box. He took a walk around the churchyard, then returned to the cottage and his family. Ada was cleaning the place to her satisfaction and smiling. Vera was asleep and the others were playing in the small garden overlooking the farm. They appeared happy, too. Life felt wonderful and Harry's cheeky grin was back again, in full force. He needed to find work, though.

Work came in Frome as a steamroller driver. He rode his motorbike to and from work daily and was home every evening. Life was normal, stable, but never boring. The children loved the village and they both knew it was safe for them to walk around, alone. They could be children at play and amuse themselves.

With the older children in school, Ada had no problems with the farm work. Vera was still sleeping a lot and was nearing her birthday when something seemed wrong with her. Ada called the doctor out and Vera was rushed to the Royal United Hospital in Coombe Down. Ada accompanied her in the ambulance.

Harry and the children followed on his motorbike and sidecar. Vera had contracted meningitis and doctors weren't optimistic about her recovery. Vera's health deteriorated overnight, and she died the next day. She hadn't reached her 2nd birthday. Life had stopped, and memories of lost family relived by Ada and Harry. How cruel was this?

Vera was buried in St Philip and St James church in Norton St Philip. Harry and Ada were distraught, they couldn't believe they had lost their little girl at such a young age. She was still a baby. Harry cried, something he had never done in public before. He had lost his daughter, how was he going to get over this? She had had everything to live for.

The whole village seemed to turn out for the funeral. They hadn't been there that long, but they all understood the heartbreak they were going through, and remembered the pretty little girl living in Town Barton. There were no secrets in the village. The children felt it too, they had lost their sister and found it hard to contain their grief.

Things were quiet for a long time afterwards. The children were all at school, and Ada continued with her farm duties. Harry carried on with his steamroller driving in Frome. Alice and Henry had moved to Upton Scudamore in Wiltshire with their son, Allan, but made occasional visits to ensure the family were okay.

Archibald and Ethel Mary also visited them and they both appreciated it, they seemed to be going through the motions of life, for the sake of the children. Blanche and Dick now had their first son, Robert, or Bob as he was known, and couldn't begin to understand how they were coping. Ada was pleased to see them. Harry spent a lot of time in the Fleur de Llys pub drowning his sorrows.

Harry wrote to his mother and his family and decided to pay a visit to Ebrington with Ada and the children. The children sat in the sidecar, whilst Harry and Ada rode on the motorbike. On reaching their destination, the whole family spent their time cherry picking in a local orchard, and all enjoyed the day. Martha and Millie were overjoyed to see the children and it was agreed at the end of the day, to make it an annual event.

Vera hadn't been forgotten, but life had to go on, and the children needed to be children again.

The cherry picking had been a resounding success and Tony, Peggy and Milly had met their grandmother, aunts and uncles. Smiles had begun to emerge at last, and Harry and Ada were hopeful for the future. Life had to become normal again.

Peggy and Milly weren't always the best behaved children. Often they would play on the steps of the George Inn, to Ada's annoyance. 'The pub is not a place to be playing,' she would say. 'Don't let me catch you there, there are other places to play.'

But they were children and didn't always listen. Ada would on occasion walk to the George Inn with her cane stick, searching for her girls, only for them to run around the back of the pub and reach their cottage before she'd returned. There would be no tea for them, and a bottle of water and some bread was quickly hidden under their pillows in preparation for it. They'd foxed their mother and had smiled to themselves.

On another occasion, after visiting the local newsagents, the girls pinched a toffee each and hid it in their pockets. They waited until they arrived home to eat it, only to be marched back to the shop again, to hand it back to the shopkeeper. 'Stealing is not allowed, don't let it happen again,' she retorted. 'I'm disappointed in you both.'

Years passed and a routine had emerged. Tony now worked in Frome making tyres. Peggy was at Coombe Down secondary school and Milly was due to start there soon. Norton St Philip was home. Harry enjoyed supping his two pints of cider in the Fleur de Llys pub, and Ada was content in doing the farm work and being there, in the countryside.

Harry's attitude towards Tony had changed. Whether it was because he was now a lot older, he was 15 now, working and had a mind of his own, or because he wasn't his son and had lost his youngest daughter; no-one knew exactly what had happened, but things weren't the same between them. Peggy and Milly were treated differently to Tony, and it was noticeable. The bond they had had when he was younger was now gone. Tony tried not to make waves and kept quiet, working and helping his mother on occasions, to keep their distance from one another.

The Second World War had begun and things weren't easy. Harry was still working in Frome and helping out as a Home Guard. You could never take the Army out of Harry, and he wanted to be of use. Ada continued her duties on the farm to ensure the rent was paid, and Harry still supped his two pints of cider at his local, regularly.

He didn't get on with his landlord, Percy Wadman, he would flirt with his wife on occasions, and Harry wasn't keen on his attitude as a person, either. He stayed away from him. He had an air about him and locals would avoid him too, for fear of him lashing out and creating a commotion. His daughter, Diane, was at school with Peggy.

Harry would occasionally visit Percy, Lily and their son, Gerald, in Tellisford. He still relished in his long walks. He would check on Vera in the churchyard on a weekend, and write to his mother frequently. The annual cherry picking event was always looked forward to and Millie now had two children of her own, Patricia and Keith, and they had moved to Bidford, not far from his mother.

Archibald and Ethel Mary had moved to a smaller cottage in East Camel in Yeovil. It still had plenty of land around it, but the living accommodation was a lot smaller. Alfred and Christopher helped attend to the land. Dorothy was still at home, but all the others were married, or had moved away, and had their own lives to live.

Frank Emms junior had married a local girl from Shipston on Stour in 1937. Her name was Phyllis May Digweed. She gave birth to a daughter, Doris May, a year later, but she had died soon after being born. Frank and Phyllis were able to hold her briefly, before the midwife took her away. Martha and the Emms family couldn't take it in. Life was so cruel. They went on to have two sons, Peter and Michael, who were perfect in every way and worshipped by their parents. They moved to Cheltenham shortly after Doris's death.

Life ticked along fine, memories would never fade, but life had to be lived and the Tracey family did just that, until Ada became ill after milking the cows on the 4th January 1943. Snow was on the ground, but she was used to climate change and working in all weathers. She had felt a bit lethargic the previous few days, but hadn't taken too much notice. She was always busy and tiredness could creep up on you. The work needed doing regardless, as it had paid the rent on the cottage.

She didn't feel at all well the next morning, so Harry had kept Peggy home from school to look after her, promising to call into the doctor's surgery on the way to work. Tony was working that morning too, and Milly was attending her first day at the "big school", Coombe Down. Ada didn't want her to miss her first day there, even though she was nervous and hadn't wanted to leave her mother. She had requested that her sister, Peggy, remain at home with her. Ada wasn't well.

Milly braved the bus alone and attended her first lessons in her new school. Tony and Harry finished their shifts and returned home. Ada wasn't any better, the doctor hadn't called until 4 o'clock that afternoon, sadly. His silent nod, when examining her, hadn't appeared good.

Peggy and Milly took turns in checking on her, and taking her food and drinks. She wasn't improving. Harry didn't know what to do. The doctor had given her medication, which she was taking, but hadn't said too much about her health problem.

It was Milly's turn to climb the stairs and see how her mother was. She walked into the room and knew something wasn't right. Her mother was still and didn't seem to be breathing. She called her name, shook her, and then shook her again. She didn't move. She shouted down the stairs to her father, who came running up to their room, along with Tony and Peggy. It was too late though, their mother was dead. She was 38 years old.

Harry contacted the doctor again, who revisited and confirmed her death. The death certificate noted pneumonia, brought on by nephretic toxaemia and cardiac failure. Her kidneys had stopped working, resulting in toxaemia and pneumonia. No-one could believe it, she had been milking the cows the day before! All the family were dumbstruck, and couldn't take it in.

Tony blamed Harry for her death. There was no reason to, as nothing he could have done differently would have changed the outcome. Ada would have still died. Their relationship was still strained, Tony was older now, and had opinions that Harry didn't altogether agree with.

No parent goes through life with their children completely agreeing with them. There's not many children who haven't had a rebellious streak as they reached puberty. He refused to speak to his father, he never ever knew he wasn't Harry's son.

Peggy and Milly were only 11 and 12 years old, had already lost their sister, Vera, and had now lost their mother. Nothing Harry said or done could calm them or give them reassurance, and he was hurting himself. He had lost his wife and his soulmate. How was he going to manage? For days the family isolated themselves in their cottage, refusing to go out or allow family and friends to enter.

Nothing anyone said to them would help. Ada was gone, and so suddenly. It wasn't fair.

CHAPTER FIFTEEN

The funeral was one of the saddest ever. All the village residents were there at the church, mostly stood outside, as there was no room inside, all the seats had been taken. They remembered the family less than 6 years previous, losing their baby daughter, Vera. Ada's family were all there, (with the exception of Ernest, who was still in the Army) and of course Percy, Lily and their son, Gerald. Dorothy and Sarah, Ada's best friends were there.

No-one could quite believe that Ada had gone, so young, and with so much to look forward to. She had been a lovely lady who had cared so much about everyone, and had never hurt anyone in her life, intentionally. She hadn't asked for much in her life, just peace and tranquillity, a loving husband and her children. They had made her happy and contented. She had never wanted more.

The church was quiet, you could hear a pin drop, the coffin was in position and the service begun. Hymns sung, tributes spoken and tears on everyone's faces. It was such an emotional occasion. Blanche tried to be brave, but couldn't hold her tears in, she'd lost yet another sister. Ethel Mary was quiet, though her face held no emotion. Her husband, Archibald, was near to collapse, and Alice had put an arm around him for comfort.

Harry stood alone, the girls held hands and Tony stood next to them. He was still blaming Harry for his mother's death, and had arranged to go and live with his aunty Alice after the funeral. Alice had agreed, but had checked with Harry first. He couldn't force Tony to stay with him, as he was old enough to make his own decisions now.

Percy Wadman, the landlord, had called into the cottage, a few days prior to the funeral. The farm work needed to continue to enable Harry to stay there. There was no way he was going to work for that man! Never in a million years. He was ignorant, egotistical, rude and impatient. He treated people like something you had spat out.

The way he had spoken to Ada at times was appalling. He didn't know how she had put up with his abusive language. No-one in the village liked him, or had any time for him. He hadn't been to work since Ada's death, either. If he had to leave the cottage, he and the girls would be homeless.

Percy and Lily agreed to having Harry and his family with them, until they could find somewhere else to live. Percy was a life saver. The furniture was loaded onto a work's van and taken to Percy's home, and made use of there. The cottage had bad memories now, their bedroom especially. Harry cried every time he entered it, and he wanted Ada back so desperately.

He knew he was losing the children's home, but couldn't help himself. His spirit had gone when Ada had died and he couldn't think straight. He wasn't able to live there any more, as the image of her lying there in their bed completely lifeless, wouldn't go away. The vision would haunt him forever if he had stayed.

The children were unable to talk to him. He didn't want to speak to anyone. He was grieving, and was oblivious to anyone else's grief. Tony was there for the girls, he was their brother and he looked after them, whilst hurting himself.

Ada was buried near her daughter, Vera, Row 6, Plot 7. The family watched in silence, as she was lowered into the ground. Harry threw a pink chrysanthemum onto the coffin, Ada's favourite flower, and one of the flowers she had carried on their wedding day. The girls followed, and so did Tony. Tears flowed for all except Harry, but his grief was obvious. He stood at the graveside for ages after everyone had gone, staring into space, totally bewildered. 'What now?' he asked himself. 'What now?'

There was no wake, Harry couldn't cope with anything more than the funeral itself. Tony went with his aunty Alice, uncle Henry, and his cousin, Allan, to Upton Scudamore; saying goodbye to Peggy and Milly, but still not speaking to Harry. Harry didn't push the issue. That was his son's choice.

Harry and the girls returned to Percy's cottage, after everyone had left the church. No-one spoke for hours, sitting at the Bridge's kitchen table, drinking tea. No reminiscing, no tears, just silence.

Eventually, the girls went upstairs to the bedroom that they would be using. Harry was sleeping on the settee in the sitting room. It wasn't ideal, but Percy and Lily hadn't minded.

The war was still going on, and Percy and Harry had volunteered to help in the Home Guards.

They felt they had a loyalty to the Army services. Percy was working, but Harry couldn't bring himself out of his shell of grief (he had cocooned himself into), to return to work as a steamroller driver. There was no money coming in, and not a lot of money left in the rainy day pot. Ada had always tried to save a little for rainy days. He didn't know how they were going to manage, and at the moment he didn't seem to care. He was closing himself down, going into his own world without a thought for anyone, except himself and Ada.

Percy and Lily looked after the girls, with their son, Gerald. They all attended the same school. Months passed and Harry had become reclusive, walking daily and returning when he felt ready to. Percy had known similar reactions from his Army days, and didn't push him in any particular direction. Only Harry could sort himself out, and in his own time.

He begun speaking at last, for which Percy was relieved. The girls needed their father more than ever now. Tony wrote to Peggy and Milly often, telling them about his life with aunty Alice and uncle Henry. He told them that he'd been thinking about joining the Navy. He hadn't quite reached his 18th birthday when he'd applied, and hadn't been completely honest about his age initially, but he was accepted. His training programme continued until he'd celebrated his birthday.

Peggy had been unwell one morning, so Milly and Gerald headed for school, leaving Peggy home to recover. Harry hadn't left for his daily walk as usual, and stayed with her. Blanche had made a visit to the Bridge's residence, to check on Harry and the girls. On seeing Peggy home from school, she'd offered to take her back home with her, and Harry had agreed.

When Milly returned home from school, she found Peggy gone, and her father told her that she'd gone to Chew Magna with her aunty Blanche. She hoped Peggy would be back when she had recovered, but she never returned. Milly missed her sister so much, and her brother too. It was just her and her father now.

It was now November, and Ada had been gone for 10 months. Milly's birthday was approaching. She would be 12. She had received mail in the post. Milly didn't usually receive any letters, except from Peggy and Tony, and thought that perhaps it was an early birthday card. It was from Ethel Mary, her step-grandmother. She was asking Milly to meet her at Yeovil train station the following week, where she was to live with her. Milly couldn't believe it. She didn't want to go to live with her. She didn't like her at all.

Showing the letter to her father, Harry had put his hands over his eyes. Tears fell, but he didn't want Milly seeing them. 'Hold yourself together,' he said to himself. 'Hold yourself together.' He had no money and was still not working, as the job in Frome had now employed someone else.

Harry had taken too long to return, after Ada's death. Sensibly, letting Milly go was the best thing for her, even though he would miss her desperately. She was all he had left.

'Do I have to go, Father?' she asked almost hysterically.

'I don't want you to go, Milly, and I will miss you terribly, but I think your step-grandmother is right. It would be best for you,' he said holding back the tears. 'My money has gone, I'm not working, and it's not fair on Percy and Lily to keep us.'

Milly cried and cried, hugging her father tightly. She had less than a week before leaving for Yeovil and the step-grandmother she detested, but couldn't do anything about it. If only her father had gone back to work, or had agreed to working the farm for Percy Wadman. They would still have their cottage then. If only their mother was still here, and hadn't died. If only her sister and brother were still here. If only, if only, if only!

Milly stood at the platform with her father, her suitcase at his feet. He handed her a post office book. 'This is yours, Milly. Your aunty Millie has been investing 10 shillings a year into it for you since you were 10.

Give it to your step-grandmother, I have informed your aunty Millie about your moving to Yeovil.'

'I don't want to go! Do I have to, Father?' she pleaded, tears in her eyes.

'I think it's for the best, I know you'll be looked after. I can't take proper care of you. I've no home, no job and I'm still not coping without your mother. You'll be better off.'

The train pulled into the station and Harry put Milly onto it, hugging her and wishing her well. He waved as it pulled away, reassuring her that someone would be at the other end waiting for her.

That someone was her grandfather, Archibald, and her aunty Dorothy, Ada's sister. Her grandfather gave her a hug and picked up her suitcase. There was a car waiting for them as he didn't drive, but her uncle Alfred did. He said hello as they got into the car.

'You'll be fine, Milly,' her grandfather said. 'We'll look after you.'

'But what about Father, is he going to be okay? He hasn't got any of us now. He's on his own,' Milly said anxiously.

'Percy and Lily will look after him. Don't you worry.' It was more of a statement than a gesture of concern, but Milly didn't say any more. They were silent until they reached the house. This was in East Camel, and Milly was to attend West Camel school. Ethel Mary had already registered her there in preparation.

Milly settled into her new life, sharing rooms with her aunty Dorothy who was 26, and was the only girl left at home. The twins were now married and living in Dorset and Phyllis was living in Frome with her husband, William, and their son, Reginald.

Roland had moved away from the area, and Ernest was still serving in the Army. Jim was still in the institution in Chard, and Alice was in Upton Scudamore. Tony continued lodging with her when he was on leave from the Navy.

Blanche and her husband, Dick, were still in Chew Magna, with their sons, Bob, Alan and daughter, Sylvia, along with Peggy. No-one was ever turned away at Blanche's, she would always find room somewhere for them. Ernest was courting Dick's sister, Hilda, whom he had known since childhood, due to his visits with Blanche to her parents' home.

They were due to get married the following year, on his discharge from the Forces.

It wasn't long before Milly's grandparents had moved to a smaller property in Somerset. This time it was to a place called Lullington, which was closer to Kathleen and Christopher's homes.

Milly would be given chores to do, before and after school. Clothes were bought second-hand for her, including boots and shoes. There was one pair of boots in particular that Milly disliked, hated in fact. They were laced up the front from foot to knee, in an awful dark brown colour, and she totally detested them. On one occasion, after tying up the cows, she purposely trod into the mud to cake the boots all over, and hid them behind the settee that was situated in the hallway. No-one ever moved the settee out to clean behind it, and when asked, Milly told her step-grandmother that she had mislaid them.

Scrubbing the kitchen floor became Milly's job and food was eaten in the scullery, never at the kitchen table with the men. She wasn't important enough for that! She would darn socks, repair clothes and endless other chores after the evening meal was finished, then off to bed ready for the next day. She enjoyed uncle Alfred's company. He was 19 and always made her feel welcome.

Her grandfather tried his best to make her feel at home, but was careful not to give her too much attention when Ethel Mary was around. Milly so loved her grandfather. Dorothy didn't go out to work and helped with the domestic duties, as all the other girls had done in the past.

When her aunty Kathleen was ready to give birth, on two separate occasions, Milly was sent to Maiden Newton for the week, to help out with her newborn babies. 'Aunty Kathleen needs all the help she can get, and it would be good practice for you in years to come,' her step-grandmother had said. Milly was actually thankful for the breaks, and her aunty and uncle treated her well. She loved helping out with the babies, too.

Her grandfather had died shortly after their move to Lullington, in 1945. After having an operation on his stomach, he had taken to hayraking the fields with his horse. The factory bell had rung, situated behind the fields, signalling the workers lunch break. Archibald's horse had taken fright and bolted and he had been thrown to the ground, opening up the stitches from his wound. He had died instantly. He had only been 65 and Milly missed him so much. Her step-grandmother was now more hostile to her than ever before.

Within the year, they were moving again, this time to Sydling in Dorset. Another cottage with some farmland. Alfred was still attending to the land and Christopher was living closer again now, and helped out, but life was very severe without her grandfather around, and Alfred was concerned at his mother's harsh behaviour towards Milly.

Harry hadn't been in contact with any of his children. He had continued with the Home Guards until the War had ended, staying with Percy and Lily. He was doing odd jobs for villagers to earn a bit of money to help out, and give Percy some keep, but had become so reclusive that he really wasn't concerned about life at all.

He thought about his children, but that was as far as it went. He visited Ada's grave daily and walked to Victoria Park in Frome, which had been her favourite park. He didn't write to the children and he had no real interest in Tony, as he wasn't his natural son. He was happy to think that the girls were well cared for, and he had no idea what Milly was going through. She was being used as a domestic slave, there was no other words for it. He never attempted to visit her as a child.

He knew Peggy would be fine. Blanche was a lovely person and had three children of her own, Peggy would be treated the same as her children. Harry thought about paying a visit to Blanche, and did one sunny day. His family had mattered, all of a sudden, and he'd wanted to know how everybody was.

He caught a bus to Bath, and another to Chew Magna. Blanche was home, but Peggy had moved to Winford Hospital, working as an auxiliary nurse and living in. She was almost 16 years old.

Harry had had no idea. Blanche told him that Peggy was okay, enjoying her job and frequently visiting them. He had promised to keep in touch more often.

He couldn't bring himself to visit Ethel Mary, he had never really liked her, and although he missed Milly dearly, he truly believed that she was being loved and cared for, as any grandchild would be. His letter writing days had gone, though he did keep promising to write to her.

Milly was now 14 years of age and not as disciplined as her step-grandmother would have liked her to be; she could be cheeky at times, and didn't always do as she was told first time. Her step-grandmother decided to put her into service in Dorchester. For her own good, Ethel Mary had said!

Mrs Methuen was a vicar's widow. She was a short, stout lady with grey thinning hair, and she wore spectacles. Her facial expressions were of surprise and inquisitiveness, and she always seemed interested in other people and their welfare; it could be seen as nosiness at times. She smiled often, unlike Ethel Mary, and Milly instantly liked her kind and caring ways. After all, Milly was her servant, and she hadn't expected it.

She had a daughter named Gladys, and her other daughter, Gertrude, was a nun and visited her mother and sister often. Their brother had died during the First World War, he had been a Lieutenant Commander and had passed away with honours. Mrs Methuen's husband, the Rev Paul Methuen, had died years earlier at 81 years of age. She was now 91 herself.

Milly had preferred her life, living in service, though it was hard work and she was only given one afternoon a week off. This she spent back in Sydling, travelling all the way by bicycle. Her step-grandmother would have listed chores ready for her. Chairs would be placed on top of the kitchen table, ready for her to scrub the floor, a basket was filled with items needing darning, and other duties needed doing outdoors. She was never given any free time to herself.

Milly never questioned the use of her free time. It would have been nice to visit the nearby park in Dorchester, or do some window shopping, or even take a bus to Winford Hospital to see her sister, but Ethel Mary made it perfectly clear that Milly was needed there, helping her aunty Dorothy.

Her step-grandmother handed over her post office book. She was now in service and any monies saved were hers in her own right. Her aunty Millie had continued to deposit 10 shillings a year into it, and she hadn't known any real money in all her life. Daring or not,

Millie withdrew some of it and purchased a pot of nail varnish and a manicure kit, a nail file and clippers in a pretty case, of all things. She had never worn nail varnish before, and had decided to treat herself. The look on her step-grandmother's face was unreadable, but she was unable to stop her.

She loved Linden Lodge. Mrs Methuen and Miss Gladys were lovely people and treated her with respect. When Miss Gertrude visited, dressed in her nun's attire, she would ask how she was, and meant it. They were a lovely family and she felt she'd had a good escape, but she missed her father dreadfully and her uncle Alfred, though he never felt like an uncle to her, more like an older brother. She wondered what her father was doing.

After the War had ended, Harry decided to visit his mother, Martha. What little monies he had left afforded him to put petrol into his motorbike. He was still living with Percy and Lily, and felt they could do with some time on their own.

He drove slowly, as the motorbike was quite old now and prone to mechanical problems. He had had no interest in keeping it in good order after Ada's death, and hardly used it. Walking was never a problem for him. He preferred walking and always had.

Martha and Frank welcomed him and apologised for not being at the funeral. They still lived at the thatched cottage in Ebrington near his uncles. Jack (John Henry) was the only sibling left at home now; everyone now referred to him as Jack.

Albert had recently married and was living in Chipping Norton with his wife Doris. Frank junior was living in Cheltenham with his wife Phyllis, and Richard (or Dick as he was now called) had returned to the neighbourhood after marrying Dorothy French from Plymouth. He had served as a prison warden in Dartmoor, Devon, before joining the Army and been imprisoned in a Stalag camp in Torun, Poland from 1942. He had also been in the Gloucester Regiment and would never forget his Army number 5182249, or his Prisoner of War number 13073.

Jim (Walter James) was living locally in Ebrington with his wife, Joan, whom he'd married a year earlier, shortly after Ada's death. He was a gamekeeper, working near Shipston on Stour. Millie and her husband Frank were still living in Bidford, with their two children.

Martha could tell from Harry's silent attitude, that he was still grieving and asked if there was anything she could do to help.

Harry replied solemnly 'I'm trying to cope, Mother, but I can't seem to function at all. My mind is on Ada constantly, I can't seem to accept she's gone.'

Martha placed a cup of tea on the kitchen table and Harry continued speaking.

'I've lost my girls, Mother. Vera died far too young, Peggy is now living in Winford hospital and working as an auxiliary nurse. Milly is with her step-grandmother and Tony is in the Navy. I couldn't get on with Tony at the end. He wasn't my son, after all.' The spark in him had gone. 'How do I cope now, Mother? I don't know how to any more!' He was at his wits end.

He drank his tea and wandered down to the church to his grandmother's grave. He sat down beside it and silently prayed, speaking quietly to her and wishing she was still with him, to give him guidance, and help show him the way forward. He called into the Ebrington Arms for a pint of cider, but his mood hadn't changed. He was lost and couldn't see a light at the end of the tunnel.

Martha had informed Millie that her brother, Harry, was home and hoped she would be able to help, but even she was unable to console him. He cried on her shoulder and she held him until there were no more tears left to shed. He was a grown man reduced to a small child. Millie was so worried about him.

He visited his uncles at Hidcote Boyce. They had stopped running the farm because they were now physically unable to continue the work. They managed the kitchen garden, kept a few chickens, cows for milk and lived in the farmhouse. The fields were rented out to an adjoining farm, so were still used and not left idle. The despair in Harry's eyes was obvious to them, and they were concerned.

'You can live her with us, Harry,' they both said at once. It had always been his home.

'There's plenty of outside work here to keep you busy. I'm sure your mother would be more than happy to have you at her cottage, too,' said his uncle Richard.

'But Ada and Vera are in Norton St Philip. I need to be near them,' Harry replied. 'A visit now and again is okay, but my place is there.'

'What about the cherry picking, Harry?' his uncle John asked. 'The girls are missing them, I'm sure. A visit to see Peggy and Milly and a day trip here would surely cheer you all up.'

Harry wasn't listening. He was wallowing in self pity and nothing could lift him out of the hole he had dug for himself. Even speaking about his children and how they must have been hurting too, couldn't change anything. No-one had any answers to give him, none that would help him, anyway.

After two weeks, Harry decided it was time to go home to Norton St Philip. That was where he belonged. Martha and Frank gave him some money, and so did his uncles. They all knew he didn't have any, or any work to earn any, for that matter. He said he was going back to Percy's, but in reality he wasn't sure where he was going. He'd felt they needed their own home back, and only rightly so. It was only supposed to be temporary, after all.

CHAPTER SIXTEEN

Back in Norton St Philip, Harry booked into a local bed and breakfast. He had the money his mother and his uncles had given him. He made a visit to Percy and Lily in Tellisford, telling them of his whereabouts. They had insisted that there would always be a home there for him, and Harry thanked them before returning to the bed and breakfast. He needed to be on his own.

He found work mowing the lawns, weeding, planting bulbs and shrubs for local residents, when the weather permitted. General labouring, plumbing, painting, anything that was needed, Harry accommodated, and although it was poorly paid he was able to keep a roof over his head.

Eventually, he sold his motorbike. It was of no use. He was happy walking and was unable to afford the petrol, anyway. The soup kitchen was available in Frome, where he often went, and he met his regular "friends" there. This saved him money as he didn't need to pay for an evening meal. Occasionally, residents would supply him with food when he was attending to their gardens, or maintaining their properties.

Harry visited the churchyard daily, checking on Ada and Vera's graves, ensuring they were litter free, weed free and occasionally placing a bunch of flowers on each plot. Victoria Park was his home now, and where he spent most of his day if he wasn't doing any odd jobs. He would sit on the bench where Ada and he had sat, and settle himself comfortably in the summerhouse, listening to the bands playing in the summertime.

He had become reclusive, but always spoke to passers by, one's who knew him before Ada's death and unknown faces looking for conversation. The mischievous grin had emerged again and he felt content living the way he was now accustomed to. No-one seemed to judge him, although he had a few glares from passing people, as his dress attire wasn't the cleanest and he now had a long white beard and unruly hair. Harry could cope with that.

Blanche would get visits on occasion, when he had earned enough money to enable him to catch the buses, and the summerhouse and shelter in Victoria Park in Frome was slowly becoming his bed, rather than the bed and breakfasts. He would only book into a local bed and breakfast when he felt he needed a bath and a good nights sleep.

Harry appeared used to living outdoors now, in all winds and weathers. But amongst it all, he still managed a smile. He would often be found holding a bottle of cider, taking a swig, smoking his pipe and admiring the views in the park, picking out the occasional weed from the flower borders, if he'd spotted any poking their heads out. He would read any newspapers left behind, so kept up to date with the politics of the world, and would then make his regular walk to the churchyard to check on Ada and Vera. He was more than content, in his own little way.

Percy would get a visit now and again. He was now used to seeing him in his vagrant state or as a gentleman of the road, which sounded much kinder. He would produce a pair of clean trousers, shoes and a jumper and offer him a hot bath. Sometimes Harry would take him up on the offer, especially where shoes were concerned, with the amount of walking he did; a hot bath hadn't gone amiss in the summertime. Lily pleaded with him to move back in with them, but Harry was stubborn and declined the offer every time.

'I'm happy as I am,' he would say and meant it. 'I've enough money for a night's bed and breakfast, if I want it.'

Peggy was now courting a lad who was also working in Winford hospital. He was a porter there and his name was Bill Sherman. They seemed to get on well and would meet up after work. Bill had lost the use of one of his arms and he was paralysed down his right side, which could be quite awkward at times. But he managed well enough, and liked his job.

Milly on the other hand, had been ordered by her step-grandmother to move back into their cottage in Sydling. She was to leave her post as servant to Mrs Methuen and return to her domestic duties there. Dorothy was getting married to a Victor Barrett and would be moving to Buckinghamshire after their wedding, on account of him being in the Army and based in that area.

Milly was to be a bridesmaid. On seeing the suit she was to wear, so drab and unfashionable, and not in the slightest bit flattering to anyone's figure, her face was a picture. A grimace adorned her face and a look of disbelief. She was 15 now and had opinions of her own. She hated the outfit, and told Peggy in her letter that she wasn't wearing it, and the only reason her step-grandmother wanted her back, was due to Dorothy leaving. She would be at her step-grandmother's beck and call, for sure.

Tony didn't write many letters to his sisters. He was still serving in the Navy and had been posted abroad, but he still kept in touch when he was able. He hadn't tried to contact his father, Harry, and was at peace with things continuing that way. He had lost his mother and he would never forget her, but Harry had no place in his life.

His last few years living at home, before his mother's death, were not ideal. He was a teenager and did not always see eye to eye with his father, but Tony was aware of a difference. He wasn't treated the same, there seemed to be hostility in his voice, something that wasn't there when he spoke to the girls. He didn't blame the girls, but they were the ones getting the praise from his father, not him.

Tony had blamed his father for his mother's death. He felt that he should have been home with her, on that dreadful day, and would therefore have been able to contact the doctor again, arranging an earlier visit.

In reality, nothing would have changed the outcome, even if Tony had been home that day too, but he needed to blame someone, so it was his father who was at fault, in his eyes, anyway.

Peggy had understood Milly's concerns at returning to their step-grandmother's to live. There was a vacancy in the hospital and she was trying to get Milly the job, and a room to live in. On Milly's afternoon off, she was to meet her at Blanche's and go with her to the hospital.

Milly carefully organised things with complete secrecy. She ensured she had clothes to take with her, without her step-grandmother noticing, and caught several buses before reaching her destination, her aunty Blanche's. Peggy was late arriving, and Milly ended up staying with her aunty instead. There wasn't room for her to stay there indefinitely, so Ernest and Hilda offered to have her with them.

Ernest was now married and lived locally in Chew Magna, with his brother, Jim. He had taken him out of the institution in Chard, on his discharge from the Army. They were looking after a property in the village, and occupied rooms in it. Neither Milly, nor Jim should have been there, but they stayed nevertheless.

It was two days before Ethel Mary realised Milly wasn't at Linden Lodge with Mrs Methuen, after she hadn't returned home on her free afternoon. She contacted Blanche, who confirmed Milly was there and would not be returning to her home. She would be looked after by family in the village. Ethel Mary didn't argue, but wasn't amused. Who was going to help her around the cottage now?

Milly absolutely loved living with Ernest and Hilda, and found work in the local dairy, a place called Dando's. Life was a lot happier and much more enjoyable. She had her cousins, Blanche's children, and Sylvia was only 9 years younger than her. She was able to socialise more and was no longer the "hired help".

The family attended Dorothy's wedding, but Milly wasn't a bridesmaid and kept her distance from her step-grandmother. No-one blamed her for running away. Alfred was happy for her and commended her for her courage and determination, and wished her well.

Ernest eventually changed jobs and was employed by Lulsgate Airport, near Bristol.

Accommodation was included with the work, and he was unable to take Jim or Milly with him. Blanche took Jim into her house, where he remained until his death, years later. Milly moved into Hilda and Dick's mother's (granny Marsh) where she remained for a good few years. She also courted her first boyfriend whilst living there. His name was Graham, and he was granny Marsh's youngest son (Dick and Hilda's brother).

It was in 1949 that Peggy and Bill had married. Milly attended with a few of the House family relatives. Tony was able to attend as he had now left the Navy, and was working locally as a compressor attendant. They had managed to obtain a mortgage on a semi-detached house and moved to Bristol, not far from Chew Magna. Peggy gave up her job and became a housewife, taking care of the domestic duties and her husband. Her house was spotless and her routine was set for the week. You could set your time by her and what domestic duties she was dealing with on a daily basis and when, but she was where she wanted to be and loved being a wife.

Harry was on his way to visit Blanche and Dick on one of his rare occasions, and had boarded the bus to Chew Magna. Milly was now a young lady, around 18 years of age and still working in Dando's. She was on the bus returning home one day, when Harry had sat down beside her.

She was so embarrassed. Harry had looked an absolute sight. His coat had seen better days, along with his trousers. His shoes had holes in the soles and it looked like he had trodden in mud and hadn't bothered to wipe the mud off them. His hair was down to his shoulders, grey and uncombed and his beard was almost to his waist, matted and caked with dirt. He desperately needed a bath.

Milly felt eyes looking at her as her father spoke to her, and she blushed. This was her own father and she was horrified. Harry was oblivious to the looks around him. It never bothered him. He was used to it, and would produce a smile whenever anyone stared at him.

They both dismounted the bus, Harry asked how she was and she told him she was doing okay.

Milly told him about her work in Dando's the dairy, and her whereabouts, living with granny Marsh. She told him of her courtship with Graham Marsh, and headed back to her home. She couldn't believe this was her father, but he seemed unconcerned and waved to her as he headed towards Blanche's dwelling.

Harry had a tear in his eye as he headed for Blanche's. Milly had grown into a lovely girl, a pretty girl. He had missed watching her grow, from a child at 11, to an adult. She was courting! His daughter had a boyfriend, his little girl. He remembered the day she had boarded the train to her step-grandmother's and her heartache at having to go. That had only seemed like yesterday.

Dick and Blanche were pleased to see him. He had sat on the bus with his daughter, he proudly told them, and asked how Peggy and Bill were. Blanche kept Harry up to date with everything, telling him that

Tony, and his girlfriend, Patricia, were due to get married soon, after his discharge from the Navy and now working near his home. He was still there in Upton Scudamore with his aunty Alice and uncle Henry. He had no interest in Tony and he shrugged his shoulders, indicating his disinterest.

Dick took Harry to the Pelican Inn, located in the centre of the small village. Dick was never one to be concerned about Harry's or anyone else's dress sense and never insisted on him changing his clothes or visiting the washroom. Harry enjoyed his pint of cider and his socialising occasionally, and he knew Dick and Blanche were concerned about him, but he also knew that his brother in law understood him completely, and had accepted the way he lived.

Blanche would search out a few items of Dick's clothes for Harry whilst they were out, and they would drive him back to Victoria Park when he was ready to return to Frome. They never judged him, and let him carry on his nomadic existence. His children were carrying on with their lives and he continued to live his, the way he wanted to.

Milly and Peggy attended Tony's wedding in September 1950. Tony was a handsome man of 23 now, and Patricia was 19. She was from Westbury in Wiltshire, a local girl living close to his aunty Alice's and uncle Henry's. He looked elated on his wedding day, dressed immaculately in his dark double breasted suit with its flared turn-up trousers. He wore a white shirt and a patterned tie and polished shoes you could see your face in. That was the Navy for you!

Patricia smiled whilst the photographs were taken, resplendent in her pale cream suit, with a pleated knee length skirt and thigh length jacket with a sweet collar and buttoned up at the front. She wore three carnations on her right lapel instead of carrying a bouquet, and her hat was adorned with feathers and netting.

Alice and Henry were there as his "parents", along with Patricia's parents. Peggy and Milly proudly showed off their partners to the family, especially those they didn't see often. The wedding was a joyous occasion, but Harry was nowhere to be seen. Ada was remembered on this wonderful day, as she always was. She would have been there rejoicing, revelling in her son's special day and wanting the best for him.

Peggy and Milly looked splendid in their outfits, though Milly's choice of hats were never her best attribute. The sun shone, giving the happy couple their blessing and another wonderful day was afforded. They lived initially in a converted barn, which had been tastefully decorated by Patricia, and a baby was on the way a year after their marriage. Unfortunately their son, Roger, died soon after his birth in September 1952.

Milly moved into the Pelican Inn in Chew Magna. She was now employed as a barmaid there, and had finished at Dando's. There was room to live in and she decided it was a good move, until she was fired! The reasons were pretty trivial, some verbal banter which offended staff and customers, it seemed, but meant she was homeless again. Back to Blanche's she went, finding work elsewhere. She was very adaptable and never out of work for long.

Eventually Milly moved into Peggy's house in Bristol and found work there. Her relationship with Graham had finished, and she was now free and single again. Her eyes were now on the next door neighbour's son, Vernon, a handsome young man who was training to be a Gentleman's hairdresser.

Vernon was the baby of 13 children. His mother, Eva Mary, had lost her first husband at an early age, after producing three daughters. His father, Frederick, had also lost his first wife the same year, and had had three young children to bring up. They had lived in Wales, in the Rhondda Valley, in neighbouring streets. Eva Mary had been born and raised there, in the Rhondda Valley. Two years after their partners' deaths, Eva and Frederick had married, producing another daughter and six more sons together. Vernon was the youngest.

Frederick was a chimney sweep and the couple had now lived in Bristol, Frederick's birthplace.

They had initially moved for work, along with their first two sons together, and the rest of the children still living at home at the time. Vernon and Cyril were the only children now left at home. Two of their sons had married the previous year and the rest had flown the nest, years before.

Milly was quite taken with the "boy" next door. He was three years younger than her, but age was immaterial, and three years wasn't a huge difference in the context of things. Peggy and Bill were aware of the attraction immediately. Vernon asked her out to the local pub and Milly was excited, similar to a teenager on her first date.

'What am I going to wear, Peggy?' she asked. 'I need to buy something new.'

'You're only going to The Venture, Milly. You don't need to dress up to go there,' Peggy answered.

'But I want to look nice. It's our first date and I want to impress him. I like him, Peggy, a lot!'

'That's pretty obvious. Have a look in my wardrobe to see if there's anything you like there,' she'd replied.

'Thanks, Peggy. You're a star.' Milly ran up the stairs, emerging from the bedroom wearing one of her sister's floral dresses. 'Well, what do you think?'

Bill walked into the house after finishing work, gazed over at Milly and looked again. 'Isn't that your dress, Peggy?' he asked. 'It looks very similar to the one I bought you a few months ago.'

'Yes it is. Milly's got a hot date in The Venture, with Vernon next door.' Peggy was secretly laughing, but hadn't shown her sister.

'Oh I see, I'm sure he could do better than take you to that place, though,' Bill laughed as he had said it, but Milly was full of excitement and took no notice at all. 'You look very nice, I made a good choice there. Have a lovely time,' he added, winking at her.

The Venture was a pub on the square in Knowle West, Bristol, merely a local for the neighbourhood residents, in minutes walking distance from Novers Park Road, where they both lived. There was a post office opposite the pub, and a primary school, with a general store and an off licence on adjacent sides. Houses, mainly Council owned, filled the rest of the square.

The area wasn't renowned for its beauty. Scenery was nothing more than streets of houses, the square and a few other shops nearby. Jarman's was an off licence serving alcohol and cigarettes and other general grocery items, behind a glass partition, and there was a fish and chip shop opposite it.

Crime was high and local children were tarred with bad names, because of their living location. It wasn't a privileged area by any means, but residents were respectful and lived according to their means. There was a children's park and the swimming baths not far away and the local Comprehensive school. Entertainment amounted to playing football in the streets, the park and walking around the area. There wasn't any money spare, after living expenses, for anything else.

Milly and Vernon enjoyed their evening out and started seeing each other regularly. Vernon had to do his National Service at Aldershot, once he had turned 21. He then continued to train as a Gentleman's hairdresser and eventually opened his own shop, after working for an employer at the start.

They were married in May 1956 at St Barnabas Church in Daventry Road, locally. With such a large family, the church was full. Peggy and Bill, Tony and Patricia, and their young daughter, Susan, were there on Milly's side. The photographs show a single missing tooth on each of Milly, Vernon, Peggy and Bill's smiles. They had all lost a tooth on the morning of the wedding. The same tooth, too!

After renting a flat in Totterdown, Milly worked in a local shop nearby until the arrival of their first daughter, Judy Ann, in October of the same year. She was a month premature, weighing only 4lb 14 oz. They had secretly hoped she would be born later, rather than sooner, as Vernon hadn't told his mother of Milly's pregnancy until after their marriage. They could then have informed her that Judy had been born early! Oops!

Vernon continued his hairdressing and eventually they moved into a property nearby with a shop front (for the barber shop) and living accommodation behind. Four more siblings followed for their daughter. Ian John, Teresa (who weighed only 4lb 4oz and was also premature), Susan Alyson and Michael Colin.

Peggy and Bill had a son, Andrew, a year after Judy's birth. They had been married for 8 years and hadn't expected his arrival, but were overjoyed, as well as surprised. Milly was frequently visiting them and Andrew was never lonely with so many cousins around. Harry now had 6 grandchildren, From his visits to Blanche, he was aware of his increasing family, but life hadn't changed for him and he rarely saw them.

Tony and Patricia had a son, Michael in 1957, the same year as Andrew, but Harry never considered their two children as his own grandchildren, and never acknowledged them at all. Michael had met him in Frome when he was older, at a cattle market event where he was helping out. Harry had met him in the tea tent, where he purchased a drink, and knew instantly that Michael was Tony's son, as the likeness was unmistakable. Harry refused to speak to him and ignored him completely.

Living in the area, they lived in Westbury, not far away, Michael had known of his grandfather's existence through photographs of him in the local newspapers. He often visited his aunty Phyllis, who lived in Frome, with his parents and sister. Michael was old enough to know what his grandfather had become, but had never actually met him, until that day.

His grandfather's ignorance was obvious and Michael was a little disappointed, but not surprised. Tony had told him about Ada's death and that Harry had been to blame. Michael wasn't born at the time, and could only believe what his own father had said to him. It wasn't the truth, but Michael didn't know any different.

Harry's mind had returned to that fatal day, the day he had lost his wife and his reason for living. Michael could have been Tony, they looked so alike, and Harry could see Ada in his features, too. It was heartbreaking. How could he speak to him? What could he say? Would he have understood? He was the same age as Tony was when Ada had died, just 15.

Instead of trying to communicate, Harry had walked away. Michael's image had stayed with him until his death. He was a part of Ada, even though he wasn't a part of him. If his wife hadn't died when she had, Michael and his sister, Susan, would have been regular visitors to their home, wherever that might have been. Ada would have insisted on it, and Harry wouldn't have been living his vagrant existence, he was certain of that.

Their six years apart, whilst he was serving in the Army had played on his mind for a long time. Sitting in Victoria Park, watching the days go by, gave him hours and hours to think about the past, and the present. If he hadn't been away for so long, Tony could have been his son, and

Michael his true grandson. That would've made a huge difference to how he felt about them. But his mind couldn't accept losing Ada, and Tony wasn't his natural son, regardless of the fact that Harry had brought him up as his own, from the age of 2.

Yes, Tony had become an awkward teenager, and Harry had been blessed with three natural daughters. Without any conscious thoughts, he had begun to treat Tony as an outsider. He was wrong, he knew that now, but whilst Ada was still alive, he had his mother and had coped. He had loved his mother.

He couldn't altogether blame Ada for Tony's existence. Six years was a long time apart and she was an attractive lady, beautiful in fact. She would have had admirers of the opposite sex, for sure. One mistake had changed their lives. Harry couldn't face returning from India initially, to Ada and a baby son that wasn't his. He opted to volunteer for China instead, giving more distance between them than ever before.

It was only on returning to his mother's in Ebrington, on his discharge from the regular Army, and her insistence that he made that eventful journey to Windsor Cottage, to discuss the possibilities of saving their marriage, were they reunited. How right his mother had been. Despite everything, he still loved Ada, and Tony was a part of her, he came with the package.

The years that followed were contented ones, hard work, not always perfect, but blissful. They were settled, and living the day to day existence of any normal family. Ada had her family, her siblings, and Harry had his, and communication was kept between them all, though visits were less frequent to Ebrington and Harry's family. Norton St Philip was the icing on the cake. They had moved around a lot beforehand, but they were comfortable there. It suited them all and the village had everything they needed, they'd not needed more.

Percy Wadman was the only major concern. Harry didn't like him, not at all, but they lived in one of his cottages and he had no choice but to be civil to him. Ada would smooth things over, when things got heated, and Harry would take a long walk and return more relaxed. The cottage was ideal, the right size and in the right area. He had tried to stay away from him, whenever possible.

Losing the cottage after Ada's death, he would always feel guilty about. He knew his children were grieving, as he was, but pride wouldn't let him work for that man. The children had no idea what was happening to them, first losing their mother, then their home. What next?

He hadn't been fair to them at all, something he'll always regret. The separation of the children was the last straw. That was something that had been taken out of his hands, though. Tony he could understand. Why would he have wanted to stay with him?

Peggy was never meant to be away permanently, it just happened that way, and Milly missed having her sister around. The letter from Ethel Mary wasn't expected either, a shock in fact. The women of the family seemed to have taken over, and there was nothing he could do about it. Well, that's not strictly true, he could have found work and made a home for them!

Harry was now on his own, all of his family gone. He didn't have the fight in him to rectify things. His grief seemed to come before anything else, despite advise from family and friends. He wasn't the only person in the world who had lost their soulmate. They had managed somehow, why couldn't he?

His life was here now, in Victoria Park. He was near Ada and Vera, and his village, Norton St Philip. He didn't want to be anywhere else, and was unaware of how much his family were hurting. They needed their father, even Tony, if he could have only but realised it. He lived his life the only way he could.

Harry's family were growing. He was missing out, was happy for them all, but still remained a gentleman of the road, spending his life between Norton St Philip and Frome. The visitors to Victoria Park weren't afraid of him, to them he was "the friendly tramp" and conversed with him as they walked around the gardens, admiring the scenery and the changing flowers of the season, in the borders around the large lawn.

The churchyard warden welcomed him daily, allowing him to look after both his wife and daughter's graves. He caused no trouble to anyone, and his mischievous grin was still apparent. The soup kitchen was used most days now, and an occasional night in one of the local bed and breakfast's afforded a bath and a little bit of luxury. He never complained about anything.

Family were readily available and willing to help, but Harry was oblivious to their concerns about the way he was living his life. He hadn't seen his mother and his siblings for years and he wasn't getting any younger himself. The winters could be cruel at times, but somehow he managed to keep himself going. Milly and Peggy had almost given up, and Blanche was concerned for his welfare. Harry was Harry, and had carried on regardless.

CHAPTER SEVENTEEN

It was October 1964 and the weather was so cold. Snow was on the ground in various areas of the United Kingdom, but Somerset hadn't received any, as yet. It was bitter though, and Harry was noticing it. He had been given a hat, scarf and gloves by the staff in the soup kitchen. They had felt sorry for him, and couldn't bear to think of him sleeping out in such awful weather.

It didn't seem to warm up at all, and by March the following year the snow was falling heavily on the ground in Somerset. By the 4th March it lay nine inches thick, and there were drifts in places, six to ten feet deep. Families were struggling to keep themselves, and their homes warm.

Dick, Vernon, and their families were concerned about Harry. How was he going to survive living outside? Milly and Vernon's roof had been damaged, resulting in them and their children living and sleeping in one room. It was so desperately cold, and they needed to keep warm.

They decided to find Harry, in an attempt to bring him home until the weather had improved. After exploring all the local places near Frome and Norton St Philip, in freezing conditions, they finally found him huddled up in the shelter in Victoria Park. His face was blue with the cold and he looked awful. He would never have survived the winter.

He was looked after at Milly and Vernon's, where he stayed for a good while. Vernon cut his hair, removed his beard and searched through his wardrobe for clothes for him, finally handing over some clean shirts and his best suit, as it was the only thing that would have fitted. Vernon had put weight on over the years, and his newer clothes were far too big.

He looked a different person, was enjoying being pampered and playing with his grandchildren.

He ate his food hungrily, supping a pint of cider in The Cumberland pub opposite, and appeared happy and contented. Milly and Peggy were relieved to see their father. He appeared to be his old self again, without his unruly hair and his beard, and he still had his pipe.

Totterdown, where Milly and Vernon lived, was a built up area with shops, a park, schools and a church in minutes walking distance. 51 St Lukes Rd was situated within a rank of shops. Vernon kept the barber's shop and alongside were Mr Wilmott's, the fruit and vegetable shop, a draper's, and a grocery store selling cold meats, cheese, bread and convenience foods.

Next to that was Bert's fish shop. He sold fresh fish and eggs mostly. The eggs were stacked in their cardboard containers of two dozen. He could be seen in the shop window rubbing away at the lion logo printed on the eggs, indicating they were battery produced, and then sold them as free range! The neighbourhood were all aware of what he was doing, and still bought his eggs. Bert was harmless and his fresh fish wasn't expensive.

There was a handyman's shop next door, which Milly and Vernon eventually bought. A newsagent and an off licence stood at the corner of the street and beyond that was the large park. The children played there after school and on the weekends, it was less than two minutes from the house.

Judy had attended the church on a Sunday, for Sunday school. She recited the books of the bible to the residents attending the Sunday service, and was rewarded with a record of Jesus wants me for a sunbeam for her efforts. Harry was proud of her.

Paper rounds were done for Flo in the newsagents, Judy ran a Sunday round, and Ian delivered the morning papers before starting school. Earning 11 shillings a week for her Sunday round, Judy saved up for her Crombie coat, a fashion of the day.

The area consisted of various nationalities; English, Welsh, Scottish, Irish, Jamaican, South African, Pakistan, Indian, to name but a few. Everyone got on, there was no racism in the area. The primary school was at the bottom of the road, under the bridge. Sid's, the sweet shop, received a daily visit from the children after the school day had finished. His frozen Mars bars were to die for!

Then there were the 99 steps! It was hard work climbing them to Richmond Street at the top, but the views from there were breathtaking. You could see most of Bristol. Judy and Ian climbed them regularly, to deliver the daily papers. Teresa, as an adult, had resided in Richmond Street for years.

The bridge at the bottom of the street was shaped like a banana. It was painted green and was a short cut for many journeys. It had always been known as the banana bridge, to locals that was.

Vernon used to take his motorbike and sidecar to one of the local pubs alongside it, until someone had stolen the vehicle whilst he was drinking a pint, or two. It was a constant talking point for years to come! Who would want to steal a motorbike and sidecar?

Harry remembered his own motorbike and sidecar, and taking Ada and the children to his mother's cottage for their annual cherry picking trip. They had been happy occasions and brought back good memories. Harry had loved his motorbike, it had been an inexpensive way of travelling to work and given him his much needed free time on his own.

Harry's grandchildren were friendly with a family in the street. They were the Edwards' children (Edmund, Janet, Jean, Steven, Paul and Brian). All were of similar ages, so they attended school together. They used to visit each other's homes and play in the park. It was a standing joke amongst the other children around. They were known as the "vegetable gang", as Vernon's surname was Green! A popular potato, the King Edward, has been grown in the UK since 1902, making it one of the oldest cultivators still grown commercially.

Harry would walk around the park, and he absolutely loved watching the children playing in their free time, remembering his own children when they were younger. Hours were spent sat admiring the views, and seeing the trains regularly cross the bridge, heading for Temple Meads train station.

Milly loved her bingo and Susan's daily school diary disclosed this. On marking her school work, the teacher would laugh at her comments. Monday- Mum went to bingo last night, Tuesday- Mum went to bingo last night, Wednesday- Mum went to bingo last night etc. The teacher knew where she used to go most nights of the week!

Michael loved his toy soldiers, and you had to carefully step over them, ensuring none were knocked down, when walking around the sitting room. He would point one soldier towards another, and the noise of guns would be enacted with his voice, then the soldier would be placed down on the floor. He was dead! He carried his box of soldiers around, even after he married. Harry would smile to himself as he watched Michael engrossed in his own war, remembering his time in the Army himself.

Teresa's party piece was always to do with food. She was a fussy eater, and Vernon insisted she ate all her food before leaving the table. Three hours later and she would still be sat there, eating one pea at a time, to her father's annoyance. Sally, the pet dog, had received most of her food without Vernon noticing.

Ian, who wasn't keen on school, would hide in the cupboard on the landing until his father had opened the barber's shop, and would then happily do as he wished in the house. That was until he was caught out and marched back to school! Ian reminded Harry of Tony, in his teenage years.

The park was a safe place to play, and had swings, sliders, roundabouts and climbing frames at one end. It was surrounded by grass, grass, and yet more grass and stretched for miles. Bonfire night was a serious affair amongst the resident children. Collecting wood and materials to build the bonfire was undertaken by every one of them, but there were two gangs. One at the top of the park and the other at the bottom end.

To ensure one gang didn't pinch each other's goods meant a night guard on the bonfires, and children slept out in tents to ensure no pilfering occurred. The aim was to build the biggest bonfire and this became an annual competition, though a healthy one. Harry recalled his competitive nature as he was growing up. He had relished a challenge then, and would have been involved in the bonfire night event, for sure.

There was a chip shop at the top of the street, which was used a lot and where Judy worked at the weekend, when she had turned 15. It was there that she had met her future husband, Adrian. He used to purchase his regular chip order after visiting the Cumberland pub, making it plainly obvious that he liked her. At first, she hadn't take any notice of him, as he was always drunk when he visited the chip shop, but eventually she agreed to date him and they were married just before she had turned 19.

Life at St Lukes Road was good, Harry liked the constant attention he had received from the family, though there never seemed to be a quiet moment in the house. Space was limited with such a large family, and it was suggested that Harry would be more comfortable staying with Peggy, Milly's sister.

Peggy and Bill had a spare bedroom and Harry lived there afterwards, playing with Andrew, their son, who was now 7 years old. Photographs of Harry sat in their garden, with Vernon's suit on and his flat cap, his pipe in his mouth and the famous mischievous grin, were precious to the family. Andrew was sat by his side, and Harry was looking contented. Everybody who knew Harry was pleased that he seemed to have settled at last, and hopeful that he would not return to his vagrant life.

Peggy had sorted out his finances and he was awarded social security benefits, something he wasn't entitled to as a gentleman of the road, as he had no residential address. He would regularly ask one of his grandchildren to visit Jarman's and purchase his tobacco and flagon of cider, though none of them were actually old enough to buy the goods. Jarman's had known the items were for Harry, so all was well. Harry was now 64, and appeared to be settled and happy, at last.

As he hadn't visited Blanche for a long time, years in fact, Peggy relayed news of his family in Ebrington. Harry's stepfather, Frank, and his mother, Martha, had died in 1959 and 1960. Millie and her husband, Henry, had insisted on them living with them in Bidford as their health deteriorated, where they were looked after until their deaths. Uncles Richard and John had also died and Harry's brother, Jack (John Henry), was now married with four children, and living in Shipston on Stour.

Millie, Harry's sister, had tried to contact him, but with no address she had no way of knowing where he was. Percy had passed away too, so his wife, Lily, and their son had moved away from the area. She finally sent a letter to Blanche, hoping Harry would call on her at some point in time.

On hearing this, his face was a blank canvas, his complexion changed to ghostly white. How could he have continued all these years thinking his family would still be there, and nothing would have changed? There was no farm to go back to, no uncles. His mother and stepfather had gone, someone else would be living in their cottage now. He'd missed out on so much, and hadn't been there to say goodbye.

He realised that he had to try to communicate more and be there for his family. He had two daughters, two son in laws and six grandchildren. They needed him, as much as he needed them. He was going to try harder, he had to, he wasn't getting any younger.

Day to day normality continued until Bill suddenly collapsed in the bathroom. He was preparing for work one weekday morning, and had felt a stabbing pain in his chest. The pain refused to go away and he dropped to the floor. Their bathroom wasn't large, and no-one had been able to enter it, as he had fallen behind the door. He was too heavy for anyone to lift or move him.

An ambulance was called and the medical team managed to eventually open the bathroom door. Bill had had a heart attack and had died instantly. He was 41 years of age. Harry remembered Ada's death in the cottage. This was so unfair, it was history repeating itself.

Andrew was still only 7 years old and had lost his father. Peggy was walking around the house in a daze, not registering her husband's death. It wasn't possible, not Bill. He had been fine the previous evening. The television had been switched on, and they were all engrossed in a documentary about Bristol and the West Country. Harry had been pointing out parts of the country where he had lived and visited. Bill hadn't complained at all, and had retired soon after the programme was over.

Harry wasn't any help at all. He became very quiet, stepped out of the house and walked, and walked, and walked. It was dark before he had returned to Peggy's.

'Where have you been, Father?' she asked. 'You've had me so worried. You didn't say you were going out.'

'Sorry, Peggy. I couldn't think straight and needed some air. Walking is second nature to me now. Is there anything I can do to help?' he finally asked.

'No. I can't believe that Bill has gone. He wasn't ill and had never complained of chest pains before. How am I going to manage?'

Harry didn't answer. He was thinking of Ada and Vera. They would be missing him. He couldn't help Peggy, he didn't know how to.

Andrew was still a child. He was crying, sat on his mother's lap. Milly, Vernon and their children arrived, as soon as they had been told of the tragedy. Andrew played cards with his cousins, tears still falling from his face, all over the playing cards. No-one knew what to say to each other. The house was deadly silent for once, completely out of character.

Harry made himself a cup of tea, loaded his pipe with tobacco and sat outside on a bench in the garden, contemplating.

The funeral was a quiet affair, but so emotional. Peggy and Bill had been so happy together, so in love. Bill was the organiser, the bill payer, and Peggy cleaned the house and looked after their son. They had been content. Harry attended the funeral, but remained in the background. Tony and his wife were there, but there was no communication between him and his father. Nothing had changed and Harry didn't try to heal the rift.

The house was so quiet at 118 Novers Park Road in Bristol. Time dragged and Harry resorted to his long walks again. Peggy was grieving for her husband, and doing her best to console her young son. But Harry had felt out of his depth, and although he desperately wanted to tell his daughter that things would be okay, he couldn't.

Vernon's father, Frederick, had died shortly after Bill, and Eva Mary was now on her own. She would call in with a hot meal for them both, and something sweet for Andrew. She was lonely, too. Milly's children had lost their favourite uncle and their grandfather, and Vernon had lost his father. Harry was aware of Milly and Vernon's grief.

It was such an emotional time and Harry couldn't cope with it all. He felt closed in, needed space and was struggling with all the grief encircling him. He couldn't support his family, he didn't know where to start. One morning, he approached Peggy, telling her that he needed to go back to Norton St Philip, to be near her mother and sister. He wasn't able to live in four walls again, not permanently, anyway.

Peggy had pleaded with him to stay. His family needed him and worried about him, when he lived his nomadic life. He was her father and she loved him dearly.

'You're not getting any younger, Father, the cold will kill you out there. How will you manage?' she asked, so concerned.

'I don't know, all I know is that I need to go back there, to what I'm used to,' he stated. 'It's where I belong, Peggy. I will visit you and Milly again, I promise.'

There was nothing she could do or say to change his mind, she shrugged her shoulders and Andrew cuddled into his grandfather. They had become so close. Fishing through her purse, Peggy handed him the notes she had. At first he'd refused them, but then accepted the money, knowing he wouldn't be able to receive any benefits again. There were still some clothes left in the wardrobe belonging to Bill, some underwear, vests, socks and a few shirts. They were put into a bag and given to him.

'You will come back again when you need us, when the weather turns too cold?' Peggy questioned, near to tears.

'I promise,' he replied. He said goodbye to his grandson, hugged Peggy and walked out of the door.

Back in Norton St Philip, Harry headed for the churchyard and Ada's grave.

'I'm sorry I've been so long, Ada. The weather was so bad last year, Vernon and Dick found me and took me to their homes. They wanted me to stay, and I was tempted, but I've been missing you and Vera. I needed to be back here. This is where I belong.' He placed a bunch of pink chrysanthemums on her grave and continued.

'We have six grandchildren, Ada. Milly has five and Peggy has a son.' There was no mention of Tony and his two children. 'They are all lovely, Andrew really took to me. I so enjoyed meeting them and playing with the younger ones. We've done well, Ada.'

After attending to Vera's grave he headed towards Victoria Park and the soup kitchen. The park had missed him, visitors expressed. They thought he had died. Harry put them straight, telling them about his daughters and his grandchildren.

'I'm back now,' he told them. 'Back to my home.'

As the years passed, Harry's health began to take its toll. He knew when he wasn't well and would visit Peggy's home, staying for a few weeks. When he felt well enough to return to his life, he would be off again. He would see Milly and Vernon, his hair would be cut and his beard would be trimmed. He didn't want his beard removed completely, for some reason.

He would look at his grandchildren, they were all growing up now, and he was pleased to see them. Weekends, for the children, were frequently spent at Blanche's, in the countryside. Playing in the large garden, running after the goose that had been bought to fatten up for the following Christmas, but had become a household pet. She hadn't had the heart to kill it! Sometimes, Harry would be there, paying a visit to Blanche.

School holidays were taken up at Ernest and Hilda's. Judy would spend two weeks with them, followed by Ian and Teresa together. Susan and Michael were both too young, but they would spend the day there, with their aunty and uncle, when Vernon collected his offspring.

Hilda became their special aunty and Judy was born on her birthday, the 29th October.

Milly and Peggy had given up on trying to persuade Harry to stay, there was no point any more. A fleeting visit now and again, a few weeks at Peggy's, and the occasional bus trip to Blanche. Back to his home he would go, as he called it, Victoria Park in Frome.

Years passed and Peggy married again, but it didn't last. Vernon and Milly continued to live in Totterdown. Judy and Ian were now working, but the others were still at school. Andrew was working and looking after his mother, she wasn't well and suffered good and bad days.

She helped clean Milly's house, whilst Milly worked in the handyman's shop next door, when she was able to, that was, and would help out with the children. Judy was struggling with a knitting pattern once, and Peggy helped her finish the garment in question. She was so grateful. Her mother hadn't had time to help her, through no fault of her own. Vernon was working away with his brother, Raymond, and the barber's shop had temporarily closed. It had reopened a few years later.

Eva Mary now lived above the handyman's shop and was looked after by Vernon, Milly and the grandchildren. The children all loved her. They would check on their nan of an evening and sit with her, watching television and keeping her company.

The grandchildren would walk her around the park occasionally. She loved her walks and the fresh air. Peggy would also visit her. Her cups of tea were always made with sterilised milk, not to everyone's taste, and she ensured Milly received her quota for the day whilst working downstairs.

Life had changed for everyone, except Harry. He was still living his life, unconcerned about anything or anyone. He was "the friendly tramp" people knew and accepted in the park and continued his walking and visiting his wife and daughter. He didn't understand "normal life", he was oblivious to it all.

Judy was 18 years of age on the 29th October 1974. She had met her future husband, Adrian, and was celebrating their engagement in the Cumberland pub opposite her house. Unbeknown to any of the family, Harry had died that day. He had been found on a park bench in Victoria Park in Frome, the bench he had sat on with Ada.

A photograph of him had appeared in the local paper, and Phyllis, Ada's sister, had noticed it when reading the newspaper. Phyllis was aware of where Peggy lived and she was contacted and told of her father's death.

Milly and Peggy travelled to Frome to identify him. He hadn't changed, he looked happy, asleep and content. The mischievous grin was still there. They had arranged for his body to be put into Ada's grave. The undertakers had cut his hair and trimmed his beard. His fingernails and toenails looked clean and manicured. He had been washed and his clothes had been removed, and he was now wearing a gown. He was 73 years of age.

The funeral was attended by just two people, Milly and Sylvia, Blanche's daughter. Peggy was having one of her bad days and wasn't well enough to attend. Vernon couldn't shut the shop and his grandchildren were either at work or at school. Any family left, that he'd had in Ebrington and the surrounding areas, were unaware of his death.

The local press wrote about Harry Tracey, a gentleman of the road. They commended him for his friendliness, his smile and his need to be near his wife. The wife he had loved so dearly and had refused to be parted from, even in death.

The certificate showed his cause of death as a Pulmonary Embolism due to Deep Vein Thrombosis. Truthfully, he had died from a broken heart, and had had to wait over 30 years to be reunited with his true love, his wife, Ada.

Ian, his grandson has inherited his mischievous grin and photographs of him in earlier years resemble photographs of Ian, now. He will never be forgotten.

EPILOGUE

On the surface, Harry appeared to be a cold person, refusing to work for Percy Wadman to keep a roof over his children's heads and then letting them go, separated from each other, after losing their mother.

That was the impression he had given to a lot of people and family, but in reality, he was lost. The women of Ada's family had taken over after her death, and worried about the children. They were sincere and sympathetic, and offering a roof over the girls' heads was kindness in itself, or so it seemed.

But finding himself on his own after losing his wife and soulmate, and then his girls, its not surprising that he had become reclusive. It had all been taken out of his hands. He was alone and had no reason to carry on, his head had told him.

He struggled to pull himself together, to return to work and find a place of his own to live. Life had no meaning any more. He had been a family man, happily working to put food on the table for his wife, stepson and three daughters.

Then Vera had died, his baby, and life seemed cruel. She hadn't had her 2nd birthday, and she didn't deserve to die. She was beautiful, was walking and talking and loved her brother, Tony. She followed him around everywhere, sat on Harry's motorbike with him, and played with the football in the garden. She would have been a tomboy if she'd lived, that's for sure.

Eventually Harry and Ada had overcame their grief, for the children's sake. Life had to carry on for them. It had taken a long time to adjust, but adjust they did. Vera was never forgotten. The smiles returned to their faces and day to day life had continued.

Norton St Philip was home and everyone appeared happy. Tony was working in Frome, in the rubber factory making tyres, and Peggy was attending Coombe Down secondary school. Milly was due to start there soon. They were growing up fast.

Then Ada had died and the world had stopped. Harry couldn't cope, even though he knew his children were grieving too. Milly had found her, after checking on her that dreadful evening. She had been out milking the cows the day before, and didn't feel well the next morning. No-one expected her to die so suddenly.

Harry closed himself off to everyone, he had done it once before, when he was in the Army.

When he had discovered Ada was carrying another man's child, he was devastated and didn't know what to do. He had loved his wife and his absence was inexcusable, but he had never expected to be in India for so long.

Harry didn't speak to anyone for weeks. He walked miles around the Army camp completely alone, and hadn't wanted company. If the horses could have spoken, they would have been the only ones who knew how he was feeling. He confided in no-one, except the animals. They understood him completely.

He hadn't had the best start in life. Being born in the workhouse to an unmarried mother, and brought up by his elderly grandparents, while his mother married and produced six more children. Harry had felt unwanted, though he loved his grandmother. He was only 4 years old when his mother had left him, and she didn't visit that often, either.

There was help for him, if he'd wanted it. His confidence was at an all time low, he was wallowing in self pity and he was grieving, not just for Ada, but for his children as well. He'd lost them and wasn't able to pull himself together, not enough to get them back.

His stepfather hadn't wanted him around, Harry wasn't his child, and now his children had been taken away from him also. He was a man, and it was the women of the families who looked after the children. Who was he to argue? What had he to offer them, anyway? He wasn't working or able to, the way he was feeling. He didn't know where to go from here, he was confused.

Becoming a gentleman of the road wasn't a conscious decision, it just happened. While the war was still on, he had helped out as a member of the Home Guards. You couldn't take the Army out of Harry. Percy had helped too, and Harry was still living with him and his wife, Lily, at the time.

Harry was a proud man, but he wasn't a dominant person. He could have visited Milly, seen how she was being treated by her step-grandmother and taken her back with him. Peggy, once recovered from her illness, could've returned to her father, but he had accepted his lot without a fight. His confidence had been destroyed.

Tony was at an awkward age, missed his mother dreadfully, and joining the Navy was a way out for him. Harry could have intervened, spoke to him, apologised even for the way he had treated him. The bond had been there from the age of 2, and Tony never knew he wasn't his natural father. Things could have been sorted, if they'd both tried.

Loneliness alone, can be a killer, but Harry was used to it from a young age. His uncles weren't the type of people to create a conversation, after work was finished for the day. It was food, then bed, there was no relaxing by the fire or small talk. Everything was so serious after his grandparents had died. His grandmother was so sorely missed.

The work dried up in the village and so did the money, but Harry needed to be near Ada's grave.

He felt safe around her. The children didn't live locally any more, and relocating didn't seem right, not appropriate. He needed to be here, in Norton St Philip. That's when he became a gentleman of the road.

Had Bill, Peggy's husband, not died when he did, Harry might have stayed with her in Bristol.

He had seemed to be doing okay, was flourishing being around the family, and they truly loved having him around. He smoked his pipe in Peggy's garden, showing off his mischievous grin and appeared so settled. Their missed years were forgotten, and they were concentrating on the future.

Losing Bill had brought Ada's death back to him and forced Harry back into oblivion. He needed to go back to his wife and daughter, as he had neglected them. There was too much grieving going on in the family.

Milly's children had lost their grandfather too, Vernon's father. He just couldn't cope.

Victoria Park in Frome became his home for the duration of his life, a park bench, the shelter or the summerhouse. The churchyard was where Ada and Vera were, where he felt safe. He did speak to people, smiled and spent his days walking, from the park to the churchyard and back. Time wasn't an issue, he could take all the time he needed.

At the end, his death on the bench in Victoria Park would have been his wish. It was Ada's favourite park and close to her and his daughter. She would have been there waiting for him. 31 years was a long time apart, but they are together now. Reunited at last, forever.

Harry's life hadn't been an easy one. Perhaps the Tracey curse had something to do with it, the curse put on the Tracey family after the death of Thomas Becket, the Archbishop of Canterbury in 1170.

'The Tracey's have always the wind in their faces.' Such is the legend.

www.ingramcontent.com/pod-product-compliance
Lightning Source LLC
Chambersburg PA
CBHW020450130626
46549CB00001B/371